KU-593-728

# ROBIN GILL

# LARDER

## FROM PANTRY TO PLATE:
## DELICIOUS RECIPES FOR YOUR TABLE

**A.**

7     INTRODUCTION

19    THE LARDER

      20    Fermented Vegetables,
            Fruits and Herbs

      31    Meat, Fish and Game
            Preservation

      42    Pickles and Jams

      51    Dairy, Butters and Oils

      58    Powders, Salts and Crisps

      61    Stocks, Sauces and
            Seasonings

69    FOR THE TABLE

      71    Bases and Blends,
            Chef's Cocktails
            and Home Brews

      85    Snacks

      123   Garden

      159   Sea

      195   Land

      241   Sweet

279   INDEX

285   ACKNOWLEDGEMENTS

# INTRODUCTION

My wife's nan, Nanna May, trusted people and generally warmed to them if they were what she called a 'good eater'. She ran the kitchen of a café in north Dublin and every now and again she would get visits from a local villain who was often in jail for one thing or another. Whenever he was out, he would always make time to pop in for a lasagne, a pot of tea and a large slice of cake. He was a 'good eater', and she genuinely thought of him as a 'lovely fella' because he ate well and finished what he ordered. I love how food and cooking for someone can have this effect on people: Nanna May, to my knowledge, was certainly anything but a heavy 'gangster godmother' type, yet these two complete opposites had a bond built by the simple process of cooking for someone.

Way back when, I was what Nanna May would have called a 'bad eater'. Until I was about 14, my relationship with food was pretty horrific. I used to love a disgusting Granby beef burger that had been cremated under a grill and slapped into a horrid white processed bun. I also ate terrible-quality frozen pizzas, alphabet spaghetti and all shapes and sizes of frozen chicken-dipper-type things. It wasn't that my parents didn't expose me to good food. Quite the opposite. But for some reason this was the sort of crap that I insisted on eating. I point blank refused to try what they were having at home, or in all the amazing restaurants around the world that I was lucky enough to be taken to. I would have been far happier with a McDonald's. I still don't know why I was like that and it's my biggest fear that my son Ziggy will follow in my bizarre footsteps.

It's much easier to tell your mum and dad that you won't try something that they have lovingly prepared for you, but when you're a guest in a mate's home, well that's different. Growing up, I spent a lot of time in my best friend Paul's house. His parents, Tom and Deirdre, were amazing cooks. It was the type of house where when you walked into the downstairs toilet you might get quite a fright, finding a brace of freshly shot birds hanging off the showerhead. There were regularly lobsters, crabs and Dublin Bay prawns that had been gifted to Tom in the local pub, and Deirdre made her own pizzas on a Friday. I pretended to have dietary problems to avoid eating certain things (how ironic, as that happens at least once every night in the restaurant ... karma, I hear you muttering!). Slowly, too embarrassed to say

no, I was exposed to all the amazing things I had been missing out on. Looking back, I now realise how much the McNerney kitchen in Clarinda Park shaped and influenced me. Paul had always wanted to be a cook; I didn't know it then but I was to follow him along many of his own chosen paths.

My father was a musician and my mother a choreographer. Both had very long, successful careers in the business and I had immense pressure to follow in their footsteps. Initially I tried music and dropped out, then dance. My father wasn't too happy about that so it didn't last long either. Then it was acting. Yep, packed that in too. I stuck at nothing! I tried all sports too – I bought the best gear – and packed it in two weeks later. Then there was school... Well, I'm sure you're seeing a pattern.

Having convinced my parents to put me into an expensive school in the centre of Dublin for my final year before college, I had reached the final flunk! I decided university wasn't for me and had a mate put me forward for an apprenticeship as an electrician. I came home to tell my parents of yet another failure, but at least this time I had a plan. My parents couldn't understand why I would want to become an electrician – as my father said, 'you can't even change a lightbulb', but he suggested cooking. I had been cooking at home and now at 17 I had a thirst for knowledge plus, finally, a decent appetite.

So, taking some advice, I decided to avoid college and get straight into it. I applied for a job in one of the busiest and highest-profile spots in Dublin. I have no regrets about passing up the chance to go to college as I felt I had some catching up to do and had wasted enough of my time and my parents' money over the years. This was my chance to show everyone that I could do something and would stick with it no matter what – hopefully with some success.

I have now been cooking professionally for 18 years and I have managed to cook in some of the best and toughest kitchens in Europe, yet I can honestly say that my first experience at that restaurant in Dublin was the most unnecessarily brutal and it has scarred me for life.

Keen as mustard with a brand new set of knives, I set foot into the kitchen, full of energy and excitement. The hustle and bustle of cooks from different lands running around frantically trying to get ready for the lunch service instantly drew me into this new world. This was the place for me. To say I was

fresh is an understatement. Within my first few weeks I had several cuts and, as my body adjusted to the 18-hour days, I would literally fall into bed at night fully clothed, only to wake up panicking about the job. I loved how much I was learning and tried to write down everything as the weeks flew by into months. I made mistakes along the way, as you would expect, but what I had not expected was the bullying.

There was a senior team of about five guys from Head Chef down to Chef de Partie. They were the pirates running the ship and seemed quite close. It started with silly pranks, like asking me to run to the basement walk-in fridge to count the produce. Upon my return they would sneer and make degrading remarks. Then there was the aggression when I had hot soup thrown at me and was forced to clean up the mess. For no apparent reason, they all seemed to dislike me. Whenever I asked a question, I was either threatened or screamed at. The quiet evenings were the worst as they had more time to be cruel. One evening they were all standing around a bucket of garlic, peeling it, and I walked up to try to take part. I reached in to grab some garlic, at which they all stopped chatting and glared at me. The horrific intimidating silence was broken by the Sous Chef calling me a 'fucking queer'. I walked away while they were all laughing and struggled to hold back the tears. This continued for months. I dealt with it by telling the stories to my pals and turning it into humour.

We were permanently understaffed because many of the new cooks who took the jobs would not last the day. I stuck with it and began to move up the ranks, to managing my own section. On a Friday lunchtime with 250 covers on the books, there was a backlog of checks that we weren't keeping up with. One of the cooks screamed at me, threw me four duck breasts and told me to get them cooking. I was nervous as I didn't know how to do this, so I threw a couple of pans on full blast heat and added two huge ladles of oil. The oil instantly started to smoke. I suddenly remembered seeing duck breasts going into a warm pan with no oil, skin side down, and went back to question the chef. He screamed at me to 'just cook the fucking things', so I panicked and threw one breast into the hot oil. A flame spurted up as I threw in the second breast. The hot oil splashed up to my neck, chin and face, covering a third of my face. I was rushed to hospital.

I was out of the kitchen for two weeks and paid for just one. The doctor told me I should take two months

off to recover. Upon my return to the kitchen the men were standing around my section reading my recipe book and making jokes. I grabbed my book back and one of them barked, 'Have you got the recipe for the duck?' They all cracked up laughing. That evening one of the waitresses was asking me about my burns when the Head Chef shouted down: 'Get the fuck away from him. He has AIDS. Just look at his fucking face.' Embarrassed, I went back to my station.

I took advice from my brother who was a manager at a restaurant in Dublin called QV2, run by a wonderful gent, Count John McCormack, and they offered me a job in the kitchen. I thanked them but I wanted to prove that I could cope and do my job before I left it. That day came when I was finishing a week where I had worked incredibly hard and had successfully smashed every service running a two-man section solo. I had cleared an area where I could lay out plates, to prepare for the slamming we were expecting. The chef grabbed me and said: 'What the fuck are you doing, you retard? Fuck off over there and strain the stocks.' That was it! I'd had enough. I threw down my apron and told him to go fuck himself and strain it himself. I went to change and gather my things, and completely broke down.

As I write this I am fighting back the tears. There is no reason for this kind of behaviour. It didn't make me a better cook. They couldn't staff the kitchen and the team all broke apart – after a few months the Head Chef walked out. If you asked me to name them I honestly couldn't; I don't remember. It's as though I've blocked them out. Thankfully this is not commonplace across the industry now, but it does happen and not only in kitchens.

From then on my career improved. I worked in better kitchens and travelled the world, and eventually started setting up my own restaurants. The businesses are run with passion and hard work but without fear. There will never be any bullying in my kitchens. I ensure there is a warm and loving atmosphere where everyone is as important as the next and everyone has a say. Ideas and creativity are embraced. The people I am blessed to work with are not my 'staff', they are my family and they know that.

Aged 19, my two pals, Paul and Ed, had landed jobs in London. Not messing about, Paul was going to Le Gavroche and Ed to Chez Nico. I didn't want to be left behind so I decided to follow. I took their advice and bought a copy of the London Michelin guide and a tube map. For two days I knocked on the back door of every kitchen that had a star or stars. I had a letter with me pleading for a position (addressed to the Chef de Cuisine, whose name I had quickly checked on the menu at the front of the restaurant). London impressed me but scared me and the tube confused me. I dropped in everywhere green as green could be. I was completely out of my depth and not too hopeful of landing a job. The last place I called into was the Oak Room Marco Pierre White. It was in Le Méridien Hotel on Piccadilly. I couldn't figure out where the back kitchen entrance was so I entered nervously through the front doors: the place just took my breath away.

Robert Reid was running the kitchen and he took the time to come and speak to me. I told him of my lack of experience and that I hadn't been to college but that I had decided to move to London and get my ass kicked there instead. He laughed and told me of the great times he had had at college and not to rush, but if I was serious I could start in a month. That was it! The three green amigos were off to London, all starting on the same day in the three top spots in the UK.

It wasn't easy. I made mistake after mistake and worked far slower than anyone else in the kitchen. I was there six days a week, getting home at 1am and back in for 8am, but every day got a little easier. Sure, I was shouted at during service and called a few names that still make me laugh, but the longer I was there, the more I became part of something, part of a team. And I developed skills that I would never forget. Robert was a fair man and became almost a father figure to me in a city that can be a very cold place at times. I spent a year and a half there, meanwhile dreaming of an easier time I'd had with my amazing friends and family in Dublin.

At 21 I returned home and took a role that I was not really ready for – as a Sous Chef at a place that I loved and had worked at before, just a stone's throw from where I grew up. It was called Brasserie Na Mara, overlooking Scotsman's Bay. I loved it there but found myself reproducing dishes I had learned to cook at the Oak Room and doing them badly. So I decided

it was time for a change again. I set off for Asia on what was supposed to be a three-week holiday but turned into a six-month stint. I became a complete hippy and told myself that I would never return to London, or anything like London, and never work in a Michelin-starred restaurant again. Life was too short and there was too much to see.

So where should I go next? Well, whenever I was lost I would always talk to Paul. At the time, he was in Naples, working in a beautiful restaurant with a Michelin star called Taverna del Capitano, right on the water in Marina del Cantone, a small fishing village. That sounded nice but I didn't want to work anywhere that had a star. I loved Italian cooking, as that's what I had started off cooking, so I set off for Naples with the romantic idea that I would be learning to make pasta with a nonna in a trattoria. I dreamed of becoming part of an Italian family, spending all my free time on a boat somewhere along the Amalfi Coast or lost in a vineyard! That might have happened but for the fact that the trattorias of that area are family-run, so unless you're local or a family member, you're pretty far down the line, and understandably so. The only option I had was to apply to a two-star place called Don Alfonso 1890 – I had a friend named Fernando who was working there and he very kindly put in a good word for me. So I landed myself in a bloody two-star working six days a week again!

The good news was that it was a family-run business, and had been since 1890. The charming and hard-working Iaccarino family who ran the restaurant had a farm overlooking Capri. It was beautiful in every way. Alfonso came from the farm every morning in a white Hiace van filled with the most wonderful produce that we got to cook with. It was my first exposure to true cooking with the seasons, when something was in such abundance and at its best and had to be put to use. It was a revelation to me. Whatever couldn't be used was preserved and kept for a season less generous. It was natural in every way.

Without realising it at the time, this made the biggest impression on how I cook today. I learned how to hold back and let the produce speak for itself. I learned for the first time what it really meant to be seasonal, not just as a slogan but to live by it. And guess what? I had the Michelin bug again. I threw out those silly hippy pants that I wore at a full-

moon party somewhere and found I had a thirst for knowledge at that level. I dreamed of Paris, having listened to the stories of Robert, who was working at Joël Robuchon, and thought that would be my next adventure. But alas, things don't always work out the way you plan them.

In our business chefs at this level are stupidly committed to the craft, taking holidays but not resting, and actually working for FREE at some highly regarded spot with glitzy accolades. In Italy I met Craig who was on such a trip. He had taken time off to travel to Don Alfonso on a break from Raymond Blanc's Le Manoir aux Quat' Saisons. He didn't speak Italian so I looked after him. Thinking about my next move, as the season was coming to a close, I wanted to know all about Le Manoir. I was intrigued, and decided that the least I could do was check it out on a similar exchange basis.

Le Manoir is a special place. I never went to catering college but I consider getting a job at Le Manoir to be the equivalent of gaining a scholarship at Oxford. The pay wasn't amazing – our industry has a bad reputation for pay and hours, and in some cases it's probably true. It is not an easy career path. But at Le Manoir I felt I was gaining knowledge in one of the most successful 'cooking schools' in the world and actually being paid for it, while many young men and women more commonly take on huge loans to attend university with no guarantee of an income. How ironic.

Well, my two-week stage turned into a minimum two-year commitment. My then girlfriend (now wife), Sarah, wasn't too happy but fully supported my decision and followed me to Oxfordshire a few months later. The two years turned into four, working with Raymond, Gary, Benoit and the amazing team. It was a disciplined place to work and the training was incredible. The kitchen had a very clear structure of who was who in the ranks, from Commis, 1/2/3, Demi, CDP (Chef de Partie), Senior CDP, Chef Tournon, Junior Sous, Senior Sous, Head Chef, Executive Chef and, finally, Raymond the Chef Patron. In the pastry section, the talented and flamboyant Benoit ran a very tight ship indeed, producing breads and some of the finest pastry in the country every day. The point I'm making is that the kitchen at Le Manoir was a huge operation with a very steep career ladder to climb. But although it was one of the most competitive environments I have ever worked in, I built some of the most sincere bonds with many of the talented individuals I got to work with and remain close to many of them to this day, following their successes all over the world. It was a very important building block for me.

I took my first head chef role in opening The Diamond Club at Arsenal's Emirates Stadium representing Raymond Blanc. This was an incredible opportunity as I was still being mentored by RB and Gary. To all my pals at home, this, ironically, was like winning the lotto and landing the luckiest job in the world. I thought it odd that when I had worked in two- and three-star places, they never gave a damn, but now this was huge.

You see, I had – and still have – zero interest in football. On one occasion, we were doing recipe testing in the private dining room kitchen in Le Manoir during the day. I still had ingredients left from some of the testing dishes that were a success, so Gary asked me to prepare them and send them out as appetisers for regulars and VIPs. This went on throughout the service until Johnson came running down, screaming, 'Robin, I need two appetisers VIP Thierry Henry'. I innocently said, 'Eh? What the hell is that? I've not cooked it before', not having a clue that this was actually a person and one of the most successful and famous footballers in the world, at the time captaining Arsenal.

I spent two years running between Le Manoir and Arsenal, and it gave me a taste of London that I hadn't had previously. I was very young when I was first working there but now I was a little older and had a little more money in my pocket, and Sarah by my side. So I decided to look for a permanent role in London. I landed a job in the City running a beautiful restaurant in The Royal Exchange building, for a forward-thinking and growing company called D&D. This was just before the financial crash. When that happened I thought it was really bad luck that I had landed a job in the City where restaurants thrive on customers with expense accounts, which were suddenly now all scrapped. I had to learn how to be frugal, to use more affordable ingredients that I had never worked with before and still make them delicious. These were challenging times but the relationships formed and skills gained became instrumental in opening my own place.

Fast forward four successful years and I had an obsessive desire to do my own thing. However, I didn't know what that was yet. During my training at Le Manoir, I had met Matt Orlando, currently of Amass in Copenhagen, who was doing an extreme cooking sabbatical. He was from San Diego and had

saved up enough cash to spend a year travelling and staging across Europe in some of the best places in the world. The idea of doing something similar never left me. I got a call from a friend who was looking to build a team to cook for a head of state from the Middle East during a visit to the UK. The salary I could earn in two months was the same as 18 months' work. Well, it was a no-brainer. The crazy, bizarre two months were exhausting but I then had a healthy bank balance. That gave me the opportunity to follow in Matt's footsteps.

I took six months off, and staged and ate in some of the finest places in Europe and Scandinavia. I visited suppliers all over the British Isles and basically studied everywhere I visited. As I was mostly travelling alone I took to writing reports on what inspired me in the design, menu ideas and wine lists, as well as the cultures in different restaurants. What inspired me most was what I called modern bistros. They were cool, laid-back dining rooms with lots of raw material, banging out great playlists. They were full of energy and creativity. Menus changed frequently with what seemed like a fearless confidence and disregard for the big guides. These places were cooking better than some three-stars I visited. They were perfectly imperfect.

I spent all my savings in those six months and I gained a few kilos. But I ended up with a sharp, clear vision of what I wanted to do. That was to take a back-to-basics approach to my cooking and to learn ancient techniques like charcuterie, baking and preserving. I wanted to work as closely as I could to being on a farm and by the coast by working directly with fishermen and farmers and buying direct.

It was at this point we came across The Dairy in Clapham. With no savings, we borrowed, begged and stole to get the business up and running, taking it from a shitty late-night bar with a terrible reputation to the restaurant it is today. The old building was originally a house and it was what I can only describe as a hoarder's paradise. Every room, from the basement to the sheds out the back and the four rooms above, were full, floor to ceiling, with absolute crap. Tractor wheels, empty sweet tins, smelly old curtains, hundreds of pillows, disgusting objects of all varieties and shapes, all worth absolutely nothing. It took us a month just to clear it.

We had £80k to get the restaurant open. Our business partner, Matt, had friends in the building trade and he called in huge favours to get things on serious mates' rates for us. Dean, Richie and Eoghann, who were dear friends and were going to be in the kitchen with me, started work six weeks before opening – not recipe-testing, which would be the norm, but sanding, painting, scrubbing and constantly cleaning up after the pretty horrifically bad-habited builders.

Getting the business to a fit opening state was traumatic. We all lost a worrying amount of weight, and I almost came to blows with the head builder who threatened to walk out unless he got more funds. Negotiations followed and we reached an agreement to get the work done. We built a herb garden on the roof and inherited some beehives from Dean's uncle. With no money left in the bank we were forced to open the doors without any form of soft opening.

Early on I had had the idea for the menu format of snacks / garden / sea / land / sweets, and I wrote the first menu. But that was as far as I got. I turned to Dean, Richie and Eoghann and explained that this was what I hoped to do. I talked them through the style and then I questioned them about how we should do it. They worked manically trying to figure out what I was trying to achieve while I struggled to get the build together. Together we pulled it off. And together is how we have approached every menu and every decision to this day.

The builders left at 5.30pm on opening day. With the smell of paint, glue and cement hanging in the air, we opened the doors of The Dairy on St Patrick's Day in 2013. We had a banging playlist, a killer menu, my amazing wife Sarah and Damiano (of Tutto wines' fame, who created our first wine list) front of house, us four cooks and an amazing KP (kitchen porter) named Depeche in the kitchen, and that was it. The cooks ran the food, and Sarah and Damiano worked the room.

Fast forward a few years and a couple more restaurants later, and we realised our dream with charcuterie room, a farm, a bread programme and a cellar filled with ferments, vinegars and miso, chutneys and jams. We are as close as you can get to being a farmhouse kitchen by the sea in almost central London, in ol' leafy Clapham Common.

**Robin Gill,**
2018

# THE LARDER

I am obsessed with forgotten traditions and the way we used to cook. My time spent in Italy, where the menu was scripted by the seasons and the produce harvested from Alfonso's farm, shook me and awakened my thirst – so much so that as I write this, we are in the process of opening our own Italian restaurant, Sorella. My years on the Amalfi Coast taught me the importance of working with the best of ingredients at their peak and preserving the excess. My restaurants are in an urban setting but my approach to cooking is an extreme version of this philosophy. We have urban gardens above the restaurants; we house beehives; our cellar is full of vinegars, miso, kimchi, charcuterie, kombucha, cordials, jams and chutneys.

Every inch of our old house is put to use with culinary experiments bubbling away. We have achieved great things from a central London location and I want to share my techniques to prove that a more traditional way of cooking is perfectly achievable in any home. The rewards and possibilities are endless. Vegetable fermentation, jam-making, pickling, curing and smoking meat and fish are but a few of the techniques that I want to share. You don't need a countryside location to stock a healthy larder, and this can be your secret weapon in creating some inspiring dishes.

# FERMENTED VEGETABLES, FRUITS AND HERBS

If you are new to this method of food preservation, I think vegetable fermentation is where you should start. It is the safest and simplest way to build up your confidence to explore the large universe of fermentation. I love the fact that you are working with something alive, and that no two batches will turn out the same. And the end product can be enjoyed fairly quickly.

It was John Lancaster, one of our regulars, who gave us a book called *The Art of Fermentation*, by Sandor Katz, because he knew we were keen to learn about fermenting and to experiment. We basically went on a fermentation rampage after that, then put our efforts out of reach and out of mind. A month later John popped in for lunch and suddenly we remembered the box of tricks we had put above the freezer. When we pulled it out and opened the jars, the smells and flavours were like nothing we'd had before. We knocked up a quick menu incorporating everything we had fermented and served it to John, hoping we wouldn't kill him (we didn't and he's still a regular). Little did he know what an impact that book would have on our approach to cooking. Now all of our cooks have a copy and use it as their go-to bible. Thank you, John.

The basic premise for vegetable and fruit fermentation is to tightly pack the chosen fruit or vegetable under a liquid to create an environment where oxygen-dependent mould and organisms cannot grow while encouraging and allowing acidifying bacteria to grow instead.

Apart from this basic principle the approach can be varied – the fermentation of fruit and vegetables has a long history, and methods and approaches have changed and developed over the years. There really is no right and wrong so long as the basic principle is observed.

In this section, I share how we approach vegetable fermentation in the kitchen at The Dairy, but that is not to say that this is the only way to do it. We have changed our own approach over the years by experimenting with different liquids, amounts of salt, methods, storage conditions and timings.

Because of this flexibility, vegetable fermentation is a good place to start if you are interested in experimenting with fermenting, in the conditions that you have available and with what works for your personal taste. The addition of spices and seasonings in these recipes is only a suggestion. Once you are comfortable with the basic principle of fermentation, you can really add whatever flavours you fancy. Ferments are pretty simple to create but can add an extra layer of flavour and balance to most dishes.

## WHEY

Whey is the liquid that separates from the solid curd as milk curdles. It is therefore a by-product of cheese-making, as well as of the production of yoghurts and other curds. The acidity of whey means that it can speed up the fermentation process.

In cheese-making, the whey is usually discarded but savvy chefs are bringing it into their kitchens and reaping the benefits. We use whey in our ferments – we have built up a strong relationship with our cheese suppliers and they are able to easily source whey for us from cheese producers. We find it to be a useful ingredient but it is not essential when fermenting at home.

Whey is growing in popularity but is still not readily available as a retail product. If you are lucky enough to live near a decent cheese shop or, even better, a cheese producer, then ask them for some and use it in your ferments. As consumers, the bigger the demand we make for something, the more likely it is to come into general circulation.

## SALT AND BRINES

One ingredient that we do rely on in our approach to fermenting is salt. It is salt that draws the naturally occurring water out of vegetables – in some recipes, such as fermented cabbage (see page 26), all that is needed is cabbage, salt and elbow grease. Salt also creates an environment that restricts the growth of some bacteria, giving lactic acid bacteria (the bacteria required here) a chance to grow. In addition salt is a natural preservative, so it is perfect for use with vegetables to prolong their shelf life.

For recipes where the ingredient is finely chopped, such as in the cabbage ferment recipe, then dry-salting is appropriate. For others where the ingredient is left whole or chopped into larger pieces, then a brine is needed. A brine is a mixture of salt and water.

The salt is added to the water and brought just to the boil to dissolve the salt, then allowed to cool before use.

We make brines of different strengths based on the amount of salt that is added. This is expressed as a percentage in relation to the amount of water. So, for example, a 2% brine means that the weight of salt added is 2% of the weight of the water. In other words, for a litre of water (which weighs 1kg) you would need to add 20g of salt.

## JARS AND EQUIPMENT

When fermenting vegetables or fruit, they need to be packed tightly into the chosen vessel as this will help eliminate oxygen. We use jars with a rubber seal such as Kilner jars at the restaurant. The ingredient is packed tightly into the jar and then any gaps are filled with liquid, which may be liquid that has naturally emerged through salting, or whey, brine or other liquid. The reason the jars have a rubber seal is so that any $CO_2$ can escape. If you are using airtight jars, it's a good idea to open them regularly during the fermentation process to allow $CO_2$ to escape and thus avoid cracked jars!

For vegetable ferments, we find the 2-litre Kilner jars with rubber seals the most useful. The 500ml jars come in handy for smaller ingredients such as herbs. Having said that, you may find some of the recipes a little large for a home kitchen, so do scale them down as you wish. For some ferments, it may be necessary to weigh down the ingredients in the jar so they stay submerged under the liquid. Lots of different things could be used, such as a large cabbage leaf, a plastic lid that fits snugly in the jar or a sealed bag of water (we use a vacuum pack bag filled with water).

One thing to note, it is important to sterilise jars and equipment and to wear clean rubber or plastic gloves when handling the ingredients. This is to avoid the introduction of any unwanted bacteria. It is especially important during the fermentation process when you are tasting the ferment to see if it is ready. Use a sterilised spoon here (simply dip the spoon into boiling water) rather than dipping dirty cutlery or hands into the jar.

## TIMING AND STORAGE

There is no right or wrong way to store ferments. Some people ferment in warm, bright locations while others insist that a cool, dark environment is best. Temperature will, of course, affect the time the fermentation takes. We store our jars at a slightly warm temperature, in a kitchen environment for example, but away from direct sunlight, as we find this works best for us.

One question that constantly comes up is how long it will take. This really is a 'how long is a piece of string?' scenario. Firstly, so many factors affect the fermentation process: the vegetable or fruit itself, the temperature, the amount of salt present, and whether you are using water as the main liquid or a more acidic substance such as whey. Secondly, personal taste also comes into play – some people prefer a lighter ferment with only a slightly acidic taste while others like a really strong and acidic punch. The best advice that I can give is to taste your ferment along the way (with a sterilised spoon). Once the vegetable or fruit breaks down slightly and there is a slightly acidic flavour, then it really is up to you when you want to use it and how much more you wish it to ferment. Fermented vegetables should taste sour not salty.

The fermentation times in these recipes are only a guideline and they fall in line with the conditions available at The Dairy. One useful tip when it comes to fermenting is to set reminders on your phone to check the jars. When you have a few ferments on the go, it is easy to forget what needs to be checked when.

When the ferment is to your taste and ready to use, it can be moved to the fridge to slow the fermentation process right down. There it can be stored unopened for up to 3 months. Once the jar has been opened, it is recommended that the ferment is used within 1 month. This applies to most of our fermented vegetables and fruits unless otherwise specified in a recipe.

## FERMENTED APPLES

**makes about 900g**

10 Granny Smith
    apples, quartered
1 litre whey
    or 500ml water
    mixed with
    500ml fresh
    apple juice)

Pack the apples into a
sterilised 2-litre Kilner jar.
Cover with whey or the
water/juice mixture and seal.
Leave to ferment at a warm
room temperature for 4
days; keep away from direct
sunlight.

When ready, the sealed jar
can be stored in the fridge
for up to 3 months. Once
opened, use within 1 month.

## FERMENTED APPLE JUICE

**makes about
780ml**

10 Granny Smith
    apples, quartered
1 litre whey (or a
    mixture of 500ml
    fresh apple
    juice and 500ml
    filtered water)

Place the apples in a
sterilised 2-litre Kilner jar,
cover with the whey (or
apple juice and water) and
seal. Leave in a warm area
of your kitchen, away from
direct sunlight, for 4 days.

Remove the apples from the
jar, draining off the whey.
(The whey can be used
again two or three times,
then discarded.) Juice the
apples in an electric juicer/
press.

The juice can be kept in
the fridge in a sealed bottle
for up to a week or it can
be frozen.

## FERMENTED ARTICHOKE

The malt barley can be purchased online from home brewing/beer brewing
companies. If not easy to source it can be omitted.

**makes about 1.5kg**

50g malt barley (optional)
1.5kg Jerusalem artichokes,
    washed and cut in half
500ml wheat beer
fine table salt

If using the malt barley, lightly toast it in a dry pan for 1–2 minutes until
slightly darkened.

Place a sterilised 2-litre Kilner jar on a kitchen scale and turn the scales
back to zero. Pack the artichokes and barley (if using) into the jar and
cover with the beer. Top up with filtered water if needed so that the
artichokes are fully submerged. Based on the weight of the contents of
the jar, calculate 2% salt. Add this, then seal the jar.

Leave to ferment at a warm room temperature for about 2 weeks; keep
away from direct sunlight. When ready, the artichokes will be slightly
softened and sour.

Store in the fridge for up to 3 months. Once opened, use within 1 month.

## POTATO FERMENT

**makes about 2kg**

2kg new/young
potatoes
250ml whey
(optional)
fine table salt

If the potatoes are small
leave them whole; cut larger
potatoes in half or into
uniform pieces. Simmer the
potatoes in whey or water
until cooked and can be
easily pierced with a knife.
Drain and allow to cool.

Set a 2-litre Kilner jar on
a set of scales and return
the scales to zero. Pack
the potatoes into the jar
and pour in the whey (if
using). Top up with water to
cover. Based on the weight
of the contents of the jar,
calculate 2% salt. Add this
to the jar. Seal the jar and
leave to ferment at a warm
room temperature for 14
days; keep away from direct
sunlight.

When ready, the sealed jar
can be stored in the fridge
for up to 3 months. Once
opened, use within 1 month.

## NETTLE FERMENT

**makes about 1kg**

1kg nettles, leaves
picked and
washed
330ml beer with
a strong hoppy
flavour
fine table salt

Place a 1-litre Kilner jar on
a set of scales and return
the scales to zero. Add the
nettles and beer to the jar
and top up with water to
cover. Based on the weight
of the contents of the jar,
calculate 2% salt. Add this to
the jar.

Seal the jar and leave to
ferment at a warm room
temperature for 10 days;
keep away from direct
sunlight. When ready, the
sealed jar can be stored in
the fridge for up to 3 months.
Once opened, use within
1 month.

## FERMENTED SORREL

**makes about 500g**

500g sorrel
1.8 litres 2% brine
(see page 20)

Pack the sorrel into a
sterilised 2-litre Kilner jar
and cover with the 2% brine.
Seal the jar and leave at a
warm room temperature
to ferment for 5 days; keep
away from direct sunlight.

When ready, the sealed jar
can be stored in the fridge
for up to 3 months. Once
opened, use within 1 month.

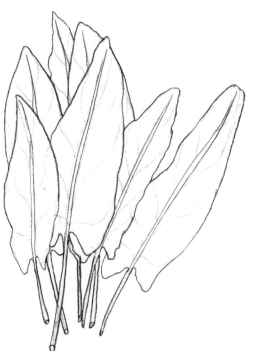

# FERMENTED BARLEY

**makes about 300g**

200g pearl barley
600ml filtered
water

Place the barley in a suitable-sized sterilised container and pour the water over the grains. Stir with a clean sterilised spoon, then cover the container with muslin. Keep in a warm part of the kitchen and allow to ferment for 4 days.

The barley is now ready to use. It can be stored, in the liquid, in an airtight container in the fridge for up to 5 days.

# FERMENTED CAVOLO NERO STALKS

**makes 800g–1kg**

cavolo nero stalks
    from approx. 5kg
    cavolo nero
about 1.5 litres
    3% brine (see
    page 20)

Pack the cavolo nero stalks into a sterilised 2-litre Kilner jar and cover with the 3% brine so that they are completely submerged.

Seal the jar and leave at a warm room temperature to ferment for 3–4 weeks; keep away from direct sunlight. The stalks are ready when they have softened slightly and taste sour.

The sealed jar can be stored in the fridge for up to 3 months. Once opened, use within 1 month.

# FERMENTED BEETROOT

**makes 2kg**

3kg raw beetroot,
    peeled and
    quartered
whey (optional)
fine table salt

Juice a third of the beetroot. Place a 2-litre Kilner jar on a kitchen scale and return the scales to zero. Add the remaining quartered beetroot to the jar and pour in the beetroot juice. Top up with a mixture of whey and water or just water. Calculate 2% of the weight of the contents of the jar and add this amount of salt to the jar. Seal the jar.

Leave to ferment at a warm room temperature for about 3 weeks; keep away from direct sunlight. Once ready, the beetroot will be slightly softened and sour. The sealed jar can be stored in the fridge for up to 3 months. Once opened, use within 1 month.

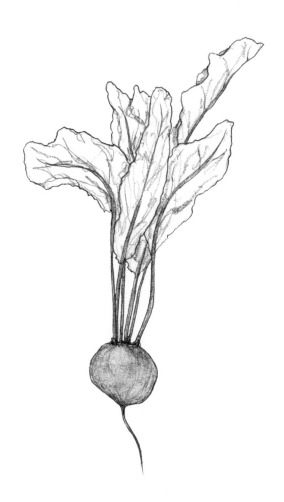

# FERMENTED DULSE

**makes 500g**

500g fresh
   dulse, washed
   really well
whey (optional)
fine table salt

Place a 500ml Kilner jar on a set of scales and return the scales to zero. Add the dulse to the jar and cover with a mixture of equal parts whey and water or just water. Calculate 2% of the weight of the contents of the jar and add this amount of salt to the jar.

Seal the jar and leave the dulse to ferment at a warm room temperature for at least 1 month; keep away from direct sunlight. The ferment is ready once the dulse has taken on strong sour and savoury notes similar to anchovies and Parmesan. When ready, the sealed jar can be stored in the fridge for up to 3 months. Once opened, use within 1 month.

# KALE FERMENT

**makes about 1kg**

1kg kale (leaves
   only), washed
   well
330ml beer with
   strong hoppy
   flavours
fine table salt

Set a 1-litre Kilner jar on a set of scales and return the scales to zero. Pack the kale into the jar and pour in the beer. Top up with water to cover the leaves. Based on the weight of the contents of the jar, calculate 2% salt. Add this to the jar.

Seal the jar and leave to ferment at a warm room temperature for 10 days; keep away from direct sunlight. When ready, the sealed jar can be stored in the fridge for up to 3 months. Once opened, use within 1 month.

# JANUARY KING FERMENT

**makes 2kg**

2 tablespoons yellow mustard seeds
1 teaspoon cumin seeds
2kg January King cabbage, quartered
3 garlic cloves, sliced
10 black peppercorns
whey (optional)
fine table salt

Toast the mustard and cumin seeds in a small dry pan until they smell aromatic.

Set a 2-litre Kilner jar on a kitchen scale and return the scales to zero. Pack the cabbage quarters, garlic, mustard seeds, cumin seeds and peppercorns into the jar and cover with a mixture of equal parts whey and water or just water. Based on the weight of the contents of the jar, calculate 2% salt. Add this to the jar.

Seal the jar and leave to ferment at a warm room temperature for 10–14 days; keep away from direct sunlight. The ferment is ready when the cabbage has taken on a sour flavour.

When ready, the sealed jar can be stored in the fridge for up to 3 months. Once opened, use within 1 month.

# CABBAGE FERMENT

**makes 900g–1kg**

1 white cabbage
fine table salt
black peppercorns
caraway seeds

Remove any tough or discoloured outer leaves from the cabbage. Cut it vertically in half, through the core, then slice thinly. Set an empty bowl on a kitchen scale and turn the scales back to zero. Put the cabbage into the bowl. Based on the weight of the cabbage, calculate 2% salt, 0.35% black peppercorns and 0.5% caraway seeds. Add these seasonings to the cabbage and stir the mixture vigorously with your hands. Set aside for 30 minutes until lots of liquid has been released, occasionally stirring with your hands.

Pack the cabbage tightly into a 2-litre Kilner jar and cover with the liquid that was released. Seal the jar and leave to ferment at a warm room temperature for 5 days; keep away from direct sunlight. The ferment is ready once the cabbage has broken down slightly in texture but still retains a bite, similar to a cooked texture. It should taste sour not salty.

The sealed jar can be stored in the fridge for up to 3 months. Once opened, use within 1 month.

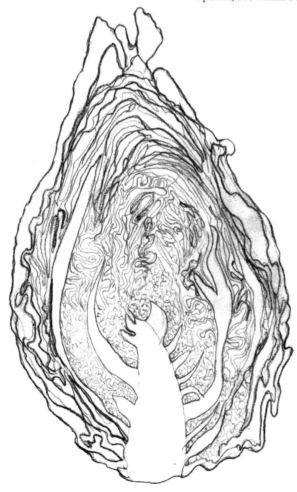

## SALSIFY FERMENT

**makes about 1.5kg**

1.5kg salsify,
    peeled
beer
fine table salt

Place a 2-litre Kilner jar on a set of scales and return the scales to zero. Add the salsify to the jar and top up with enough beer to cover. Calculate 2% of the weight of the contents of the jar and add this amount of salt to the jar.

Seal the jar and leave the salsify to ferment at a warm room temperature for about 14 days; keep away from direct sunlight. The ferment is ready once the salsify has broken down slightly in texture but still retains a bite, similar to a cooked texture. It should taste sour not salty.

When ready, the sealed jar can be stored in the fridge for up to 3 months. Once opened, use within 1 month.

## SLOE FERMENT

**makes about 1kg**

1kg sloes
30g fine table salt

Mix the sloes with the salt in a large bowl. Set aside for 1 hour so they release liquid.

Decant the contents of the bowl into a 1-litre Kilner jar. Weigh down the sloes so that they are submerged under the liquid, then seal the jar. Leave to ferment at a warm room temperature for 10 days; keep away from direct sunlight. The sloes will completely soften and break down.

Push the sloe pulp through a drum sieve; discard any stones. Mix the pulp with the liquid that was released from the sloes. Decant the mixture into a sterilised jar and seal. Store in the fridge for up to 3 months. Once opened, use within 1 month.

## SWISS CHARD FERMENT

**makes about 2kg**

2kg Swiss chard, washed
3 garlic cloves, sliced
15 black peppercorns
whey (optional)
fine table salt

Roughly chop the chard stalks; keep the leaves whole. Place a 2-litre Kilner jar on a set of scales and return the scales to zero. Add the chard, garlic and peppercorns to the jar and cover with a mixture of equal parts whey and water or just water. Calculate 2% of the weight of the contents of the jar and add this amount of salt to the jar.

Seal the jar and leave to ferment at a warm room temperature for 10–14 days; keep away from direct sunlight. The ferment is ready once the chard has taken on a sour flavour. When ready, the sealed jar can be stored in the fridge for up to 3 months. Once opened, use within 1 month.

# KIMCHI

**makes about 1.8kg**

2 Chinese cabbages (we use wong bok),
  thinly sliced
½ carrot, peeled and grated
2 garlic cloves, sliced
1 spring onion, sliced
15g root ginger, grated
fine table salt
caster sugar
fish sauce
light soy sauce
shrimp paste
Korean chilli powder

Set a large mixing bowl on a set of scales and return the scales to zero. Mix together the cabbages, carrot, garlic, spring onion and ginger in the bowl. Based on the weight of the contents of the bowl, calculate 2% salt. Add this to the bowl. Stir the mixture vigorously with your hands. Set aside for about 1 hour, occasionally mixing vigorously as before, until lots of liquid has been released.

Calculating from the weight of the mixture in the bowl, in a separate bowl weigh out 4% caster sugar, 2% fish sauce, 2% light soy sauce, 2% shrimp paste and 3% Korean chilli powder. Mix these ingredients together to form a paste, then mix the paste into the cabbage mixture.

Pack the mixture tightly into a 2-litre Kilner jar, with all the liquid that was released. Seal the jar and leave to ferment at a warm room temperature for about 3 weeks; keep away from direct sunlight.

When ready, the sealed jar can be stored in the fridge for up to 3 months. Once opened, use within 1 month.

# VEGAN KIMCHI

This is a spicy kimchi! If you can't handle the heat, reduce the amount of chillies.

**makes 900g**

10 green chillies
2 sweetheart cabbages (if unavailable,
  other cabbages can be used)
2 cinnamon sticks
2 star anise
20g Szechuan peppercorns
fine table salt

Char the chillies on a hot barbecue or ridged grill pan until completely blackened on all sides.

Cut the cabbages into wedges. Place an empty 2-litre Kilner jar on a set of scales and return the scales to zero. Pack the cabbage into the jar with the cinnamon sticks, star anise, peppercorns and charred chillies. Cover with water. Based on the weight of the contents of the jar, calculate 3% salt. Add this to the jar. Seal the jar.

Leave to ferment at a warm room temperature for about 3 weeks; keep away from direct sunlight. When ready, the sealed jar can be stored in the fridge for up to 3 months. Once opened, use within 1 month.

# FENNEL KIMCHI

**makes about 1.8kg**

40g fennel seeds
40g black peppercorns
10g pink peppercorns
30g cumin seeds
6 bulbs of fennel
about 300ml fresh apple juice
about 300ml whey or filtered water
fine table salt
4 garlic cloves, sliced
12 star anise

Toast the fennel seeds, peppercorns and cumin seeds in a dry pan, then grind in a mortar and pestle or spice grinder to a powder.

Trim the fennel bulbs and remove the outer layer. Using an electric juicer, juice these outer layers and the trimmings along with one whole fennel bulb (alternatively you can blend the fennel in a blender or food processor until as liquid as possible, then strain through a fine sieve into a bowl). Measure the fennel juice and mix it with an equal amount of apple juice and an equal amount of whey or water.

Set an empty 2-litre Kilner jar on a set of kitchen scales and turn it back to zero. Cut the remaining 5 fennel bulbs into 1cm slices and pack into the jar. Add the juice and whey/water mixture and top up with water to cover. Based on the weight of the contents of the jar, calculate 2% salt. Add this along with the garlic, star anise and ground spices.

Seal the jar and set aside at room temperature, away from direct sunlight. The kimchi will take 2–3 weeks to ferment (it can be left to ferment for up to 2 months; the flavour will only improve). Give the jar a shake each day for the first few days.

The kimchi is ready when the fennel has softened slightly but retains a little bite and has a sour taste. Store in the fridge for 3 months. Once opened, use within a month.

# PRESERVED AMALFI LEMONS

**makes 12**

12 Amalfi lemons
coarse sea salt
fresh lemon juice (if required)

Cut each lemon into quarters lengthways but leave a couple of centimetres uncut at one end so that the quarters remain attached. Pack gaps between the quarters with salt. Pack the lemons tightly into a sterilised 2-litre Kilner jar. Fill any gaps in the jar with more salt until the lemons are completely covered. Seal the jar. Leave at room temperature, out of direct sunlight – a garage/cellar would be ideal but a store cupboard will suffice.

Juice will start to be released after 1–2 days of the preserving process, which will dissolve the salt. If the lemons become exposed, top up the jar with fresh lemon juice. Preserving time is dependent on many factors including temperature, but it will take at least 3 weeks. Turn the jar occasionally during the process to disperse the salt and juice. The lemons are ready once the peel has softened. After this, they can be stored in the fridge for up to 9 months.

# SOUR ONIONS

**makes about 1.2–1.4kg**

10–12 Roscoff
    onions, quartered
whey or filtered
    water
fine table salt

Place an empty sterilised 2-litre Kilner jar on a set of kitchen scales and turn the scales back to zero. Pack the onions into the jar and cover with whey or water so that the onions are completely submerged. Based on the weight of the contents of the jar, calculate 2% salt and add it.

Seal the jar and leave at warm room temperature to ferment for about 1 month; keep out of direct sunlight. The onions will be ready when they have started to break down a little and are sharp and acidic in taste.

The sealed jar can be stored in the fridge for up to 3 months. Once opened, use within 1 month.

# MEAT, FISH AND GAME PRESERVATION

I consider being a chef no different to being a carpenter. We both have tools and we both build and create. The only difference is that my creations are eaten moments after completion. Chefs are craftsmen, and there are many different types of craft within the cooking world. One of these is ancient and yet still so relevant: the art of curing meats. You need butchery skills as well as patience and an understanding of how and why the process works.

At the Basque restaurant Asador Etxebarri I had one of the most beautiful, eye-opening experiences of my career – just by having dinner there. Everything was primitive; everything was cooked over coal and wood, with a delicate touch using ingredients taken from the surrounding Basque hills. It all blew me away with its honesty. But the one thing I will never forget is Victor's chorizo. It was soft and slightly smoky, with a subtle kick of chilli and smoked paprika, and an intense acidity reminiscent of lemons from Amalfi. We have all tried the mass-produced 'chorizo' in supermarkets worldwide so I did not expect for this to have such an impact on me. The difference was unbelievable. From that moment I made it my mission to learn the craft of meat preservation.

Over the past three years at The Dairy we have been experimenting and improving. We are blessed with a cellar with naturally perfect conditions, which means we need to work less hard for a better product, but we are still learning every time we make a new batch. You should not be afraid to try it yourself. The process of curing meat is simple although it needs time, patience and love. I can honestly say it is one of the most rewarding and satisfying crafts to learn. The moment you cut into your creation, your gleaming pride will be difficult to hide!

You need to take great care with meat and fish preservation and follow instructions to the letter, because it is a little more fragile than the fermentation and preserving of fruit and vegetables. There is a slightly higher risk of it not working out due to the nature of meat and fish. I am in no way trying to put you off but it is worth doing some research in advance. There are many useful books and online resources on the topic. Below is a basic introduction to our approach at The Dairy, which outlines some exact conditions that need to be adhered to.

In vegetable preservation, the goal is often to remove any oxygen present so that certain types of moulds and organisms could not grow. Similarly, in meat and fish preservation, moisture is removed to deprive these organisms of the water that they need to survive. We use a mixture of methods to remove the moisture: dry-curing, salting and smoking.

## DRY-CURING/MAKING CHARCUTERIE AT HOME

There are some useful tips and pieces of equipment to consider if you fancy giving dry-curing a try in your kitchen.

1. For some recipes, you will be required to mince or grind the meat. For occasional use, the mincer attachment on a stand mixer will be perfectly acceptable.

2. One of the key points to remember for dry-curing is the environment that needs to be created for the hanging period. These three conditions are key:
   - a temperature of 15–18°C
   - 60–70 per cent humidity
   - air circulation

   There are no small domestic appliances on the market currently for dry-curing meat so you would need to create this environment in another way. There are many creative tutorials and videos online showing multiple ideas for this. For example, a drying chamber could be created in an old mini fridge or wine fridge set to a high temperature of somewhere between 15–18°C (the fridge would need to have a fan to keep the air circulating). To create the correct humidity, you could simply place a pan of heavily salted water in the bottom of the fridge. There are, of course, plenty of other creative ways to create this environment. So long as all three conditions are adhered to, then dry-curing at home is achievable.

3. Regarding the storage of charcuterie, over time any exposed surfaces will dry out and become less pleasant to eat. So once it is ready, wrap the charcuterie in greaseproof paper, then cover well in clingfilm and keep in the fridge. If

wrapped well, most dry-cured meat can be kept for up to 5 months, but use your discretion when it comes to shelf life. Look out for telltale signs: if at any stage it has dried out too much and is an unpleasant texture as a result, or if there is a rancid or bitter scent or flavour, it is best not to keep it.

4. As some of our recipes make a large quantity, it is always a nice idea to share the end result with family and friends. You'll prove popular, I promise!

## SMOKING

Some of our recipes require smoking, which is achievable in a home environment. Cold-smoking takes place at a temperature of 32°C or lower, which means that the meat or fish is smoked but not cooked. Therefore, there cannot be a heat source underneath it. The heat required for the smoke needs to be separate and away from the meat or fish, which must be enclosed in a chamber that can then be filled with smoke.

If the meat or fish only needs to be cold-smoked for a few minutes, this can be achieved quite simply: spread woodchips in a flat tray such as a deep roasting tray and place a flat steamer rack over the chips. Warm the tray over a medium heat until the chips start to smoke. Remove from the heat and place the fish or meat to be smoked on the steaming rack. Completely cover the top and sides tightly with oven-safe clingfilm so the smoke is sealed inside with the fish or meat and leave to smoke for the required time.

If you want to cold-smoke for a longer time, you need to create a smoking chamber. There are plenty of creative ways to do this – again, there are some informative tutorials online – but the basic premise

is that the heat source is separate from the chamber and the smoke is fed between the two with a tube.

Other recipes require hot-smoking, which is smoking that takes place at a temperature of up to 93°C. So that the meat is both smoked and gently cooked at the same time. Reasonably priced stovetop and outdoor smokers are available from many online sources.

## SALTING

Salting is often used in the preservation of fish but also can apply to meat, especially offal, as it too works to draw out moisture through osmosis while also acting as a preservative itself. The ingredient is packed in salt, or a mixture made mostly of salt, and allowed to cure. After the curing, the ingredient could be smoked to dry it out even further or it could be stored in oil.

# FENNEL SALAMI

**makes about 2kg**

3kg boneless pork shoulder,
    trimmed and diced
300g hog casing

**1ST STAGE CURE**
15g pink curing salt
150g Maldon sea salt flakes
30g dextrose

**2ND STAGE CURE**
½ bulb of garlic, cloves peeled
50ml olive oil
300ml white wine
30g fennel seeds
5g dried chilli flakes

To make the 1st stage cure, mix the salts and dextrose. Toss the meat with this mixture in a freezer bag and seal. Leave to cure in the fridge for 48 hours.

For the 2nd stage cure, cook the garlic in the olive oil until soft. Boil the wine in a pan until reduced by half; cool. Put the garlic, olive oil and wine into a blender or food processor and blend until smooth. Toast the fennel seeds in a dry pan until fragrant, then grind finely to a powder. Stir the fennel seeds and chilli into the garlic and oil mix.

Drain any excess liquid from the pork, then pass the meat through a mincer attachment. Mix the 2nd stage cure paste through the mince.

Tie off one end of the hog casing. Pipe the meat into the hog casing to make sausages approximately 300g in weight and tie off the ends. Weigh the sausages. Hang them in a suitable place – at 15–18°C with 60–70% humidity and a good airflow (see page 31) – until they lose 30% of their original weight. This usually takes about 3 weeks.

Once ready, wrap the sausages in clingfilm or place in a dry airtight container. Store in the fridge and slice as needed. (See page 31 for guidance on storage.)

# GOOSE HAM

**makes 2 (cuts into about 60 slices)**

2 boneless goose breasts (skin on)
Maldon sea salt flakes
caster sugar
pink curing salt
10 black peppercorns
2 star anise
a pinch of dried chilli flakes
2 garlic cloves, crushed
3 sprigs of thyme, leaves picked

Weigh the goose breasts (together), then calculate the seasonings: you want 2.25% sea salt, 1.5% caster sugar and 0.5% pink curing salt.

Toast the peppercorns and star anise in a dry pan until fragrant, then crush quite finely. Mix with the sea salt, sugar, curing salt, chilli flakes, garlic and thyme leaves. Distribute the seasonings evenly over the goose breasts and rub in on both sides. Place the breasts in freezer bags and seal well. Leave to cure in the fridge for 7 days, turning the bags over every 2 days.

Remove the goose breasts from the bags, rinse and pat dry. Wrap them in muslin and tie the ends. Weigh each breast. Hang in a suitable place – at 15–18°C and with 60–70% humidity and a good airflow (see page 31) – until the meat loses 30% of its original weight. This usually takes about 3 weeks.

Once ready, wrap the goose hams in clingfilm or place in a dry airtight container. Store in the fridge and slice as needed. (See page 31 for guidance on storage.)

# BRESAOLA

**makes about 1.3kg**

1.2kg coarse sea salt
800g demerara sugar
1 x 2kg silverside beef joint, sinew removed
red wine

Mix together the salt and sugar. Pack the beef in the salt mixture in an airtight container so that the meat is completely surrounded by salt and sugar. Cover the container tightly and leave in the fridge for 6 days, turning the beef each day.

Remove the beef from the sugar and salt mixture, rinse and place in a clean, snug-fitting airtight container. Cover with red wine and seal. Leave in the fridge for 3 days.

Remove the beef from the wine and weigh it. Wrap it in muslin and hang it in a suitable place – 15–18°C with 60–70% humidity and a good airflow (see page 31) – until it loses 30% of its original weight. This will take 10–14 days.

Once ready, keep the beef, well wrapped, in the fridge and cut thin slices as required. It can be stored in the fridge for up to 5 months. (See page 31 for guidance on storage.)

# COPPA

**makes about 1.5kg (cuts into 500 slices)**

rock salt
1 pork coppa joint (comprising neck,
   shoulder and loin)
15 black peppercorns
15g fennel seeds
5g smoked paprika

Rub lots of salt evenly all over the coppa, then place it in a freezer bag and seal tightly. Place on a rimmed tray and set another heavy tray over the coppa with some weights on top. Place in the fridge and leave to cure, allowing 1 day per kilo weight of meat. Turn the coppa every day to help distribute the salt.

Remove the coppa from the bag and rinse off the salt in cold water. Pat dry. Toast the peppercorns and fennel seeds in a dry pan until they smell fragrant. Crush these coarsely and mix with the paprika. Dust the spices evenly over the meat.

Wrap the coppa in muslin and tie it with butcher's twine to form a nice round shape. Weigh it, then hang in a suitable place to dry – 15–18°C, with 60–70% humidity and a good airflow (see page 31) – until the meat loses 30% of its original weight. This usually takes 3–4 weeks.

Once ready, wrap the coppa in clingfilm or place in a dry airtight container. Store in the fridge for up to 5 months and slice as needed. (See page 31 for guidance on storage.)

# LOMO

**makes about 1.3kg**

1 x 2kg boned rack of pork
Maldon sea salt
white wine
espelette pepper

Remove the skin and most of the fat from the pork, leaving just a thin cap of fat over the meat. Weigh the trimmed meat. Roll it in coarse sea salt so it is completely covered, then place it in a sealable bag and seal. Place a weight on top of the bag and leave it in the fridge for 24 hours per kilo.

Rinse off the salt and place the pork on a plate. Put it back into the fridge, uncovered, and leave for 24 hours.

Weigh the meat again. Brush all over with white wine, then roll in espelette pepper to coat. Wrap the meat in muslin and hang it in a suitable place – at 15–18°C with 60–70% humidity and a good airflow (see page 31) – until it loses 30% of its original weight.

Keep, well wrapped, in the fridge and cut into thin slices as required. The lomo can be stored in the fridge for up to 5 months. (See page 31 for guidance on storage.)

# NDUJA

**makes about 2.5kg**

2kg skinless fresh pork belly, cut into
    large dice
250g hot paprika
150g smoked sweet paprika
50g Maldon sea salt
5g dextrose
5g pink curing salt
10g Bactoferm (or other live starter culture)
2 tablespoons distilled water
300g hog casing, soaked in tepid water for
    at least 20 minutes and rinsed

Partially freeze the pork belly, then pass it through a fine mincer twice. Put it into the bowl of a stand mixer and add the hot and sweet paprika, salt, dextrose and curing salt. Mix on a medium speed for 1 minute. Dissolve the starter culture in the distilled water, add it to the meat and mix until well distributed.

Tie off one end of the hog casing. Stuff the mixture into the casing and tie off into 12cm sausages. Hang the sausages for 24 hours at room temperature.

Cold-smoke the sausages for 4 hours (see page 32).

Hang the sausages in a suitable place – at 15–18°C with 60–70% humidity and a good airflow (see page 31) – for 1 week. After this, the nduja can be kept, well wrapped, in the fridge for up to a month and used as required.

# PANCETTA

**makes about 1.3kg**

1 skinless fresh pork belly (about 2kg)
Maldon sea salt
white wine
cracked black pepper
dried thyme

Weigh the meat. Roll it in coarse sea salt so it is completely covered, then place it in a sealable bag and seal. Place a weight on top of the bag and leave it in the fridge for 24 hours per kilo.

Rinse off the salt and place the pork on a plate. Put it back into the fridge, uncovered, and leave for 24 hours.

Weigh the meat again. Brush all over with white wine, then roll it in black pepper and thyme to coat. Wrap the meat in muslin and hang it in a suitable place – at 15–18°C with 60–70% humidity and a good airflow (see page 31) – until it loses 30% of its original weight.

Keep, well wrapped, in the fridge and cut into thin slices as required. The pancetta can be stored in the fridge for up to 5 months. (See page 31 for guidance on storage.)

# SMOKED BONE MARROW

The amount of bone marrow you will get from marrow bones will be about 10 per cent of the weight of the bones. If you need 50g bone marrow, for example, you need to start with about 500g marrow bones.

**yield will depend on how many marrow bones you begin with (see introduction)**

marrow bones (ask your butcher to split the bones down the middle)
7% brine (see page 20)
applewood chips
Maldon sea salt and freshly ground black pepper

Soak the bones in cold water for 5 hours to soften the marrow before scooping out. Place the marrow in the 7% brine and leave for 5 hours in the fridge. Remove from the brine.

Preheat the oven to 120°C fan/140°C/Gas Mark 1.

Take a tray with a steam insert (such as a deep roasting tray that will hold a flat steaming rack) and spread applewood chips over the bottom of the tray. Warm it over a medium heat until the chips start to smoke. Remove from the heat. Place the marrow on a heatproof tray in the steam insert and completely cover the top and sides tightly with oven-safe clingfilm so the smoke is sealed inside with the marrow. Leave to smoke for 10 minutes.

Uncover the smoked marrow and place it on its heatproof tray in the oven. Roast the smoked bone marrow for 10 minutes. Transfer to a blender or food processor and blend until smooth. Season with salt and pepper.

The bone marrow can be used straight away, or kept in the fridge for 1–2 days or frozen.

# WILD GARLIC AND SUNFLOWER SALAMI

**makes about 2kg**

3kg boneless pork shoulder, trimmed
    and diced
300g hog casing (for casing the sausages)

**1ST STAGE CURE**
15g pink curing salt
150g fine table salt
30g dextrose

**2ND STAGE CURE**
600g wild garlic leaves
120g sunflower seeds
300ml white wine

To make the 1st stage cure, mix the salts and dextrose. Toss the meat with this mixture in a freezer bag and seal. Leave to cure in the fridge for 48 hours.

Meanwhile, for the 2nd stage cure, dry the wild garlic leaves in a dehydrator, or oven at its lowest setting, until completely dry – this will take 2–3 hours. Once dried, blend to a powder. Gently simmer the sunflower seeds in the white wine until the liquid has evaporated and the seeds have softened; allow to cool.

Drain off any excess liquid from the pork. Pass the meat through a mincer attachment. Fold the wild garlic powder and sunflower seeds through the minced meat.

Tie off one end of the hog casing. Pipe the meat into the casing to make sausages approximately 300g in weight and tie off the ends. Weigh the sausages. Hang them in a suitable place – at 15–18°C with 60–70% humidity and a good airflow (see page 31) – until they lose 30% of their original weight. This usually takes about 3 weeks.

Once ready, tightly wrap the salami in clingfilm or place in a dry airtight container. Store in the fridge and slice as needed. (See page 31 for guidance on storage.)

# BOTTARGA

Bottarga is dried cod's roe that is used to season dishes. While it can be purchased from fine Italian delicatessens, this can work out to be quite expensive. We decided to make our own at the restaurant as cod's roe is so often thrown away. Bottarga is an amazing way to use this often discarded ingredient. It is possible to make bottarga at home but you will need to be able to create the correct conditions for the hanging process. Some notes on how to create these conditions can be found on page 31. If you are unable to make your own bottarga, or to source it, then anything with a deep savoury note can be used instead to season dishes – bonito flakes, for example, would be a suitable alternative.

**makes 30–40% of the weight of the cod's
roe you start with**

1.5 litres water
450g rock salt
500g–1kg cod's roe

Bring the water and salt to the boil and simmer until the salt has dissolved into the water. Pour into a bowl and allow to cool completely (this is a 30% brine). Submerge the roe in the brine, place in the fridge and leave for 2 hours.

Remove the roe from the brine and gently place it on a wire rack set over a tray near the fan in your fridge. Leave for 7 days to dry out. Carefully wrap the roe in muslin and hang in a suitable drying chamber – 15–18°C with 60–70% humidity and a good airflow (see page 31) – for 2–3 weeks.

Once ready, the bottarga can be kept in an airtight container in the fridge for up to 6 months and shaved off bit by bit for use. (See page 31 for guidance on storage.)

# CURED SALMON

The salmon can be cured in this manner and used as is, or it can then be smoked to add extra depth to the flavour.

**makes about 1.5kg**

40g fennel seeds
40g black peppercorns
40g juniper berries
800g fine table salt
160g caster sugar
160g demerara sugar
280g soft brown sugar
zest of 8 lemons
16 sheets of dried nori (3g each), cut into small pieces with scissors
1 side of salmon, pin-boned and skinned
applewood chips, for smoking

Lightly toast the fennel seeds, peppercorns and juniper berries in a dry pan until they smell fragrant. Crush them lightly in a pestle and mortar. Combine the crushed spices with all the other ingredients, apart from the salmon and applewood chips, in a bowl and mix thoroughly.

Lay a double layer of clingfilm, roughly four times the width of the salmon, across a worktop. Spread half of the spice cure evenly over the clingfilm, following the outline of the fish. Place the salmon on this and scatter the remaining cure over the top. Wrap the clingfilm around the fish, sealing in the cure. Set in a suitable-sized tray and leave in the fridge for 4 days, turning the fish over every 24 hours.

Unwrap the fish, rinse under cold water and pat dry. This cured salmon can be kept in the fridge, wrapped well in clingfilm, for up to 3 weeks.

To lightly smoke the salmon for dishes such as Loch Duart Salmon (see page 182): spread some applewood chips over the bottom of a large, deep roasting tray. Warm the tray over a medium heat until the chips start to smoke. Place the fish on a heatproof tray set on a flat steamer rack. Remove the roasting tray from the heat. Place the steamer rack directly over the smoking chips. Completely cover the top and sides tightly with oven-safe clingfilm so the smoke is sealed inside with the fish, then leave to smoke lightly for 7 minutes.

To fully smoke the salmon, it would need to be placed in a smoking chamber (see page 32) for 7 hours.

Once smoked, store the salmon, wrapped well in clingfilm, in the fridge.

# CURED SARDINES

These will keep in the fridge in a sealed jar, covered in olive oil, for up to a year so it is worth making a big batch starting with at least 1kg of sardines. They can be used in a very similar way to anchovies in the seasoning of dishes.

**makes about 700g**

20g fennel seeds
150g parsley (leaves and stalks)
zest of 2 lemons
3 garlic cloves (peeled)
200g coarse salt
1kg sardines, heads removed and gutted
olive oil (for storage)

Toast the fennel seeds in a dry pan until fragrant. Tip into a blender or food processor and add the parsley, lemon zest and garlic cloves. Blend together to make a coarse paste. Add the salt and blend again.

Spread some of the paste over the bottom of a clean container, then layer up the sardines and the remaining paste so that the fish are completely covered. Cover with an airtight lid and leave to cure in the fridge for 5 days.

Remove the sardines from the paste, rinse well and pat dry. Fillet the sardines. Pack them into a jar, cover with olive oil and seal. Store in the fridge. When you remove sardines from the jar, ensure that the rest remain covered with olive oil.

# SMOKED COD'S ROE

**makes about 700g**

1 large, very fresh cod's roe
fine table salt
applewood chips, for smoking

Cut the roe away from the membrane. Place in a sieve and rinse under cold running water for 30 minutes. Drain and weigh the roe. Calculate 2% of this weight: this is the amount of salt to add. Season the roe with the salt.

Take a flat tray with a steam insert (such as a deep roasting tray that will hold a flat steaming rack) and spread the applewood chips over the bottom of the tray. Warm it over a medium heat until the chips start to smoke. Meanwhile, place a tray of ice cubes on the steam insert and put the roe on a tray over the ice. Remove the tray of smoking chips from the heat and set the steam insert over it. Completely cover the top and sides tightly with oven-safe clingfilm so the smoke is sealed inside with the roe. Leave to lightly smoke for 10 minutes.

Decant the smoked roe into an ice-cold sterilised jar and seal. It can be kept in the fridge for 3–5 days.

# SMOKED MACKEREL

**makes 6 fillets**

20g fennel seeds
150g flat-leaf parsley (stalks and leaves)
zest of 2 lemons
3 garlic cloves (peeled)
200g coarse sea salt
3 medium mackerel
applewood chips, for smoking

Toast the fennel seeds in a small dry pan until they smell fragrant. Blend the fennel seeds with the parsley, lemon zest and garlic in a food processor to make a paste. Add the salt and blend again.

Gut the mackerel and remove the gills. Rinse well to remove any blood. Pack the cavities with some of the salt mixture, then completely cover the fish with the salt mixture on a tray. Leave in the fridge for 6 hours.

Rinse away the salt mixture and pat the fish dry. Return to the clean tray and leave to dry out, uncovered, in the fridge overnight.

You now need to cold-smoke the mackerel, which can be done in a smoking chamber (see page 32) for 3 hours or using the quick cold-smoke method. For this, take a flat tray with a steam insert (such as a deep roasting tray that will hold a flat steaming rack) and spread the applewood chips over the bottom of the tray. Warm it over a medium heat until the chips start to smoke.

Meanwhile, place a tray of ice cubes on the steam insert and put the mackerel on a tray over the ice. Remove the tray of smoking woodchips from the heat and set the steam insert over it. Completely cover the top and sides tightly with oven-safe clingfilm so the smoke is sealed inside with the fish. Return the tray to a low heat and leave to smoke for about 1 hour – keep an eye on the fish to be sure it is smoking and not cooking, and adjust the heat under the tray if necessary. Replace the ice and replenish the wood chips as required during the smoking.

Fillet and pin-bone the fish. Char the skin side of the fillets with a blowtorch, on a barbecue or under a hot grill. The cured mackerel fillets can be stored in an airtight container in the fridge for a couple of weeks.

# PICKLES AND JAMS

Pickles and jams are an easy way to preserve fruits and vegetables through the use of acid or sugar, or a mixture of the two. There is a simple joy in this kind of preservation. Certain times of the year are more bountiful than others and preservation of this kind means that we can capture fruits and vegetables in their prime to enjoy again in another form during the colder months. There is something very uplifting about opening larder cupboards during the darker days to be greeted by rows of vibrant jars.

### PICKLES

When it comes to pickling, there are endless methods, from simple cold pickles – where the raw ingredient is just submerged in vinegar – to gastriques, where shallots are gently sweated in wine and then vinegar. In this section, I have included a mixture of methods. The one that we rely on the most uses a standard 1:1:1 pickling liquor made with equal parts of water, caster sugar and vinegar. These are heated together so that the sugar dissolves, then brought to the boil and poured over whatever is being pickled. The type of vinegar used varies,

depending on the flavour wanted and the pickled ingredient itself.

Most pickles can be stored in a cool, dark place for up to a year and then, once opened, in the fridge for 3 months, unless otherwise specified in the individual recipes. You can use any jars that you have for pickles, but it is best practice to sterilise them. For the restaurant we make our pickles in big batches although the recipes here can be scaled down as required. There is no need to be too prescriptive – if you have a glut of an ingredient then get pickling. It doesn't matter how large or small a batch you make, the principle is the same.

### JAMS

Jams rely on sugar as the preservative. Again, any sterilised jars that you have can be used. Some fruits do not contain enough natural pectin to ensure the jam sets. In this case, we use jam sugar, which contains pectin.

# BEER-PICKLED ONIONS

**makes 1kg**

600ml strong hoppy beer
330ml cider vinegar
270g honey
2 sprigs of thyme
3 bay leaves
1 tablespoon Maldon sea salt
36 black peppercorns, coarsely crushed
1kg cipollini onions or other small
    onions (peeled)

Put all the ingredients, except the onions, into a suitable-sized pot and bring to the boil. Add the onions and simmer until they are just tender. Remove from the heat and allow to cool at room temperature.

Store in sealed sterilised jars in a cool, dark place for a year. Once opened, keep in the fridge and use within 3 months.

# CELERIAC PICKLE

**makes about 250g**

½ celeriac
150ml white wine
    vinegar
300ml water
10g fine table salt
10 juniper berries,
    crushed
8 black
    peppercorns,
    crushed

Peel the celeriac and slice it on a mandoline as thinly as possible. Put the slices in a bowl.

Bring the vinegar, water, salt and spices to the boil, then pour the hot liquor over the celeriac. Cover with clingfilm or a lid and leave to steam for 5 minutes. Decant into a sterilised 500ml jar and seal. This pickle can be kept in the fridge and used over a 3-week period.

# CARROT AND CARAWAY PICKLE

**makes about 1kg**

40g caraway seeds
1kg mixed heritage
    carrots
200ml cider
    vinegar
200ml water
200g caster sugar

Toast the caraway seeds in a dry pan until they smell aromatic. Set aside.

Peel the carrots, then slice into thin rounds on a mandoline.

Combine the vinegar, water, sugar and caraway seeds in a suitable-sized pot. Bring to the boil, then add the carrot slices and remove from the heat immediately. Decant into a sterilised 2-litre jar and seal.

The pickle can be stored for 1 year in a cool, dark place. Once opened, keep in the fridge for up to 3 months.

## NASTURTIUM CAPERS

**makes 250g**

250g nasturtium
buds
coarse sea salt
250ml water
200ml white wine
vinegar
50g caster sugar

Pack the nasturtium buds in coarse salt in a jar so that they are completely covered. Seal the jar and leave it in a cool, dark place for 1 month.

Remove the buds from the jar and rinse well in a sieve. Pour the water and vinegar into a suitable-sized pan and add the sugar. Bring to the boil, stirring to dissolve the sugar. Add the buds and immediately remove from the heat. Decant into sterilised jars and seal.

Store in a cool, dark place for up to a year. Once opened, keep in the fridge and use within 3 months.

## WILD GARLIC CAPERS

**makes about 250g**

250g picked wild
garlic buds
coarse sea salt
500ml water
100g caster sugar
400ml white wine
vinegar

Pack the wild garlic buds into jars with the salt so that they are completely covered. Seal the jars and leave them in a cool, dark place for 1 month.

Remove the buds from the salt and rinse well.

In a suitable-sized pan, bring the water, sugar and vinegar to the boil. Add the buds and remove from the heat immediately. Decant into sterilised jars and seal. The garlic capers can be stored in a cool, dark place for up to a year. Once opened, keep in the fridge and use within 3 months.

## LOVAGE SEED PICKLE

**makes about 150g**

150g lovage seeds
50ml cider vinegar
50g caster sugar
50ml water

Put the seeds in a sterilised 200ml heatproof jar. Combine the cider vinegar, sugar and water in a pot and bring to the boil. Remove from the heat and pour the boiling liquid over the seeds. Seal the jar and allow to pickle for 5 days.

The sealed jar can be stored in a cool, dark place for up to a year. Once opened, keep in the fridge and use within 3 months.

## WILD GARLIC PICKLE

**yield will depend
on how many
stalks you begin
with**

wild garlic stalks,
finely diced
pickling liquor:
equal parts
water, white wine
vinegar and
caster sugar

Place the wild garlic in a sterilised jar. Combine the ingredients for the pickling liquor in a pan – you need enough liquid to cover the garlic – and bring to the boil, stirring to dissolve the sugar. Pour the boiling liquor over the wild garlic and seal the jar.

The pickle can be stored in a cool, dark place for up to a year. Once opened, keep in the fridge and use within 3 months.

## PICKLED WAKAME

**makes about 100g**

35ml rice wine
   vinegar
35ml water
35g caster sugar
50g dried wakame

Put the vinegar, water and sugar in a pan and bring to the boil, stirring to dissolve the sugar. Pour this boiling pickling liquor over the wakame and allow to cool.

Decant into a sterilised jar and seal. Store in a cool, dark place for 3 months. Once opened, keep in the fridge and use within a month.

## PICKLED RADISHES

**makes 1.5kg**

300ml water
300ml white wine
   vinegar
300g caster sugar
1.5kg radishes

Combine the water, vinegar and sugar in a pan and bring to the boil, stirring to dissolve the sugar. Pour this boiling pickling liquor over the radishes in a bowl. Allow to cool, then decant into sterilised jars and seal. The radishes are ready to use straight away or can be stored in the fridge for up to 2 months.

## PICKLED ELDERBERRIES

**makes about 400g**

400g elderberries
   (picked off
   the stem)
100ml Cabernet
   Sauvignon
   vinegar
100g caster sugar
100ml water

Put the elderberries into a 500ml sterilised heatproof jar. Combine the vinegar, sugar and water in a pot and bring to the boil. Remove from the heat and pour the boiling liquid over the berries. Seal the jar and leave in a cool place to pickle for 5 days.

The sealed jar can be stored in a cool, dark place for up to a year. Once opened, keep in the fridge and use within 3 months.

## PICKLED WHITE PEACHES

**makes about 800g**

500ml water
500ml white
   wine vinegar
300g caster sugar
16 coriander seeds
16 black
   peppercorns
2 cinnamon sticks
4 star anise
2 cloves
a pinch of
   ground mace
10 ripe white
   peaches, peeled

Combine all the ingredients, except the peaches, in a pan. Bring to the boil, then simmer for 5 minutes.

Put the peaches into two sterilised 2-litre heatproof jars. Pour in the hot spiced liquid and seal the jars. Leave to pickle for at least 7 days before use.

The sealed jars can be stored in a cool, dark place for up to a year. Once opened, keep in the fridge and use within 3 months.

## ROCK SAMPHIRE PICKLE

**makes 600g**

600g rock
    samphire
170ml rice wine
    vinegar
170g caster sugar
170ml water

Pack the rock samphire into a sterilised 1-litre heatproof jar. Combine the vinegar, sugar and water in a pot and bring to the boil. Remove from the heat and pour the boiling liquid over the rock samphire. Seal the jar and leave in a cool place to pickle for 5 days.

The sealed jar can be stored in a cool, dark place for up to a year. Once opened, keep in the fridge and use within 3 months.

## SHALLOT VINEGAR

**makes 500ml**

500g banana
    shallots,
    finely diced
500ml red wine
    vinegar

Put the shallots in a sterilised jar and cover with the red wine vinegar. Seal and leave in the fridge to pickle for at least 3 days before using. The vinegar can be kept for up to 3 months in the fridge.

## RED WINE
## SHALLOT GASTRIQUE

**makes about 1kg**

1kg shallots,
    finely diced
500ml red wine
300ml red wine
    vinegar
Maldon sea salt
    and freshly
    ground black
    pepper

Put the shallots into a pan with the red wine. Bring to a simmer and reduce until all the liquid has evaporated. Add the red wine vinegar, bring to a simmer and reduce until the liquid has evaporated. Season with a pinch each of salt and pepper. Allow to cool.

Decant into a sterilised jar and seal. Store in a cool, dark place for up to 1 year. Once opened, keep in the fridge and use within 3 months.

## WHITE WINE
## SHALLOT GASTRIQUE

**makes about 1kg**

1kg shallots,
    finely diced
500ml white wine
300ml white
    wine vinegar
Maldon sea salt
    and freshly
    ground black
    pepper

Put the shallots and wine in a pan, bring to a simmer and reduce until all the liquid has evaporated. Add the vinegar, bring back to a simmer and reduce until the liquid has evaporated. Season with a pinch each of salt and pepper. Allow to cool.

Decant into a sterilised jar and seal. Store in a cool, dark place for up to a year. Once opened, keep in the fridge and use within 3 months.

# ARTICHOKE PICCALILLI

This is an amazing variation on a traditional piccalilli. I love it with all types of cold meats such as ham, game terrines and any type of pie. It works particularly well with the Rabbit Feast on page 205. I have deliberately given quantities for a large batch as the piccalilli really is so versatile and also makes a lovely present.

**makes about 2kg**

**FOR THE PICCALILLI**

1.5kg Jerusalem artichokes, scrubbed clean

4 white-skin onions

600g red peppers, stalks and seeds removed

60g fennel seeds

10g celery seeds

50g black peppercorns

20g cumin seeds

2 litres cider vinegar

75g plain flour

100g English mustard powder

400g caster sugar

30g ground turmeric

a pinch of saffron threads

**FOR THE BRINE**

500g fine table salt

4.5 litres water

Dice the artichokes, onions and peppers so they are roughly in uniform-sized pieces.

For the brine, put the salt and water in a pan and bring to the boil, then simmer until the salt has completely dissolved. Remove from the heat, pour into a bowl and cool. Add the vegetables to the brine, cover the bowl and leave in the fridge for 24 hours.

Toast the fennel seeds, celery seeds, peppercorns and cumin seeds in a dry frying pan until aromatic. Tip into a mortar and crush coarsely with the pestle.

Put 200ml of the cider vinegar, the flour and mustard powder in a small bowl and whisk into a paste. Pour the remaining vinegar into a large pan and add the sugar, crushed spices, turmeric and saffron. Bring to the boil, then simmer over a medium to high heat. Gradually stir in the flour-mustard paste and continue cooking, stirring, for about 12 minutes or until the liquid has thickened.

Drain the vegetables from the brine and pack into sterilised Kilner jars. Pour the hot pickling liquor over the vegetables, leaving a 2cm gap at the top. Seal the jars. The piccalilli can be stored for 6 months in a cool, dark place (leave it for a minimum of 2 weeks before eating). Once opened, keep in the fridge for up to 3 months.

# ONION TREACLE

**makes about 100ml**

10 large white onions, quartered
1 sachet (8g) pectin powder
50g caster sugar
Maldon sea salt

Place the onions in a large pressure cooker, or a large pot, and fill halfway up with water. Seal the pressure cooker, or cover the pot with foil and then a lid so that no steam can escape. If using a pressure cooker, steam the onions for about 3 hours. If using a pot, steam over a very gentle heat for 6–7 hours until the onions have completely softened but have not coloured.

Pour the onions into a sieve set over a bowl and place a heavy weight on the onions so that all the liquid will be drained from them and pass through the sieve. Discard the onions.

Measure the strained liquid, then pour it into a pan. Boil to reduce by 80%. Add the pectin and sugar and simmer for about 5 minutes, whisking constantly, until the mixture reaches 107°C. Season lightly with salt to taste. Allow to cool before pouring into a sterilised container. Seal, then store in the fridge for up to 2 months.

# APRICOT AND LEMON THYME JAM

**makes 6 x 228ml jars**

1kg fresh apricots
50ml water
50ml fresh lemon juice
600g jam sugar
100g unsalted butter, cut into cubes
100g honey
3 sprigs of lemon thyme, leaves picked
1 teaspoon Maldon sea salt

Before you begin making the jam, put three or four small plates in the freezer. Cut the apricots in half and remove the stones, then cut each half into quarters. Place the apricots and water in a large pot and cook over a medium heat for 10 minutes to soften. Stir in the lemon juice and sugar and bring the mixture up to 104°C.

Reduce the heat and allow to simmer, stirring now and again, for a further 20 minutes or until the jam has reached soft setting point – use the wrinkle test to check. To do this, take the pan off the heat and carefully spoon a little jam on to one of the cold plates. Let it stand for a minute, then push the blob of jam with your finger. If the surface of the jam wrinkles then it has reached setting point; if it is still quite liquid, then put the pan back on the heat and boil the jam for another couple of minutes before testing again, using different plates from the freezer.

Meanwhile, make a brown butter by melting and heating the butter cubes in a pan over a high heat until the butter starts to foam and brown and gives off a nutty aroma. Once this occurs, remove from the heat immediately and cool quickly by setting the base of the pan in cold water, to stop the butter from burning.

Put the honey in another pan and cook over a medium heat to a dark caramel colour. Remove from the heat and stir in the brown butter. Add to the apricot jam while still warm. Stir through the lemon thyme leaves and salt. Ladle the warm jam into sterilised jars and seal.

The jam can be stored in a cool, dark place for up to 6 months. Once opened, keep in the fridge and use within 6 weeks.

# BLOOD ORANGE MARMALADE

**makes about 2.5kg**

3.5kg blood oranges
150ml fresh lemon juice
1.2kg demerara sugar
1.2kg dark muscovado sugar

Peel two-thirds of the oranges and julienne the peel.

Using an electric juicer/press, juice all the oranges in two batches – first the oranges that have been peeled and second those that haven't. Keep the fruit pulp and the juice from each batch separate.

Pour the fruit pulp from the second batch (unpeeled oranges) into a pan and cover with water. Bring to the boil, then put on the lid and simmer for 1 hour. Strain the liquid into a jug or bowl; discard the fruit pulp.

Mix all the blood orange juice (from both batches) with the lemon juice and measure the mixture. Pour into a pan and add enough of the reserved strained liquid from the boiled fruit pulp to make the total liquid up to 3 litres. Add the sugars and the julienned zest. Wrap the reserved fruit pulp from the peeled oranges in a piece of muslin, tie the ends together to make a bag and add to the pan. Slowly bring the mixture up to 110°C, stirring constantly.

Allow to cool slightly before removing the muslin bag; squeeze any juice from the bag into the marmalade. Decant the marmalade into hot sterilised jars and seal. The marmalade can be stored in a cool, dark place for a year. Once opened, keep in the fridge and use within a month.

# FORCED RHUBARB, HIBISCUS AND GINGER JAM

**makes 6 x 228ml**

1.5kg forced rhubarb, cut into 1.5cm pieces
zest and juice of 2 lemons
5g root ginger, grated
5g dried hibiscus flowers
150ml water
500g jam sugar

Put the rhubarb, lemon zest and juice, ginger, hibiscus flowers and water in a pan over a medium heat and cook for about 10 minutes or until the fruit softens. Stir in the sugar, then simmer, stirring regularly, for about 45 minutes or until a thick consistency – use the trail test to check for setting. To do this, take a spoonful of the jam and allow it to fall back into the rest; it should fall slowly, forming a trail that will hold its shape on the surface of the jam in the pan for a minute or so.

Remove from the heat and allow to cool for 5 minutes before ladling the warm jam into sterilised jars; seal.

The jam can be stored in a cool, dark place for up to 6 months. Once opened, keep in the fridge and use within 6 weeks.

# SOUR TOMATO JAM

**makes about 1.5kg**

10 shallots, thinly sliced
5 garlic cloves, sliced
2.5kg overripe tomatoes (with their vines),
   roughly chopped
5 bay leaves
150ml olive oil
1 litre tomato juice
fresh horseradish, finely grated
whey or extra tomato juice
fine table salt and cracked black pepper

Gently sweat the shallots, garlic, tomato vines and bay leaves in the olive oil until the shallots have softened. Add the tomatoes and cook until all excess liquid has evaporated.

In a separate pan, reduce the tomato juice down to a purée consistency.

Mix together the reduced tomato juice and the tomato mixture and allow to cool. Discard the tomato vines and bay leaves.

Weigh the tomato mixture and calculate 1.5% salt, 1% fresh horseradish and 25% whey or extra tomato juice. Stir these into the mixture with pepper to taste. Decant into sterilised jars and seal. Leave to ferment at a warm room temperature for 5 days; keep away from direct sunlight.

When ready, the sealed jars can be stored in the fridge for up to 3 months. Once opened, use within 1 month.

# WILD BLACKBERRY
# AND LEMON VERBENA JAM

**makes 6–8 x 228ml jars**

1.5kg wild blackberries
400ml water
1.5kg jam sugar
2 tablespoons fresh lemon juice
50g picked lemon verbena leaves

Before you begin making the jam, put three or four small plates in the freezer. Put the berries into a large pan with the water, set on a medium heat and cook for 10 minutes to soften the fruit. Stir in the sugar and lemon juice, turn up the heat and cook rapidly for 15 minutes or until at setting point – use the wrinkle test to check the consistency. To do this, take the pan off the heat and carefully spoon a little jam on to one of the cold plates. Let it stand for a minute, then push the blob of jam with your finger. If the surface of the jam wrinkles then it has reached setting point; if it is still quite liquid, put the pan back on the heat and boil the jam for another couple of minutes before testing again, using different plates from the freezer as necessary.

Cut the lemon verbena leaves into small pieces and stir through the jam. Allow to cool for 5 minutes, then ladle the warm jam into sterilised jars and seal.

The jam can be stored in a cool, dark place for up to 6 months. Once opened, keep in the fridge and use within 6 weeks.

# DAIRY, BUTTERS AND OILS

Butter has become quite the obsession since our opening. Our bone marrow butter has become a cult classic, Dean's chicken skin butter legendary and Simon's sour smoked whiskey butter a revelation. I find it fascinating how certain fats and oils take to new flavours and lift dishes to the next level. For example, the aroma from dulse butter when it hits a pan, finishing a roast piece of monkfish, is quite something. The intense flavour ember oil gives to a tartare or yoghurt is mind-boggling! I think it's worth always having a number of oils in the cupboard as well as some flavoured butters in the fridge. Then you can effortlessly enhance a simple dish cooked at home.

# BONITO BUTTER

For this recipe, we use the skin from smoked eel as we don't want anything in the kitchen to go to waste. However, you can use the skin of any smoked fish such as mackerel. Alternatively, the butter can be made without the fish skin, in which case increase the bonito flakes to 10g.

**makes about 500g**

500g unsalted butter, cut into small cubes
80g skin from smoked fish
5g bonito flakes

Melt the butter in a pan over a high heat and cook until the butter starts to foam and takes on a really golden colour. Reduce the heat, add the fish skin and sweat for 1–2 minutes. Remove the fish skin, then transfer the butter to a blender or food processor and add the bonito flakes. Blend together. Allow to cool.

Store in an airtight container in the fridge for 1 month, or freeze for 3 months.

# CHICKEN AND SAVORY BUTTER

**makes about 600g**

500g Cultured Cream (see page 54)
10g herb savory, leaves picked
100g chicken or duck fat
½ garlic clove, crushed
a small bunch of thyme
zest of ½ lemon
40g fine table salt

Whisk the cultured cream until it separates into butter and buttermilk. Strain the buttermilk into a bowl and reserve the butter in the sieve. Blend the savory into the buttermilk really well in a blender or food processor, then strain through a fine sieve.

Put the chicken or duck fat, garlic, thyme and lemon zest in a pot and heat to 90°C. Remove from the heat and allow to infuse for 20 minutes, then strain the mixture into the bowl of a stand mixer fitted with the paddle attachment and allow to cool.

Add the butter from the cultured cream. Whip the two fats together. Add the buttermilk and salt and whip until combined. Store, wrapped in clingfilm, in the fridge for up to a month or freeze for longer storage.

# CULTURED BUTTER

**makes 750g**

1 litre double cream
200ml buttermilk
about 5g fine table salt

Pour the cream into a pan and heat to 35°C. Stir in the buttermilk. Pour into a container and cover with a piece of muslin secured with an elastic band or string. Leave in a warm, dry area of your kitchen to ferment for 24 hours.

Season the mix with the salt and refrigerate. Once chilled, transfer the mixture to a stand mixer fitted with a whisk attachment. Whisk on a medium-high speed for about 15 minutes. It is ready when the liquid (buttermilk) separates from the solid butter.

Strain the buttermilk from the butter through muslin into an airtight container. Pack the butter together into a block and wrap in greaseproof paper or put into another container. Store both in the fridge for up to 3 months.

## NORI BUTTER

**makes about 250g**

2 sheets of dried
  nori (3g each)
5g dried wakame
  flakes
1 black peppercorn
250g unsalted
  butter, cut into
  small cubes

Preheat the oven to 150°C
fan/170°C/Gas Mark 3–4.
Toast the nori and wakame
with the peppercorn on a
baking tray in the oven for
10 minutes.

Melt the butter in a pan over
a high heat and cook until
it starts to foam and takes
on a really golden colour.
Immediately remove from
the heat and cool quickly
to stop the butter cooking
further.

Blend the toasted
ingredients with the
butter in a blender or food
processor. Allow to cool,
then store in an airtight
container in the fridge for a
month, or freeze for
3 months.

## SMOKED BUTTER

**makes 250g**

200g applewood
  chips
250g unsalted
  butter, diced
  and frozen

Take a flat tray with a steam
insert (such as a deep
roasting tray that will hold
a flat steaming rack) and
spread the applewood chips
over the bottom of the tray.
Warm it over a medium heat
until the chips start
to smoke. Remove from the
heat.

Place the frozen butter on
a tray on the steam insert/
steaming rack and set this
over the smoking chips.
Completely cover the top
and sides tightly with
oven-safe clingfilm so the
smoke is sealed inside with
the butter. Leave to lightly
smoke for 10 minutes.

Store in an airtight
container in the fridge for up
to 6 weeks.

## SMOKED BONE MARROW BUTTER

**makes 275g**

250g Smoked
  Butter (see
  above), at room
  temperature
25g Smoked Bone
  Marrow (see
  page 37)
Maldon sea salt

Put the smoked butter in
a stand mixer fitted with a
paddle attachment. Turn the
mixer to a high speed, add
the bone marrow and mix
to incorporate. Add salt to
taste.

Store in an airtight container
in the fridge for up to 1 week.
Remove from the fridge 10
minutes before serving.

## WHISKEY CULTURED BUTTER

**makes 750g**

about 4 teaspoons
  whiskey
750g Cultured
  Butter (see
  opposite), at room
  temperature

Fold the whiskey into the
butter until fully combined.
Taste and add more whiskey
if you like. Store wrapped
in greaseproof paper or in
an airtight container in the
fridge for up to 3 months.

# FRESH CURD

Be sure all the ingredients are cold before starting.

**makes about 800ml**

1.25 litres whole milk
60ml double cream
25ml buttermilk
1 teaspoon fine table salt
5g vegetable rennet

Put all the ingredients in a bowl and whisk together to combine. Pour into a pan and set over a gentle heat. Bring the mixture to 36°C, then remove from the heat and allow to cool to room temperature.

If you are looking for a loose, light curd then this is now ready to use. If you want a thicker, more stable curd, line a large sieve with a piece of muslin and set it over a deep bowl, then pour the mixture into the sieve. Gather up the edges of the cloth and secure. Leave in the fridge overnight.

The next day, the thicker curd will be left in the cloth and some whey will have passed into the bowl (this whey can be reserved and used for ferments). The curd can be seasoned, smoked or flavoured with herbs and spices as desired.

Both the loose and thick curd can be stored in an airtight container in the fridge for up to 3 days.

# CULTURED CREAM

**makes about 600ml**

500ml double cream
100ml buttermilk

Place the cream in a pan and heat to 35°C. Stir in the buttermilk. Pour the mixture into a sterilised container (a plastic container is fine) and cover with muslin secured with an elastic band or string – the cream needs to breathe, hence the cloth covering. Leave in a warm, dry place to culture for about 4 days. The mixture will thicken and become sour. Once ready, the cultured cream can be stored in the fridge in an airtight container for up to 2 weeks.

# KEFIR

**makes about 2.4 litres**

2 litres whole milk (unpasteurised if possible)
100g kefir grains
400ml double cream

Gently warm the milk to approximately 30°C, then add the kefir grains (they are dormant and the heat will activate them). Stir in the cream. Decant into a sterilised plastic, glass or crockery container and cover with muslin secured with a rubber band or string. Leave in a warm spot in the kitchen to culture until the mixture becomes quite thick and the aroma is pleasant and acidic. This will usually take about 24 hours.

After culturing is complete, strain the grains out of the finished kefir (the grains can be used again to make more batches of kefir). The finished kefir will keep in the fridge in a sealed container for 2–3 weeks.

# BEN'S BEESWAX CREAM

This recipe was developed by Ben, who thought of the idea one day while maintaining the hives on the rooftop of The Dairy. He was blowtorching the wooden frames of the hives, to clean them, and was taken by the incredible aroma that was released. This is a delicious accompaniment to the Hibiscus Doughnuts on page 274 or to spoon over a dessert just as you would cream.

**makes about 500g**

75g comb from honey, broken up to release
  the honey
375ml UHT double cream
60g honey
100g egg yolks

Using a blowtorch, burn the exterior of the comb on all sides for about 2 minutes or until you start to smell the honey caramelising. Put the comb in a suitable-sized pan with the UHT cream. Slowly, while stirring with a wooden spoon, bring the mixture to the boil. As soon as it starts to boil, remove from the heat and allow to infuse for 10 minutes.

Place the pan back on the heat and bring just to the boil again. Remove from the heat and pass the cream through a fine sieve into a deep bowl, pushing hard on the comb to release as much of the honey as possible through the sieve. Leave to stand and the mix will produce a skin. Skim this off the top. Allow a skin to form again three further times and remove it each time. (Doing this will prevent the beeswax cream from cracking during baking.)

In a small pan, caramelise the honey to a light amber colour. Allow to cool until it is just warm, then mix it with the egg yolks. Whisk the egg yolk mixture with the cream mixture until combined – try to avoid whisking in any air bubbles. If bubbles do appear, bang the bowl on a hard surface to deflate them.

Preheat the oven to 95°C fan/115°C/Gas Mark ¼. Pour the mixture into a baking dish. Bake for 1 hour. Allow to cool at room temperature, then keep in the fridge until required.

# CRAB OIL

**makes about 350ml**

800g–1kg crab shells, cleaned
200ml vegetable oil
50g fennel seeds
50g coriander seeds
a pinch of dried chilli flakes
2 bay leaves
200ml rapeseed oil
zest of 2 lemons
20g dried wakame

Smash the crab shells into small pieces using a mallet or hammer. Put the shells and vegetable oil into a medium-sized pan over a high heat. Cook for 3–5 minutes, scraping the bottom of the pan, until the shells are nicely toasted. Add the spices and bay leaves for the last 2 minutes of cooking so they get toasted too. Lower the heat and add the rapeseed oil. Bring up to just below a simmer (85°C), then cook for 45 minutes.

Remove from the heat and add the lemon zest and wakame. Cover the top of the pan with clingfilm and leave to infuse for 1 hour. Strain the oil and decant into jars. Keep in the fridge – the oil can be used straight away – for up to a week, or in the freezer for up to 3 months.

## HERB OIL

**makes about 200ml**

a bunch of flat-leaf parsley, leaves picked and chopped

3-4 sprigs of tarragon, leaves picked and chopped

½ bunch of chervil, leaves picked and chopped

a bunch of chives, chopped

a bunch of spring onion tops (the green part), chopped

200ml extra virgin olive oil

Maldon sea salt

Blend the herbs and onion tops with the oil in a blender or food processor. Pour the mixture into a pan and warm over a high heat, stirring constantly. Season with salt. Pour the mixture back into the blender or food processor and blend for 1 minute.

Strain the oil through a piece of muslin into a tray set over ice so it cools quickly. The oil can be kept in an airtight container in the fridge for a week or in the freezer for 3 months.

## GARLIC OIL

**makes 1 litre**

1 litre extra virgin olive oil

5 garlic cloves, finely sliced

Put the oil and garlic into a pot and heat to 70°C. Remove from the heat and allow to infuse for 1 hour at a warm room temperature.

Strain the oil, then decant into an airtight jar or bottle. Keep in the fridge for up to 1 month.

## KOMBU OIL

**makes 150ml**

100g dried kombu

150ml grapeseed oil

Preheat the oven to 110°C fan/130°C/Gas Mark ½–1. Toast the kombu in a small tray in the oven for 1 hour.

Blend the toasted kombu with the oil in a blender or food processor, then strain through a fine sieve. The oil can be stored in a sealed jar in the fridge for up to 3 months.

## EMBER OIL

Please prepare this recipe with care because dealing with burning hot embers can be dangerous.

**makes 1 litre**

1 litre vegetable oil

1 ember of white-hot charcoal from a barbecue or fire

Pour the oil into a large pot. Wearing heavy barbecue gloves and using appropriate tongs, gently place the burning hot ember into the oil. Cover with a lid and leave to infuse as it cools. Once cool, strain through a fine sieve. Store in an airtight container or jar in a cool, dark place.

# NORI OIL

**makes about 350ml**

350ml grapeseed oil
5 sheets of dried nori (3g each), cut into
    small pieces with scissors
a bunch of parsley, leaves picked
a bunch of chervil, leaves picked
a bunch of tarragon, leaves picked
a bunch of dill, leaves picked

About 2 hours before required, put the oil into the freezer to chill.

Preheat the oven to 180°C fan/200°C/Gas Mark 6. Toast the nori on a baking tray in the oven for 5 minutes.

Blanch the herb leaves in boiling water for 2 minutes; refresh in iced water and drain well. Chop the herbs roughly.

Put the oil and toasted nori into a blender or food processor and blend for 2 minutes. Add the herbs and blend again for 2 minutes. Strain the mixture through a fine sieve into a bowl set over ice (keeping the oil cool helps to retain the bright green colour).

Store the nori oil in a sealed container in the fridge for 1 month or in the freezer for 3 months.

# SICHUAN OIL

This is not for the faint-hearted! It is best to make it outdoors or in a very well-ventilated area, and please prepare with extreme care because dealing with oil at this temperature can be dangerous.

**makes about 500ml**

500ml vegetable oil
1 cinnamon stick
4 star anise
200g Sichuan pepper
100g dried chilli flakes
2 garlic cloves, finely sliced

Pour the oil into a pan and add the cinnamon stick, star anise and Sichuan pepper. Heat to 220°C. Carefully (wearing protective gloves) pour the hot oil over the chilli flakes and garlic in a heatproof bowl. Leave to cool to room temperature.

The oil is ready to be used straight away. Decant into an airtight container or jar and store in the fridge for up to a month.

# LOBSTER OIL

**makes about 350ml**

800g–1kg lobster shells, cleaned
200ml vegetable oil
50g fennel seeds
50g coriander seeds
a pinch of dried chilli flakes
2 bay leaves
200ml rapeseed oil
zest of 2 lemons
20g dried wakame

Smash the lobster shells into small pieces using a mallet or hammer. Put the shells and vegetable oil into a medium-sized pan over a high heat. Cook for 3–5 minutes, scraping the bottom of the pan, until the shells are nicely toasted. Add the spices and bay leaves for the last 2 minutes of cooking so they get toasted too. Lower the heat and add the rapeseed oil. Bring to just below a simmer (85°C) and cook for 45 minutes.

Remove from the heat and add the lemon zest and wakame. Cover the top of the pot with clingfilm and leave to infuse for 1 hour. Strain and decant into jars. Keep in the fridge – the oil can be used straight away or stored for up to a week – or in the freezer for up to 3 months.

# POWDERS, SALTS AND CRISPS

Everyone should have a dehydrator – they are cheap as chips on eBay. Dehydrating, or drying something out completely, can add a serious depth of flavour to all kinds of food, from fruits and vegetables to fish. Try slicing a scallop thinly and dehydrating it overnight at around 65°C: the natural sugars caramelise and you end up with a super-intense, sweet scallop crisp that could be crumbled over a ceviche to intensify the flavour.

That is why we dehydrate things – it intensifies flavours. We add dried mushrooms to a game broth and the earthy flavours go off the charts. Poach a quince, then stick it in a dehydrator for 6 hours and see what you think! You will not be disappointed.

Drying also means you avoid waste. I used to throw away lemons in the fridge that were not being used up, but now I peel them and dehydrate the peel. Once I have built up a large batch I blend the peel with some salt and fennel seeds to make the most amazing aromatic salt to season lamb, chicken or fish. When we prepare wild mushrooms, we keep all the trimmings and dry them. Then, when we have a good batch it is blended into a powder. This is a premium product generated from WASTE! Have a look at how much it will cost you to buy a pack of mushroom powder in your local supermarket! The price should be encouragement enough to try making your own at home.

## SEAWEED CRACKERS

**makes 300–400g**

900ml water
190g tapioca pearls
15g Nori Powder (see page 60)
5g Maldon sea salt
vegetable oil for deep-frying

Pour the water into a pan and bring to the boil. Add the tapioca and cook over a gentle heat, stirring constantly, until thick and translucent. Stir in the nori powder and salt. Pour on to a baking tray lined with greaseproof paper or a silicone mat and spread out into a thin layer. Leave to dry out at a warm room temperature (or in your oven at the lowest setting or in a dehydrator). Once completely dry, break into crackers. If not frying straight away, the crackers can be kept in an airtight container.

Just before serving, heat oil in a deep pan or deep-fat fryer to 200°C and deep-fry the crackers until puffed and golden. Drain on kitchen paper.

# LEVAIN CRISPS

This is a great way to use up any excess levain/sourdough starter. Ideally use a really sour levain here.

**makes about 250g**

250g levain/sourdough starter
½ teaspoon fine table salt

Preheat the oven to 250°C fan/its highest setting. Line a baking tray with a silicone mat, or greaseproof paper brushed with oil, and place in the oven to heat up.

Put the levain and salt in a blender or food processor and blend with enough water to create a double cream consistency. Spread a really thin layer of the mixture on the hot lined tray and bake until it just turns golden. Remove from the oven and allow to cool slightly before breaking into crisps.

Repeat with the remaining mixture. The crisps can be kept in an airtight container for up to 1 week.

# PUFFED BARLEY

**makes about 200g**

200g pearl barley
vegetable oil for deep-frying
Maldon sea salt

Put the barley in a pot and cover with water. Bring to the boil, then simmer until completely overcooked and soft – this will take about 40 minutes. Drain the barley in a sieve and rinse to remove excess starch.

Spread out the barley grains on a large tray in one layer. Dry out completely in a dehydrator, or in the oven at its lowest setting (this will take about 6 hours). If not frying straight away, the dried grains can be stored in an airtight container at room temperature.

Just before serving, heat oil in a deep pan or deep-fat fryer to 250°C and deep-fry the barley grains for 30 seconds or until puffed. Drain on kitchen paper and sprinkle with a pinch of salt.

# FRIED BREAD

**makes about 300g**

300g yesterday's sourdough
50ml olive oil
1 garlic clove, crushed
zest of 1 lemon
3 sprigs of lemon thyme, leaves picked
Maldon sea salt

Chop up the bread, then dry out completely in a dehydrator, or in the oven at its lowest setting, for 3–4 hours. Blend the dried bread in a food processor to a breadcrumb consistency.

Set a wide-bottomed pan on a medium heat and add the olive oil followed by the breadcrumbs. Toast, using a whisk to stir the crumbs, for about 10 minutes or until golden brown. Add the crushed garlic, lemon zest and thyme with a pinch of salt and mix in. Tip the mixture on to a flat tray lined with kitchen paper to cool. Store in an airtight container for up to 5 days.

## NORI SALT

**makes about 110g**

2 sheets of dried
  nori (3g each)
100g Maldon
  sea salt
5g dried wakame

Preheat the oven to 160°C fan/180°C/Gas Mark 4. Place the sheets of nori on a baking tray and toast in the oven for 5 minutes.

Blend the toasted nori with the salt and wakame in a blender or food processor until finely ground. Store in an airtight container in your store cupboard.

## NORI POWDER

**yield depends on how many nori sheets you begin with**

sheets of dried nori
  (use a minimum
  of 4 sheets as
  fewer will not
  turn in the
  blender)

Preheat the oven to 160°C fan/180°C/Gas Mark 4. Place the sheets of nori on a baking tray and toast in the oven for 5 minutes. Allow to cool completely.

Cut the sheets into small pieces. Put into a blender or food processor (make sure the bowl is really dry) and blend to a fine powder. Store in an airtight container in your store cupboard.

## SPICED SALT

**makes 120g**

10g caraway seeds
10g black
  peppercorns
100g fine table salt

Toast the caraway seeds and peppercorns in a small dry frying pan until aromatic. Crush coarsely in a mortar and pestle. Blend the spices through the salt in a blender or food processor. Store in an airtight container at room temperature.

## MUSHROOM POWDER

**makes about 100g**

500g chestnut
  mushrooms,
  finely sliced

Spread the mushroom slices on a large baking tray in a single layer. Place in a dehydrator, or the oven set at about 70°C fan/90°C, and leave to dry out completely. This should take about 8 hours.

Once completely dry, tip the mushrooms into a high-speed blender and blend to a fine powder (if your blender is not high-speed, blend as fine as possible, then pass through a sieve to remove any lumps). Store in an airtight container in your store cupboard.

## BLACKBERRY LEAF POWDER

**makes about 100g**

2 shopping bags
  of unsprayed
  blackberry leaves

Rinse the leaves well in a colander under cold running water, then shake or spin dry.

In a dehydrator, or your oven set to the lowest heat, dry out the leaves completely – this will take 6–8 hours. Allow to cool, then blend to a fine powder in a blender or food processor. Store in an airtight container in your store cupboard.

# STOCKS, SAUCES AND SEASONINGS

### BROWN CHICKEN STOCK

**makes about 3 litres**

4kg chicken wings
1 pig's trotter, split
5 litres water
1 bulb of garlic, cut in half (horizontally)
3 banana shallots, cut in half

Preheat the oven to 220°C fan/240°C/Gas Mark 9. Roast the wings and trotter in large roasting trays for 35 minutes.

Tip the wings and trotter into a large stock pot. Deglaze the roasting trays with some of the water by bringing to the boil, stirring and scraping. Add to the stock pot with the remaining water. Bring to the boil and skim. Reduce to a gentle simmer and cook for 3 hours, skimming regularly.

Add the garlic and shallots. Simmer for a further 1½ hours.

Strain the stock into a large container. Set the sieve containing the chicken wings and trotter over a bowl and place a weight on top. Leave for 1 hour to extract all the juices. Add these to the strained stock. Strain through a fine sieve.

The stock can be stored in the fridge for a couple of days but can also be frozen in portions to be used at a later date.

### LAMB STOCK

**makes about 2.5 litres**

2kg lamb bones, chopped
a drizzle of white wine
vegetable oil
500g lamb trimmings (not too fatty
    if possible), diced
3 litres Brown Chicken Stock (see above)

Preheat the oven to 220°C fan/240°C/Gas Mark 9. Roast the lamb bones in two large roasting trays for 20–30 minutes or until golden. Remove the bones and set aside. Skim off any fat from the roasting juices left in the trays, then deglaze with the white wine by bringing to the boil, stirring and scraping. Save these deglazed roasting juices.

Heat about 1cm of vegetable oil in a wide-based pan over a high heat. Add the lamb trimmings, in batches, and brown to a dark golden colour.

Place the browned lamb trimmings, the roasted bones and reserved roasting juices in a large pot and add the brown chicken stock. Bring to the boil and skim, then simmer gently for 5 hours, skimming as required. Remove from the heat and allow to sit for 2 hours before straining this lamb stock through a fine sieve.

If not needed straight away, the stock can be stored in the fridge for a couple of days or frozen.

# LAMB SAUCE

**makes about 500ml**

2kg lamb bones, chopped
1 bottle of white wine
vegetable oil
1.25kg lamb trimmings (not too fatty
    if possible), diced
3 litres Brown Chicken Stock (see page 61)
60ml fresh lemon juice
zest of ½ lemon
a sprig of rosemary
2 garlic cloves, crushed

Preheat the oven to 220°C fan/240°C/Gas Mark 9. Roast the lamb bones in two large roasting trays for 25–30 minutes or until golden. Remove the bones and set aside. Skim off any fat from the roasting juices left in the trays, then deglaze with half of the white wine by bringing to the boil, stirring and scraping. Save these deglazed roasting juices.

Heat about 1cm of vegetable oil in a wide-based pan over a high heat. Take the leanest 500g of the lamb trimmings and brown, in batches, to a dark golden colour. If the oil catches badly while you are browning the lamb, clean out the pan and use fresh oil for the next batch.

Place these browned lamb trimmings, the roasted bones and reserved roasting juices in a large pot and add the brown chicken stock. Bring to the boil and skim, then simmer gently for 5 hours, skimming as required. Remove from the heat and allow to sit for 2 hours before straining this lamb stock through a fine sieve.

Brown the remaining lamb trimmings in batches in a wide-based pan as before, starting with the fattiest trimmings and a little oil, then keep reusing the fat to brown the rest, ensuring the fat doesn't burn. Once all these trimmings are browned, drain off the majority of the fat before deglazing the pan with the lemon juice.

Put all the trimmings back into the pan and add 1 litre of the lamb stock and bring to the boil. Skim the surface. Reduce the heat slightly and allow to reduce until the liquid is no longer covering the lamb trimmings. Add the remaining lamb stock and allow it to reduce once again by half.

Boil the remaining wine to reduce by half. Add to the sauce. Remove from the heat and add the lemon zest, rosemary and garlic. Leave to infuse for 10 minutes before straining through a fine sieve. The sauce can be kept in the fridge for a couple of days or it can be frozen in portions to use at a later date.

# VENISON SAUCE

**makes about 200ml**

1kg venison bones, cut into small pieces
1 litre Brown Chicken Stock (see page 61)
5 juniper berries
200g venison trimmings
50ml vegetable oil
50g unsalted butter
200ml Madeira
2 garlic cloves, sliced
2 sprigs of thyme
1 tablespoon Cabernet Sauvignon vinegar

Preheat the oven to 220°C fan/240°C/Gas Mark 9. Roast the venison bones in a roasting tray for 35 minutes.

Meanwhile, bring the brown chicken stock to the boil and reduce by a quarter. Toast the juniper berries in a small dry pan until they smell aromatic, then lightly crush them; set aside.

Add the roasted venison bones to the reduced stock. Deglaze the roasting tray with a little stock from the pot and pour back into the pot. Bring back to the boil, then simmer for 1½ hours. Leave to cool for 20 minutes with the bones in, then remove them and strain the stock.

While the stock is simmering, caramelise the venison trimmings in a very hot pan with the vegetable oil. Add the butter and continue to cook, scraping the bottom of the pan, until the meat has taken on a dark, roasted colour. Remove the meat from the pan (reserve it). Strain off the fat (reserve it), then deglaze the pan with the Madeira and reduce by half.

Add the venison stock and two-thirds of the caramelised meat to the Madeira reduction. Bring to the boil and skim, then keep on a light rolling boil for 20 minutes.

Strain into a clean pan and add the remaining caramelised venison trimmings. Reduce by a third to a glossy sauce. Add the juniper berries, garlic, thyme and vinegar. Stir in the reserved fat (from caramelising the venison trimmings) to taste. Allow to infuse for a couple of minutes, then strain the sauce through muslin and chill quickly over an ice bath so that the fats emulsify.

If not using straight away, keep in the fridge and warm through before serving.

# MISO

Miso is something that you might not necessarily choose to make at home but it is interesting to see the process behind it. If you do want to try making it, then really any carbohydrate can be mixed with the 'koji' (the fermentation culture) to create different flavours. We have experimented with everything from beans to bread. During the process of making the koji and miso, it is important that the environment is very clean and the equipment sterilised so as not to introduce the wrong type of bacteria. In any recipes in this book where miso is used, it is perfectly acceptable to use your favourite shop-bought variety if you haven't made your own!

## KOJI

**makes about 670g**

500g plump white rice
10g koji spores/starter (2% of dry
    rice weight)

Soak the rice in cold water overnight. Drain the rice and spread in a thin layer in a steamer tray. Place this tray over a roasting/baking tray of water. Cover with a lid or foil and gently steam the rice for 1½ hours – it should be quite dry and barely cooked. Set aside on the steamer tray.

Put the koji spores in a small blender and blend to a dry powder. When the rice has cooled to about 35°C, sprinkle over the koji powder and mix well. Spread out the rice in a thin layer on the steamer tray. Set this over a tray of room-temperature water. Cover the top of the steamer tray with clingfilm and wrap around the bottom tray so that the rice is sealed in with the water. Pierce a few holes in the film. Leave in a warm, moist environment such as a kitchen for 5 days, stirring the rice occasionally.

A white mould should appear on the rice, similar to the mould found on the outside of brie, and the rice will kind of break down. The rice and mould are the koji. Once it reaches this stage, it can be used straight away or stored in the fridge, tightly wrapped, for up to 4 days.

## MISO

**makes about 1kg**

500g dried white beans (we use haricot
    beans), soaked in water overnight
500g Koji (see above)
fine table salt

Drain the beans and place in a pot. Cover with water and bring to the boil, then simmer the beans, skimming occasionally, until they are overcooked and starting to fall apart. Drain and cool down to a temperature of about 35°C.

Mix in the koji. Weigh the mixture and calculate 7% of this – this is the amount of salt to add. Mash or mince the mixture to a rough paste. Spoon into a sterilised container, packing tightly to remove any air bubbles. Top with a layer of salt. Place a sterilised weight over the top of the mixture, then cover the container with muslin. Leave in a cool, ambient environment (a cellar is ideal) for at least 30 days or until the saltiness is taken over by sweet and umami flavours. Once ready, store in an airtight container in the fridge.

## HERB MISO

This is a variation of our traditional miso. We add 500g of mixed herbs and they get pushed through the mincer with the bean and koji mixture. A mixture of chervil, parsley and tarragon is a good place to start but most herbs will work and it is a good way to use leftovers. The rest of the process remains the same.

## ONION MISO

This is another variation on the original but this time 250g spring onion tops and 250g wild garlic leaves get minced into the mixture. The rest of the process remains the same.

## BREAD MISO

This variation is a bit different. Tear 500g stale bread into chunks, then soak in water for about 2 hours so that the bread completely softens. Drain and squeeze out as much water as possible. Mix the bread with the koji, then weigh the mixture and add 5.5% salt. The rest of the process remains the same. Once ready, if the mixture is very sloppy, it can be very gently cooked in a pan to evaporate some of the liquid.

## ROAST GARLIC MISO PURÉE

**makes about 650g**

350g garlic cloves (peeled)
a drizzle of vegetable oil
demerara sugar
175g unsalted butter, cut into small cubes
150ml sherry vinegar
175g sweet white miso
175g malt extract

Preheat the oven to 180°C fan/200°C/Gas Mark 6. Toss the garlic cloves in the oil and coat them in demerara sugar. Wrap the cloves loosely in foil to create a parcel. Roast for 25 minutes. Open the parcel and return to the oven to roast for a further 5 minutes. Tip the garlic into a food processor and blend the cloves to a smooth purée.

Put the butter into a pan set over a high heat and cook until the butter starts to foam, brown and take on a nutty aroma. Immediately remove from the heat and cool quickly to stop the butter from burning.

Boil the vinegar in another pan until reduced to 75ml.

Add the brown butter, vinegar, miso and malt extract to the garlic purée and blend until smooth. Cool. The purée can be stored in the fridge in an airtight container for up to 1 month.

# DASHI

**makes about 1 litre**

25g dried kombu
1 litre distilled water, boiled and cooled (or
    use filtered water or still mineral water)
1 sheet of dried nori (about 3g)
15g bonito flakes
2 teaspoons white soy sauce
10 wild garlic leaves (if unavailable use 2
    sliced garlic cloves)
Maldon sea salt

Add the kombu to the water in a pan and bring to a very gentle simmer (do not boil). Simmer for 1 hour.

Strain the liquid through a fine sieve into a jug. Season with the nori, bonito flakes, soy sauce, wild garlic leaves and a pinch of salt. Allow to infuse for 5 minutes. Taste to check the seasoning and adjust as required: the dashi should be salty and savoury with umami. Strain the dashi through the fine sieve.

Once cooled, it can be stored in a sealed container in the fridge for 2–3 days.

# WHITE ONION DASHI

**makes about 1.5 litres**

1.5 litres water, boiled and cooled (or use
    filtered water or still mineral water)
20g dried kombu
1 medium white onion, sliced
10g bonito flakes
white soy sauce
Maldon sea salt

Combine the water, kombu, onion and bonito flakes in a pan. Bring to a very gentle simmer (do not boil), then cover with a lid and keep at a very low simmer for 1 hour.

Strain and season with white soy sauce and salt to taste. Once cooled, the dashi can be stored in a sealed container in the fridge for 2–3 days.

# ELDERFLOWER VINEGAR

The cider vinegar in this recipe is optional but will speed up the process.

**makes about 2 litres**

280g caster sugar
2 litres water
500g elderflower stems
1 tablespoon cider vinegar (optional)

Put the sugar and water in a pot, set over a medium heat and bring to the boil. Lower the heat and simmer gently for a few minutes until the sugar has completely dissolved. Allow to cool (this is a 14% sugar syrup).

Pour the syrup into a sterilised container and add the elderflower stems. Cover the top with muslin. Keep at room temperature for about 2 weeks, agitating the liquid each day by stirring with a sterilised spoon or moving the container.

After 2 weeks, some bubbles should have started to appear and the liquid should be sour. Add the cider vinegar if you are using it. Again, leave at room temperature, covered with cloth – it is a matter of taste how long you leave the vinegar to sour, so taste it regularly with a sterilised spoon.

When it reaches your desired acidity, strain it and decant into sterilised narrow-necked bottles. Seal the tops of the bottles well (we use a wax seal). Allow the vinegar to mellow in the bottle in a cool, dark place for 6 months to a year before use.

# MAYONNAISE

**makes about 300g**

3 egg yolks
1 teaspoon Dijon
    mustard
1 teaspoon white
    wine vinegar
250ml rapeseed oil
50ml water
    (if needed)
fine table salt

Put the egg yolks, mustard and vinegar in a blender or food processor and blend together. Drizzle in the oil while blending to emulsify to a mayonnaise. Let it down with a little water if it gets too thick. Season with a pinch of salt to taste.

The mayonnaise can be stored in the fridge, covered, for a couple of days.

# SICHUAN MAYONNAISE

**makes about 300g**

3 egg yolks
1 teaspoon
    Chardonnay
    vinegar
250ml rapeseed oil
50ml water
    (if needed)
fine table salt
Sichuan Oil (see
    page 57)

Put the egg yolks and vinegar in a blender or food processor and blend together. Drizzle in the rapeseed oil while blending to emulsify to a mayonnaise. Let it down with a little water if it gets too thick. Season with a pinch of salt and Sichuan oil to taste.

Store in an airtight container in the fridge for up to 2 days.

# SMOKED COD'S ROE EMULSION

**makes about 400g**

150g cod's roe
7% brine (see page 20)
applewood chips for smoking
50g sourdough bread, crusts removed
whole milk
5g Dijon mustard
½ garlic clove (peeled)
250ml vegetable oil
50ml water (if needed)
fresh lemon juice
Maldon sea salt

Brine the roe in a 7% brine in the fridge for 3 hours. Remove from the brine.

Take a flat tray with a steam insert (such as a deep roasting tray that will hold a flat steaming rack) and spread the applewood chips over the bottom of the tray. Warm it over a medium heat until the chips start to smoke. Remove from the heat. Place a tray of ice cubes on the steam insert and put the roe on a heatproof tray over the ice. Set over the smoking chips. Completely cover the top and sides tightly with oven-safe clingfilm so the smoke is sealed inside with the roe. Leave to smoke for 2–3 minutes.

Repeat the process, heating the woodchips and smoking the roe for another 2–3 minutes.

While the roe is being smoked, soak the sourdough in milk.

Squeeze the liquid from the sourdough, then put the bread in a blender or food processor. Add the roes, mustard and garlic and blend until smooth. Drizzle in the vegetable oil while the blender/food processor is running until emulsified to a mayonnaise consistency. Let down with a little water if the emulsion is too thick. Season with lemon juice and salt to taste.

The emulsion can be stored in the fridge, in an airtight container, for a couple of days.

# FOR THE TABLE

I have created a healthy selection of larder recipes in the first part of this book, certainly more than you might find at the back of most cookbooks. For me, our larder is the backbone of our recipes, it is our secret weapon. In my opinion, the better you stock your larder the easier it is to create interesting and exciting dishes without breaking a sweat, and as such, most if not all the recipes in this second half of the book will refer to a recipe from the larder chapter.

I have broken this section into chapters that reflect what we do in our restaurants – snacks, garden, sea, land and sweet – and the recipes flow from spring and summer into autumn and winter.

I hope you enjoy cooking the recipes. Don't worry if things don't always go to plan, some of our greatest dishes were created by accident!

'Mistakes are almost always of a sacred nature. Never try to correct them. On the contrary: rationalise them, understand them thoroughly. After that, it will be possible for you to sublimate them.'
–Salvador Dali

# BASES AND BLENDS, CHEF'S COCKTAILS AND HOME BREWS

# BASES AND BLENDS

## SALT SOLUTION

Some of our cocktails benefit from a spray of this salt solution over the top before serving. It adds a nice balance of flavour between sweet and savoury notes.

**makes 200ml**

100g Maldon
  sea salt
100ml water

Dissolve the salt in the water in a pan over a medium heat. Allow to cool. Decant into a spray bottle or atomiser and keep at room temperature.

## SUGAR SYRUP

**makes about 500ml**

250g caster sugar
250ml water

Dissolve the sugar in the water in a pan over a low to medium heat. Ensure that the sugar is fully dissolved. Allow to cool. The syrup can be stored in a sealed jar or bottle in the fridge for 6 months.

## BLACKBERRY SYRUP

**makes about 700ml**

250g blackberries
250g caster sugar
250ml water

Combine the blackberries, sugar and water in a pan and simmer gently until the fruit has completely softened and the sugar has dissolved. Strain through a fine sieve, pressing on the fruit in the sieve so that all the juice passes through. The syrup can be stored in a sealed jar or bottle in the fridge for 2 weeks.

## BROWN SUGAR SYRUP

**makes about 500ml**

250g demerara
  sugar
250ml water

Dissolve the sugar in the water in a pan over a low to medium heat. Ensure that the sugar is fully dissolved. Allow to cool. The syrup can be stored in a sealed jar or bottle in the fridge for 6 months.

## DILL SYRUP

**makes about 350ml**

175g caster sugar
175ml water
10g dill

Dissolve the sugar in the water in a pan over a low to medium heat. Bring to the boil, then remove from the heat and add the dill. Clingfilm the top of the pan and leave the syrup to cool and become infused with the dill flavour for 3 hours. Strain through a fine sieve, pressing down on the dill in the sieve to ensure that all the flavour passes through. The syrup can be stored in a sealed jar or bottle in the fridge for 2 weeks.

## BLACKBERRY SHRUB

**makes 875ml**

500ml Blackberry
  Syrup (see
  above)
375ml apple cider
  vinegar

Mix the syrup with the vinegar. Store in sealed sterilised jars in a cool, dark place for 2 months before use.

## SORREL SYRUP

**makes about
200ml**

200g sorrel
50ml Sugar Syrup
   (see page 72)
50ml fresh
   lemon juice
100ml cloudy
   apple juice

Blanch the sorrel in a pan of boiling water for 10 seconds. Drain and refresh in iced water. Put into a blender or food processor with all the other ingredients and blend together until as smooth as possible. Strain through a fine sieve, then pass through muslin. Store in a sealed jar or bottle in the fridge for a couple of days.

## THYME SYRUP

**makes about
500ml**

250g caster sugar
250ml water
a bunch of thyme
   (about 15g)

Dissolve the sugar in the water in a pan over a low to medium heat. Bring to the boil, then remove from the heat and immediately add the thyme. Allow to cool to room temperature. Strain the syrup through a fine sieve, pressing on the thyme in the sieve to ensure that all the flavour passes through. The syrup can be stored in a sealed jar or bottle in the fridge for up to 2 weeks.

## APPLE PURÉE

**makes about
800g–1kg**

10 Chantecler
   apples, or other
   sweet apples,
   quartered
   and cored
200ml Sugar Syrup
   (see page 72)

Cook the apple quarters on a barbecue, or hot ridged grill pan, until slightly charred for flavour. Tip them into a pan and add the sugar syrup. Simmer gently until the apples break down. Purée in a blender or food processor, then pass through a fine sieve. The purée can be stored in an airtight container in the fridge for up to 2 days, or frozen.

## RHUBARB PURÉE

**makes about 350g**

300g rhubarb, cut
   into uniform-
   sized pieces
50g caster sugar
20g Ultratex
Maldon sea salt
   and freshly
   ground black
   pepper

Put the rhubarb and sugar into a pan, cover and cook over a gentle heat until the rhubarb is soft. Pour into a blender or food processor and blend to a smooth purée with the Ultratex. Season with a pinch of salt and black pepper to taste. Store the purée in an airtight container in the fridge for up to 2 days or freeze.

## ELDERFLOWER CORDIAL

**makes about 5 litres**

300g fresh elderflowers
2 lemons
3.6 litres water
2kg caster sugar
1 teaspoon citric acid

Remove the elderflowers from the stalks, picking off all the leaves. Rinse the flowers gently. Peel the lemons and remove the pips. Put the water, sugar and citric acid in a large pot and bring to the boil. Once the sugar has dissolved, add the lemon flesh and elderflowers. Remove from the heat and leave to macerate for 2 hours.

Strain the liquid, then pour into sterilised bottles and seal. Store in a cool, dark place for up to a year. Once opened, keep in the fridge and use within 3 months.

# DEAN'S GREEN TEA KOMBUCHA

Dean's obsession with kombucha is quite infectious. As I walk round the restaurants I can see terrifying-looking jars of scoby with people's names on them, because many of the team want to have their own concoction on the go. One of our guys was suffering quite badly with some stomach pains that wouldn't go away. Doctors and antibiotics had no impact. He started his own kombucha and the problem disappeared. They are currently looking at launching their own brand together. Bravo and best of luck to them!

**makes about 3 litres**

3.5 litres filtered water
12g unbleached green teabags
300g caster sugar, plus extra to add
    at the end
1 kombucha scoby

Bring the water to the boil and boil for 10 minutes. Strain 3 litres of the water into a sterilised large, heatproof glass jar. Cool until the temperature reaches 68°C, then add the teabags. Leave to infuse for 40 minutes.

Add the sugar and stir to mix well, then strain into a sterilised large, wide-mouthed glass jar. Add the kombucha scoby. Place a cloth over the top of the vessel and leave at room temperature for 3–5 days until the liquid reaches an acidity of 3.8ph on a PH meter.

Strain out the scoby (it can be kept and used again). Measure the liquid and add ½ tablespoon of caster sugar per 1 litre. Mix well. Pour into bottles that can hold pressure, such as beer bottles, leaving about a 4cm gap at the top. Seal the bottles and leave for at least 3 days at room temperature (15–20°C). Then store in the fridge.

# FAT-WASHED WHISKEY

**makes 750ml**

250g unsalted butter, cut into small cubes
750ml Irish whiskey

Make a brown butter by melting and heating the butter cubes in a pan over a high heat until the butter starts to foam and brown and gives off a nutty aroma. Once this occurs, remove from the heat immediately and cool quickly by setting the base of the pan in cold water, to stop the butter from burning.

While the butter is still warm, add the whiskey and stir. Clingfilm the top of the pan and allow to cool and set for 3 hours, then leave in the freezer overnight. The next day, lift off the layer of butter from the top and strain the whiskey through a fine sieve into a glass jar. Store the whiskey in the fridge. The butter can be kept (in the fridge) and used in the parfait for Old-Fashioned Ice Cream Sandwiches (see page 272).

## ROSEMARY CIDER BRANDY

**makes 750ml**

4 sprigs of
    rosemary
750ml apple
    cider brandy or
    Calvados

Add the rosemary sprigs to the brandy in a large jar, seal and leave to infuse for 2 days in a cool, dark place. Strain through a fine sieve, pressing down on the rosemary in the sieve to ensure all the flavour passes through. Store the brandy in a sealed jar or bottle at room temperature.

## BLACKBERRY BRANDY

**makes about 1 litre**

400g blackberries
750ml brandy
150g caster sugar

Place the blackberries, brandy and sugar in a large sterilised jar. Seal and store in a cool, dark place for at least 2 months before use. During the first 2 weeks, give the jar a shake every 1–2 days. After this, give the jar a shake once a week.

## PEA GIN

**makes 750ml**

750ml gin
2 handfuls of
    fresh peas (in
    their pods)

Pour the gin over the peas in a large jar, seal and leave to infuse for 4 days in a cool, dark place. Strain through a fine sieve, pressing the peas in the sieve to ensure all the flavour passes through. Store the gin in a sealed jar or bottle in the fridge.

## BEETROOT GIN

**makes 750ml**

4 raw beetroots,
    peeled and diced
750ml gin

Add the diced beetroot to the gin in a large sterilised jar, seal and leave to infuse in a cool, dark place for 3–4 days. Strain through a fine sieve. Store the gin in a sealed jar or bottle in a cool, dark place.

## ROSEMARY GIN

**makes 750ml**

4 sprigs of
    rosemary
750ml gin

Add the rosemary sprigs to the gin in a large jar, seal and leave to infuse for 2 days in a cool, dark place. Strain through a fine sieve, pressing down on the rosemary in the sieve to ensure all the flavour passes through. Store the gin in a sealed jar or bottle at room temperature.

## RHUBARB LIQUEUR

**makes about
900ml**

300g rhubarb,
    chopped
200g caster sugar
1 vanilla pod
zest of ½ orange
750ml vodka

Put the rhubarb and sugar into a jar, seal and leave for 24 hours. Add the whole vanilla pod and orange zest, then pour in the vodka to cover everything. Seal the jar again and shake well. Leave in a cool, dark place for about 2 months before use; during the first few days, give the jar a shake each day to encourage the sugar to dissolve. After 2 months, strain the mixture and bottle the liqueur.

# CHEF'S COCKTAILS

Mixologists and cooks think in the same way: it's all about the perfect balance of flavours. At The Dairy, the bar runs into the kitchen, so breaking a barrier. The bar is always checking out what's on the menu and questioning what's in season. Chefs will interact and consult, and are rewarded with taste tests. Cocktails at The Dairy are a complete collaboration between the bar and the kitchen, working together on flavours and ingredients. A perfect example of this is the Kerry G Old-Fashioned (see page 80) and our Ice Cream Sandwiches (see page 272). In the process of making the cocktail, we fat-wash the whiskey with butter, then we use the butter to make the parfait for the dessert.

## DILL OR DIE

**serves 1**

1 thumb-sized piece
  of cucumber, diced
4 sprigs of dill
50ml Hendrick's gin
25ml fresh lemon juice
35ml Dill Syrup (see page 72)

Muddle the cucumber and 3 sprigs of dill together in a mixing glass, pressing and crushing lightly. Add the gin, lemon juice and syrup with some ice and shake. Fine-strain the mixture into a martini glass. Garnish with the remaining sprig of dill.

## CIDER WITH ROSIE

**serves 1**

2 sprigs of rosemary
25ml Rosemary Cider Brandy
  (see page 75)
25ml Chase Marmalade vodka
15ml fresh lemon juice
25ml Sugar Syrup
  (see page 72)

Muddle one of the rosemary sprigs in a mixing glass, pressing lightly to release the aromatic oil from the herb. Add the brandy, vodka, lemon juice and sugar syrup. Shake with ice, then fine-strain into a martini glass. Garnish with the remaining sprig of rosemary.

## DAIRY-QUIRI

**serves 1**

35ml dark rum
15ml falernum
25ml fresh lime juice
40ml Apple Purée
  (see page 73)
a wedge of lime, to garnish

Shake all the ingredients together in a mixing glass with ice. Fine-strain into a martini glass. Garnish with a wedge of lime.

## PEA AND MINT SOUR

**serves 1**

1 egg white
25ml fresh lemon juice
25ml Sugar Syrup (see page 72)
6 mint leaves, chopped
50ml Pea Gin (see page 75)
Salt Solution (see page 72),
   to finish

Dry-shake all the ingredients together in a mixing glass. Add some ice and shake again. Fine-strain into a martini glass. Atomise with a spray of salt solution.

## PANIC! AT THE PISCO

**serves 1**

15ml La Diablada pisco
35ml Belsazar white vermouth
15ml fresh lemon juice
25ml Sugar Syrup (see page 72)
25ml Rhubarb Purée
   (see page 73)
a strip of orange peel (pith
   removed), to garnish

Shake all the ingredients together with ice in a mixing glass. Fine-strain into a martini glass. Gently twist the orange peel over the glass to release the essential oils, then drop it into the drink.

## SORREL BELLINI

**serves 1**

20ml Sorrel Syrup (see page 73)
20ml gin
5ml Elderflower Cordial
   (see page 73)
chilled Champagne or
   prosecco

Shake together the sorrel syrup, gin and elderflower cordial in a mixing glass. Fine-strain into a champagne flute. Top up with Champagne or prosecco.

## APPLE AND FENNEL
## HENDRICK'S

**serves 4**

3 small Granny Smith
   apples, quartered
1 bulb of fennel (reserve the
   fennel fronds to garnish)
½ cucumber
juice of 1 lime
140ml Hendrick's gin (35ml
   per person)

Using an electric juicer/press, juice the apples,
fennel and cucumber. Add the fresh lime juice
straight away to keep the juice a bright, fresh
green colour.

Divide chunky ice cubes and gin among four
glasses, add the juice and stir. Garnish with the
fennel fronds.

## BRING THAT BEET BACK

**serves 1**

50ml Beetroot Gin
   (see page 75)
20ml Blackberry Syrup
   (see page 72)
3 dashes of cocoa/
   chocolate bitters
cacao nibs, to garnish

Stir the gin, syrup and bitters together in a mixing
glass with ice. Strain over fresh ice in a small rocks
glass. Garnish with cacao nibs.

## THYME FOR ANOTHER

**serves 1**

100ml tonic water
50ml Botanist gin
25ml Thyme Syrup
   (see page 73)
25ml cloudy apple juice

Simmer the tonic water until reduced by half; cool.

Stir all the ingredients together in a glass with ice. Strain into a chilled martini glass and enjoy!

## KERRY G OLD-FASHIONED

**serves 1**

50ml Fat-Washed Whiskey
   (see page 74)
20ml Brown Sugar Syrup
   (see page 72)
3 dashes of Angostura bitters
a strip of orange peel
   (pith removed), to garnish
Salt Solution (see page 72),
   to finish

Stir the whiskey, syrup and bitters in a mixing glass with ice, then strain over fresh ice in a small rocks glass. Gently twist the orange peel over the glass to release the essential oils, then drop it into the drink. Atomise with a spray of salt solution.

## ROSIE AND GIN

**serves 1**

2 sprigs of rosemary
35ml Rosemary Gin
   (see page 75)
10ml Campari
5ml gin
35ml grapefruit juice
10ml fresh lemon juice
15ml Sugar Syrup (see page 72)

Muddle one of the rosemary sprigs in a mixing glass, pressing lightly to release the aromatic oil from the herb. Add the rosemary gin, Campari, gin, juices, syrup and some ice and shake together. Fine-strain the mixture into a martini glass. Garnish with the remaining sprig of rosemary.

## RAMBLE IN THE BRAMBLE

**serves 1**

25ml Blackberry Brandy (see
    page 75)
25ml apple brandy (Somerset
    Pomona) or Calvados
1 egg white
25ml fresh lemon juice
a wedge of lemon, to garnish
a blackberry from the brandy,
    to garnish

Dry-shake all the ingredients together in a mixing
glass. Then add some ice and shake again. Strain
on to fresh ice in a rocks glass. Garnish with a
lemon wedge and one of the blackberries from the
brandy.

## VODKA AND COFFEE AFFOGATO

**serves 7–8**

| **VODKA AND MILK** | **COFFEE GRANITA** |
| --- | --- |
| 100ml milk | 300ml espresso |
| 100ml vodka | coffee |
| 100g caster sugar | |

Mix together the milk, vodka and sugar. Cover and
leave at room temperature for 4 days. The milk will
curdle slightly. Pass through a fine sieve and store
in the freezer.

For the granita, freeze the coffee until solid. Break it
up with a fork to create a granita texture.

To serve, put a spoonful of the vodka and milk
mixture in each glass and top with a spoonful of
coffee granita (approximately 40g of each mixture).
Serve each glass with a spoon on the side.

## THE DAIRY AMERICANO

**serves 1**

50ml Vergano Mauro
    Americano
25ml white vermouth
soda (to top up)
a strip of orange peel (pith
    removed), to garnish

Mix together the Vergano Americano and white
vermouth. Pour over ice in a rocks glass. Top up
with soda and stir gently. Gently twist the orange
peel over the glass to release the essential oils,
then drop into the drink.

# HOME BREW BEER

Big shout out here to Will and Wesley, a classic example of teamwork and passion. These guys actually come in on their days off to experiment and develop beer recipes together. I'm sure they enjoy the tasting too! Someone's gotta do it!

When it comes to making your own beer, the possibilities are endless. There are many sources for research, and it is always a good idea to do some reading before investing in equipment. One of the key points to remember is to keep all equipment and areas sterilised throughout the process. To get started with beer-making, the following equipment is required: a very large pan, a temperature probe, a fermentation bucket with an airlock, a hydrometer, a bottling wand, a beer capper, bottles and caps. The recipes here are for large quantities but they can, of course, be scaled down to your requirements.

## GINGER BEER

**makes about 4 litres**

### GINGER BUG

500ml water
175g caster sugar
175g root ginger, finely grated

Pour the water into a suitable-sized, sterilised container. Add 25g of the caster sugar and 25g of the ginger. Cover the top of the container with muslin. Leave at room temperature for 7 days, feeding it each subsequent day with the same quantities of sugar and ginger.

### GINGER BEER

5 litres water
1kg caster sugar, plus some extra
   to be added at the end
250g root ginger, finely chopped
juice of 2 limes
juice of ½ lemon
a Ginger Bug (see above)

Bring the water and sugar to the boil in a large pan, stirring to dissolve the sugar. Add the ginger and simmer for 10 minutes. Remove from the heat and allow to cool to about 40°C, then stir in the lime and lemon juices. Cool to room temperature before adding the ginger bug.

Strain through a fine sieve into a fermentation bucket and seal. Leave at room temperature for about 3 weeks. During this time, test regularly with a hydrometer – the sugar level should be dropping. Once it levels off and stops dropping, the liquid is ready for the next step.

Weigh the liquid and calculate 10% of this – this is the amount of sugar you will need to add. Decant 700ml of the liquid into a pan and add the sugar. Bring to the boil to dissolve the sugar, then cool before pouring back into the rest of the liquid. Using a bottling wand, decant into sterilised bottles, cap and seal. Allow to condition at room temperature for one week, then store in the fridge until required.

# PUMPKIN BEER

**makes about 23 litres**

3 pumpkins (we used Delicia)
500g Marisota malt barley
25 litres water
3kg dry malt extract
40g Equinox/Ekuanot hops
1 sachet English ale yeast (7g)
1 cinnamon stick
2 cloves
a thumb-sized piece of root ginger (peeled)
granulated sugar

Preheat the oven to 160°C fan/180°C/Gas Mark 4. Peel two of the pumpkins and discard the seeds and fibres. Dice the flesh and spread on a large baking tray. Roast for 20 minutes or until soft. Allow to cool.

Cut the remaining pumpkin in half and remove the seeds and fibres, then juice it (with the skin on) through an electric juicer. Set the juice aside.

Wrap the roasted pumpkin and the Marisota malt barley in a piece of muslin and tie the top. Add this parcel to 6 litres of the water in a large pan and allow to stew over a low heat, keeping the water at 72°C, for 30 minutes.

Remove the parcel and give it a good squeeze over the pan, then discard. Add the remaining water to the stewing liquor and bring to the boil. Whisk in the malt extract while the liquid is boiling. Add 15g of the Equinox hops, then leave to boil vigorously for 1 hour.

Cool to 80°C, then add the remaining Equinox hops and the raw pumpkin juice. Cool rapidly to 20°C in sterilised trays set over ice. Pour into a fermentation bucket, whisk to add in air, whisk in the yeast and seal the bucket. Leave to ferment at room temperature.

On day 4, remove a little of the liquid and pour into a sterilised pan. Add the cinnamon, cloves and ginger, and bring to the boil. Allow to cool before pouring the whole lot back into the fermentation bucket.

On day 7, check the sugar levels with a hydrometer. Do the same on day 8. If the level is the same then the liquid is ready. If not, repeat the checking each day until the level stops dropping and is the same 2 days in a row.

Once ready, measure the liquid and calculate 4.5g of granulated sugar per litre. Decant a small amount (about a litre) into a pan and add the sugar to this. Bring to the boil just to dissolve the sugar, then remove from the heat and allow to cool before adding back to the rest of the liquid, stirring to mix.

Using a bottling wand, decant into sterilised bottles, cap and seal. Allow to condition at room temperature for 3 weeks and then store in the fridge until required.

# SNACKS

# FERMENTED POTATO FLATBREAD

## NDUJA AND CULTURED CREAM

serves 12

Potato flatbreads feature in many cuisines. In my own Irish culture, there are a lot of recipes but none call for the potato to be fermented. In Ireland fermented potatoes were (and still are) used to distil a lethal drink called poitín, or poteen, which could range anywhere from 40 per cent to 90 per cent ABV (alcohol by volume)! In fact, the Irish word for a hangover is póit. We find that adding fermented potato gives this light flatbread an incredible sour flavour that is very welcome. We serve it with cultured cream and our own nduja, but it is a really versatile bread that can be served with just about anything, from hummus to a fried egg at breakfast.

### FERMENTED POTATO FLATBREAD

15g fresh yeast
225ml tepid water
125ml buttermilk
430g strong white flour
15g rye flour
a large pinch of fine table salt
250g Potato Ferment (see page 23), lightly crushed with the back of a fork
a pinch of Maldon sea salt

Mix the yeast with a small amount of the water. Add this to the rest of the water and the buttermilk in the bowl of a stand mixer fitted with a paddle attachment and mix until smooth. Add the flours and table salt and mix/knead for about 5 minutes to make a smooth dough. (Alternatively, you can mix and knead the dough by hand.) Cover the dough with a towel or clingfilm and leave to rise in an ambient part of the kitchen (20–24°C) for 40 minutes.

Fold the dough over on itself to knock out the air, then leave to rise for 40 minutes. Fold again to knock out the air, then leave to rise for another 40 minutes. Repeat the process so that the dough has four rises and four folds in total. Once the dough has had its final fold, chill it until it reaches 8°C (use a temperature probe to check).

Remove the dough from the fridge and roll it out on a lightly floured surface into a large rectangle about 3cm thick. Place on a large baking tray. Scatter the potatoes and Maldon salt over the top. Leave to prove in an ambient part of the kitchen until the dough rectangle has almost doubled in thickness.

Preheat the oven to 250°C fan/its highest setting. When the bread is ready to be baked, place a baking tray filled with water in the bottom of the oven, then slide the bread, on its baking tray, on to a higher shelf. Bake for 10 minutes. Remove the tray of water, lower the oven temperature to 180°C fan/200°C/Gas Mark 6 and bake the bread for a further 6 minutes or until it sounds hollow when tapped on the bottom. Cool on a wire rack.

### ASSEMBLY

Cultured Cream (see page 54)
Nduja (see page 36)
picked marjoram leaves

Warm the potato flatbread in the oven or on a barbecue. Tear into portions. Serve with a ramekin of cultured cream and a ramekin of nduja topped with marjoram on the side.

# BREAD COURSE

On a trip to Stockholm I visited Restaurant Frantzén. I spent a couple of days in the kitchen there and then had dinner. This consisted of twenty-plus courses, all of which were incredible, but the one thing that stood out and made me think was the bread. When you sit down at your spot for dinner (mine was at the counter peering into the kitchen), there is a little box in your place setting. Inside I found some bread dough that was proving. It was explained to me that I would have the bread later when it was ready, but they wanted to stress the process and its importance.

About 45 minutes and eight or so courses later, they produced the bread fresh from the oven with a number of accompaniments. I took time to relax, break bread and think.

For many years in zillions of restaurants bread has been a gap-filler once you sit down – usually stale, unseasoned, bought from a mass producer. You get my point. Offering bread is one of the oldest and most sacred traditions in the world that has been bastardised for too long by too many.

When we opened The Dairy it was our mission to create the best bread serving we could. We had a terrible gas lower-deck oven that enabled us to bake only one tray at a time, which caused fights over oven space. But we made it happen. Our bread is one of the things that keeps our customers coming back. We decided that it should not be offered the moment guests sit down but a few courses later, served in baskets made by my mum. Our guests have to tear the warm crusty bread with their hands, which makes them stop for a minute to relax and enjoy that sacred and intimate tradition of breaking bread with each other.

# TOMATO AND BUCKWHEAT PANCAKES

This is our version of a tomato tart, gluten-free and very light. We use second-grade beef tomatoes (which basically means overripe) to make the chutney. It may seem odd to barbecue the tomatoes for it, but this does add a real depth to the flavour profile. The chutney can be made in advance and you'll have quite a large amount. The recipe could be halved but it is worth making a big batch as it keeps well in the fridge and can be used to jazz up anything from oily fish like mackerel, smoked eel and sardines to roast lamb, chicken or quail. If you don't have access to a barbecue, you can forgo the barbecuing step and instead smoke the chutney at the end. Sometimes at the restaurant, having barbecued the tomatoes, we taste the chutney and are not happy with the intensity of the smokiness, so we smoke it as well.

*serves 4–6*

## BBQ TOMATO CHUTNEY

80ml Chardonnay vinegar
10 beefsteak tomatoes
1 shallot, finely diced
50g chives, finely chopped
Onion Treacle (see page 48)
capers, drained
Maldon sea salt and freshly ground
  black pepper

Boil the vinegar in a small pan to reduce to about 20ml (4 teaspoons).

Fire up a barbecue (or alternatively, smoke the chutney at the end; see below). When there is plenty of smoke, place the tomatoes on the grid over a low heat and cook until they start to break down and the skins start to blister.

Transfer the tomatoes to a pan set over a low heat and cook until the liquid from the tomatoes has evaporated. Remove from the heat and stir in the shallot and chives. Season to taste with the vinegar, onion treacle, capers, salt and pepper.

If you want to smoke the chutney rather than barbecuing the tomatoes, spread the chutney in a thin layer on a heatproof tray and place this into a steel steaming tray. Cover with oven-safe clingfilm, sealing in the top and allowing gaps for the smoke to come through. Place some wood chips in a baking tray and heat over a medium heat until the chips start to smoke. Place the steaming tray over the smoking chips and smoke the chutney for 10 minutes.

## BUCKWHEAT PANCAKES

95g buckwheat flour
1½ teaspoons baking powder
1 teaspoon bicarbonate of soda
a large pinch of fine table salt
190ml buttermilk
1 egg, separated
15g unsalted butter, melted, plus butter
  for frying
buckwheat groats, for sprinkling

Mix together the flour, baking powder, bicarbonate of soda and salt. In a separate bowl, mix together the buttermilk, egg yolk and melted butter. Whisk the egg white to stiff peaks. Whisk the buttermilk mixture into the flour mixture until smooth, then fold in the egg white.

Melt a small knob of butter in a large frying pan set over a medium heat. Ladle about half of the batter into the pan to make a pancake about 1cm. When the pancake is cooked about three-quarters of the way up, sprinkle the top with some buckwheat groats. Allow to cook a little more,

*...continued on page 90*

then turn the pancake over to finish cooking on the other side. Remove from the pan. Repeat with the remaining batter.

Allow the pancakes to cool, then use a round cutter of your chosen size to cut out small discs.

## ASSEMBLY

a selection of small seasonal tomatoes
   (we use Datterini when available), cut
   in half
a drizzle of olive oil
bronze fennel fronds
tarragon leaves
chervil leaves
basil leaves
hard goat's cheese (we use Tymsboro),
   frozen and grated
grated fresh horseradish
Maldon sea salt and freshly ground
   black pepper

Warm the small pancakes on a baking tray in a hot oven for 1–2 minutes or until they are just heated through. Season the fresh tomatoes with a drizzle of olive oil, salt and pepper. Top each pancake with a little of the tomato chutney, followed by the fresh tomatoes, herbs and goat's cheese, and finish with a little horseradish.

# TRUFFLE BARON BIGOD

## FIG AND WALNUT TOAST, ROOFTOP HONEY

This is a very special 'Dairy' recipe, one of only a few that we cannot ever dare to take off the menu (we did this once and it was met with tears and anger from our guests; my wife, aka 'Boss Lady', stepped in and it was put swiftly back on the menu, never to be tampered with again). We initially used a Brie de Meaux but as we became increasingly confident about British and Irish cheese we looked for a substitute. Our friends in Neal's Yard Dairy put us on to a lovely couple who produce Baron Bigod. In my opinion it is one of the greatest cheeses on the planet, not just in Europe. You don't need to make your own bread but we thought you might like to try.

serves 4–6

### TRUFFLE BARON BIGOD

200g Baron Bigod cheese
80g mascarpone
10g fresh black truffle, grated
2–3 drops of truffle oil
Maldon sea salt and freshly ground
   black pepper

\* This is best prepared 24 hours in
   advance to allow the cheese to take on
   the truffle flavour.

Cut the Baron Bigod in half horizontally. Season the mascarpone with the fresh truffle, truffle oil, salt and pepper. Spread this mixture across the bottom cut side of the Baron Bigod, then put the top half on to make a sandwich. Wrap in clingfilm and store in the fridge for at least 24 hours.

### FIG AND WALNUT BREAD

**Makes 2 small or 1 large loaf**

75g walnut halves
300g Campaillou bread flour or other
   strong white flour, plus extra for dusting
75g strong wholemeal flour
50g chestnut flour
10g fresh yeast
10g salt
30g honey
30g full-fat plain yoghurt
120ml semi-skimmed milk
50ml apple juice
75g dried figs, soaked in green tea for
   30 minutes, then drained
75g golden sultanas

Lightly toast the walnuts in a dry pan, then crush them slightly.

Put the flours, yeast and salt into a large stand mixer fitted with the paddle attachment and mix for 3–4 minutes. Add the honey, yoghurt, milk and apple juice and continue mixing/kneading on a low speed for 10–15 minutes, scraping the sides of the bowl if the mixture catches. The resulting dough should be sticky but retain its shape and have a slight bounce to the touch. Add the figs, sultanas and walnuts and mix for 3 minutes. (Alternatively, you can mix and knead the dough by hand.)

Using a dough scraper, tip the dough on to a floured surface. Divide in half if you want to make two loaves. Fold the dough and tuck under the ends to create a rectangular loaf. Dust with Campaillou flour and slash the top with a sharp knife. Place on a floured baking tray and leave in a warm place to prove until almost doubled in size.

Preheat the oven to 250°C fan/its highest setting. Bake the bread for 6 minutes. Transfer from the baking tray to the oven rack. Lower the oven temperature to 180°C fan/200°C/Gas Mark 6 and bake for a further 20

...continued on page 94

minutes or until the bread sounds hollow when tapped on the bottom. Cool on a wire rack.

**ASSEMBLY**

good-quality honey, for drizzling
10g fresh black truffle

Remove the cheese from the fridge about 1 hour before serving to allow it to soften.

Preheat the grill. Slice the bread and toast the slices. Top each slice of toast with a slice of the cheese and melt under the grill for about 30 seconds. Drizzle with honey and grate over a little fresh truffle, then serve.

# CHICKEN LIVER PARFAIT

## APRICOT GEL AND TOASTED SOURDOUGH

serves 10–12

This is one of the very first recipes I learned at Marco Pierre White's legendary restaurant, The Oak Room. During my time there the recipe had 50 per cent foie gras and a small fortune's worth of Perigord truffle grated in! If you can afford it, why not, eh? For years, we kept the foie gras in and Richie questioned the necessity of it. He claimed that if we made sure the chicken livers were the absolute best quality that could be found, the foie gras would not be missed. He was absolutely right. Not only was it as delicious, if not more, it was hugely cheaper and considerably less controversial. It meant that we then became a foie gras-free restaurant. This may not seem like a big deal but I spent ten years of my training in restaurants that spent thousands of pounds a month on the stuff! I was lucky enough to be able to work with the world's most expensive ingredients on a daily basis, but what I have now come to realise is that cost is not always an assurance of flavour. Here the humble chicken liver beats the big, fat, overfed goose liver. You'll see I still like the finer things in life though and have grated a heap of black truffle over the top. I couldn't help myself…

### CHICKEN LIVER PARFAIT

650g fresh chicken livers
pink curing salt
fine table salt
450g unsalted butter, softened
5 eggs (at room temperature), beaten

### MARINADE

5 medium shallots, sliced
250ml Madeira
250ml port
100ml red wine
50ml Cognac
2–3 bay leaves

First make the marinade. Put all the ingredients in a pan and cook on a low heat until all the liquid has evaporated. Allow to cool, then keep in the fridge until required.

Set a large empty bowl on a set of kitchen scales and turn the scales back to zero. Combine the marinade and livers in the bowl. Based on the weight of the contents of the bowl, calculate 0.5% pink salt and 0.5% salt (about 3.5g of each). Add these and mix in. Tip the mixture into a freezer bag, seal tightly and refrigerate for 12 hours.

Place the butter in another freezer bag and seal. Warm both bags at the same time by placing them under hand-hot running water at about 40°C (make sure the bags are well sealed so that no water gets in). Once the butter has melted, the chicken livers should be at the correct temperature.

Decant the chicken livers and marinade into a blender or food processor and blend until smooth. Add half the eggs and blend again. While blending, add the melted butter at a steady pace. Finally, blend in the remaining eggs. Pass the mixture through a fine sieve.

Preheat the oven to 80°C fan/100°C/Gas Mark low. Transfer the mixture to terrine moulds (or loaf tins). Cover each mould with a folded piece of foil and top with a lid (cover loaf tins with extra foil). Set the moulds in a bain marie, or roasting tray of hot water, and place in the oven to cook for about 35 minutes – the core temperature of the parfait needs

*…continued on page 96*

to reach 68°C, so use a temperature probe to check this before removing the moulds from the oven. Allow to cool, then keep in the fridge until required.

## APRICOT GEL

300g fresh apricots, stones removed
   and roughly diced
35g caster sugar
20g Ultratex
sherry vinegar
freshly ground black pepper

Combine the apricots and sugar in a pan, cover and cook over a gentle heat until the fruit is soft. Transfer to a blender or food processor and blend to a smooth purée with the Ultratex. Season to taste with sherry vinegar and black pepper.

## ASSEMBLY

fresh black truffle (optional)
fresh apricots, stones removed and sliced
2 slices of sourdough bread per
   person, toasted
Maldon sea salt and freshly ground
   black pepper

Whisk the parfait in a stand mixer fitted with a balloon whisk attachment, or using a hand-held mixer, until light and aerated. Taste and season with salt and pepper as required. Spread a little of the apricot gel in each bowl and top with a spoonful of the whipped chicken liver parfait. Grate over fresh black truffle, if using. Serve sliced apricots and toasted bread on the side.

# BRAWN

To give utmost respect for Mary Holbrook's beautiful pigs, every bit of them must be put to good use. This is our version of a pig recipe that most cooks like to put their own stamp on. It's best to follow our technique but you can be creative with the spices, herbs and seasonings. I would always recommend serving brawn with something sharp and fresh to cut through the fat. That's the only rule.

serves 10–15
(depending on size
of the pig's head)

1 pig's head, split down the centre
7% brine (see page 20)
1 litre white wine
1 white onion, cut in half
1 bunch of celery, cut in half (across)
1 carrot, cut in half
4 bay leaves
1 clove
1 bulb of garlic, cut in half (horizontally)
6 allspice berries
a handful of white peppercorns
2 handfuls of flat-leaf parsley
    leaves, chopped
50ml fresh lemon juice
wholegrain mustard
Dijon mustard
Maldon sea salt

Remove the brain from the pig's head. Remove the ears from the head. Clean the head and the ears well using an abrasive sponge. Burn the hairs off both using a kitchen blowtorch. Brine them in a 7% brine in the fridge, or a cool place, for 8 hours.

Drain the head and ears from the brine. Preheat the oven to 120°C fan/140°C/Gas Mark 1.

Pour the wine into an ovenproof pot or flameproof casserole that the head and ears will fit into snugly. Bring to the boil and boil for 2 minutes to evaporate some of the alcohol.

Slightly char the onion, celery and carrot on a barbecue, or on a hot ridged grill pan, for flavour, then add to the pot. Add the bay leaves, clove, garlic, allspice berries and peppercorns. Finally, add the pig's head and ears and top up with water to cover. Put a lid on the pot and place in the oven to cook for 5–6 hours or until the meat is falling off the bone.

Remove the head and ears from the stock. Strain the stock into another pan and boil to reduce it by two-thirds so that it is highly seasoned and strong in gelatine.

Pick the meat off the head. Roughly chop half of the skin and fat from the head and mix with the meat. Slice the ears into thin strips and mix in. Season the meat mixture with the parsley, lemon juice and mustard to taste. Mix some of the reduced stock through the mixture so that it has a stew-like consistency. Taste and season with salt if required.

Pour the mixture into a terrine mould lined with clingfilm. Cover the top with clingfilm and weigh down with a light weight, just to press the brawn gently into shape. Leave to set in the fridge overnight.

About 20 minutes before serving, turn the brawn out of the terrine mould and remove the clingfilm. Slice the brawn into 2–3cm pieces. Leave to come up to room temperature.

...continued on page 100

## ASSEMBLY

breakfast radishes
radish tops
Pickled Radishes (see page 45)
capers, drained
miner's lettuce
Dijon mustard
toasted sourdough or fresh warm bread

Serve a slice of brawn on each plate with a side of radishes, radish tops, pickled radishes, capers and miner's lettuce. Serve a spoonful of Dijon mustard in a small ramekin at the side. This dish is delicious with some slices of toasted sourdough or fresh warm bread.

# SPICED POLLOCK GOUGÈRES

This is a fine example of taking something that in most cases is thrown away and turning it into something outrageously elegant. Gougères can be a vessel to use up all sorts of things – we make a beautiful mousse from cheese trim and rinds to fill gougères, or to fill mushrooms. Here a filling based on cooked fish is piped into gougères, which are topped with a rich mornay sauce. Any type of cooked white fish could be substituted for the pollock. Served warm, the gougères are a welcoming mouthful to start off an evening. In the restaurant this is often the first snack. Our guests stop and take a bite, then settle in, feeling comfortably at home.

**Makes about 30**

### GOUGÈRES

100g unsalted butter
130ml whole milk
120ml water
1 teaspoon fine table salt
a pinch of espelette pepper
150g plain flour
110g Cheddar (preferably Isle of Mull), grated
4 eggs
egg yolk, to glaze

Preheat the oven to 180°C fan/200°C/Gas Mark 6.

In a pan, bring the butter, milk, water, salt and espelette pepper to the boil. Stir in the flour and cook over a medium heat for about 5 minutes, stirring. Transfer to a stand mixer fitted with a paddle attachment, or a bowl if using a hand-held electric mixer, and add the grated cheese. Mix in the cheese until evenly incorporated. Allow the mixture to cool slightly, then mix in the eggs one at a time to make a smooth choux paste.

Spoon the choux paste into a disposable piping bag. Pipe into small rounds on a baking tray lined with greaseproof paper, allowing about

*...continued on page 102*

a heaped tablespoonful of mixture per gougère. Leave space between the rounds to allow for spreading. Dip your finger in beaten egg yolk and gently smooth out the peaks and round off the tops.

Bake for 30 minutes. Lower the oven temperature to 160°C fan/180°C/ Gas Mark 4 and bake for a further 5 minutes. Cool on a wire rack.

## POLLOCK FILLING

270g cooked skinless pollock fillet
35g White Wine Shallot Gastrique
 (see page 46)
50g Mayonnaise (see page 67), seasoned
 with a pinch of smoked paprika
½ bunch of chives, chopped
Tabasco sauce
fresh lemon juice
Maldon sea salt

Mix together the pollock, shallot gastrique, mayo and chives. Season with a few drops of Tabasco, lemon juice and salt to taste. Spoon the mixture into a disposable piping bag and keep in the fridge until required.

## MORNAY SAUCE

20g unsalted butter
20g plain flour
160ml whole milk
40g strong Cheddar, grated
2 teaspoons Dijon mustard
25g egg yolks
40ml double cream, whipped
 until slightly thick

Melt the butter in a pan and add the flour. Cook out the flour for 1–2 minutes, stirring. Whisk in the milk. Continue to whisk over the heat until the sauce has thickened. Remove from the heat and mix in the cheese and mustard. Allow the mixture to cool slightly, then stir in the egg yolks and cream. Decant into a disposable piping bag.

## ASSEMBLY

espelette pepper
chopped chives

Preheat the oven to 180°C fan/200°C/Gas Mark 6 and heat the grill to high. Poke a small hole in the bottom of each gougère and pipe in the pollock filling. Arrange the gougères on a baking tray and warm in the oven for a couple of minutes. Pipe the mornay sauce over the top of each gougère, then flash under the hot grill until golden. Serve hot, dusted with espelette pepper and garnished with chopped chives.

# SALT COD BRANDADE

## SQUID INK AND SORREL

serves 6

Every chef I know has their own interpretation of brandade. I first learned Raymond Blanc's version while working in his kitchen on the fish section many moons ago. Brandade is best made on the day and kept warm, never hitting the fridge – we had to make it fresh for every service and I admit that I had a tendency to make a little too much every time. I loved to scrape the pot clean with some torn bread (don't tell RB). The quality of the olive oil is key. There are so many horrific varieties on the market, you will feel quite rightly devastated if your dish is ruined by cheap, poor-quality oil. We use an Arbequino oil that is slightly sweeter than most and not as peppery. My advice is to search for your favourite and stock up.

### COD BRANDADE

200g rock salt
500g good-quality waxy potatoes
300g skinless cod fillet
250ml whole milk
250ml water
3 garlic cloves (peeled)
¼ white onion
1 bay leaf
4 black peppercorns
70ml extra virgin olive oil
fresh lemon juice
Maldon sea salt and freshly ground
    black pepper

Preheat the oven to 190°C fan/210°C/Gas Mark 6–7. Sprinkle a little of the rock salt on a baking tray and add the potatoes, spreading them out on the salt. Bake for about 45 minutes or until cooked through. While the potatoes are cooking, cover the cod in the remaining rock salt and marinate for 8 minutes, then rinse in cold water and pat dry.

Combine the milk, water, garlic cloves, onion, bay leaf, peppercorns and a pinch of salt in a pot. Bring to a simmer and gently poach the garlic until it is soft. Strain the liquid into another pot. Keep the garlic; crush it and set aside.

Add the cod to the strained hot liquid and poach gently for 12 minutes. Remove from the heat and leave to cool in the liquid for 10 minutes.

While the potatoes are still hot, scoop out their flesh and pass through a drum sieve or fine mesh chinois into a mixing bowl. Drain the cod (reserve the liquid) and gently fold into the warm potato along with the crushed garlic. Stir in the olive oil and season to taste with lemon juice, salt and pepper. Loosen the brandade with some of the reserved poaching liquid.

### SQUID INK DRESSING

10g squid ink
50ml extra virgin olive oil
juice of 1 lemon
a pinch of smoked paprika

Put the squid ink in a mixing bowl and whisk in the oil, lemon juice and paprika.

### ASSEMBLY

a bunch of sorrel leaves
olive oil

Spoon the brandade into a round on each plate and top with sorrel leaves. Drizzle with the dressing and a little olive oil on the side.

# PÂTÉ EN CROÛTE

serves 10–12

I find cooking at home to be therapeutic and stress-free. I move at a slower pace, a glass of wine in hand. This pâté en croûte is one of the recipes I like to make, taking my time by spreading the work over a couple of days. The flavour of the pâté will only improve if you make it a day ahead. So if you're entertaining at the weekend, start to prepare this on the Wednesday by slicing the pancetta, making the pastry, cooking the onions and weighing the mix. Bake on Thursday to enjoy on Saturday, and finish any left over on Sunday.

## FILLING

625g pork belly mince
2 teaspoons white wine
1 tablespoon port
1 garlic clove, finely chopped
½ allspice berry, crushed to a powder
2 sprigs of thyme, leaves picked
15g Maldon sea salt
1 white-skinned onion, diced
25g lard or unsalted butter
75g sunflower seeds
1 teaspoon Madeira
30g flat-leaf parsley, leaves picked
    and chopped
1 egg
1 egg yolk
½ green apple (such as Granny Smith),
    cored and diced
125g pork liver, cut into 1cm dice
125g pork back fat, diced

Mix together the pork belly mince with the white wine, port, garlic, allspice, thyme leaves and salt in a large bowl. Cover tightly with clingfilm and leave in the fridge overnight.

Sweat the onion in the lard or butter until completely softened but with no colour. Fold in the sunflower seeds and Madeira. Remove from the heat and allow to cool before mixing into the pork belly mixture. Stir in the parsley, egg, egg yolk, apple, pork liver and back fat.

## PASTRY

285g strong white flour
1 teaspoon baking powder
2 teaspoons fine table salt
50g duck fat
45g unsalted butter, diced
1 egg
1 teaspoon white wine vinegar
about 50ml whole milk

Put the flour, baking powder, salt, duck fat and diced butter into a stand mixer fitted with the paddle attachment (or into a food processor) and mix to a breadcrumb consistency. Mix the egg with the vinegar and add to the flour mixture. Add enough milk to make a smooth dough that is dry to the touch.

(If making the pastry ahead of time, it can be wrapped in clingfilm and kept in the fridge. Bring it to room temperature for an hour before required.)

...continued on page 108

## ASSEMBLY

unsalted butter for greasing the mould
400g thinly sliced pancetta (see page 37)
    or smoked bacon rashers
1 egg, beaten, for glazing
3 sheets/leaves of silver leaf gelatine
300ml fresh apple juice
50g Onion Treacle (see page 48)

Grease a 1-litre terrine mould (35.5 x 11cm, 12cm deep) with butter. Roll out the pastry on a lightly floured worktop away from you into a rectangle about 5mm thick that is large enough to line the entire mould and fold over the top as a lid. Place the terrine mould on the rolled-out pastry parallel to one short side and about three-quarters of the way down the rectangle. Cut lines in the pastry diagonally towards each corner of the mould.

Now line the mould with the pastry, sealing up any gaps at the corners. You will have a long overhang of pastry on one side, which will be folded over the top (reserve the pastry trimmings). Line the pastry case with the pancetta or bacon, laying them crossways so there is an overhang on each long side. Spoon the pork filling into the centre and fold the overhanging bacon over the top. Finish by folding the pastry overhang over the top and sealing well by crimping the edges.

Cut three holes in the lid down the length of the terrine. Make three small funnels out of foil and fit them into the holes. Roll some of the pastry trimmings into three thin sausage shapes and place at the base of the funnels to secure them in the pastry. Brush the entire pastry lid with beaten egg. Put into the fridge and leave to set for at least 2 hours.

Preheat the oven to 210°C fan/230°C/Gas Mark 8. Bake the pâté en croûte for 15 minutes. Lower the oven temperature to 170°C fan/190°C/Gas Mark 5 and bake for a further 15–20 minutes or until the core temperature reaches 58°C. Allow to cool in the mould to room temperature, then place in the fridge to set overnight.

To make the jelly, soak the gelatine in cold water to soften it. Warm the apple juice and onion treacle together. Drain the gelatine and stir into the warm liquid until completely melted. Allow to cool to about 10°C, then pour through the funnels into the pâté en croûte. Remove and discard the funnels. Place the mould back in the fridge and leave to set for 2 hours.

Remove the pâté from the mould. Slice and serve with any pickles that you have, some Dijon mustard and a nice peppery leaf salad.

# BEEF TARTARE

## SOUR ONIONS, NASTURTIUM CAPERS AND ROCK OYSTER

For this tartare, we use quite a funky 100-day-aged beef rump at the restaurant but
I have also used onglet, fillet and sirloin. When you buy your beef, ask your butcher for
a nice aged piece of whatever he has. There are big punchy flavours in this dish, ticking
all the boxes with acidity, heat and spice, so you need a cheesy well-aged piece of beef
to stand up for itself. We use nasturtium capers, made from flowerbuds that we collect
from our farm, but garlic capers or regular capers will do just fine too. This dish is really
a belter and an all-year-rounder.

**serves 8–10**

*...continued on page 110*

## OYSTER EMULSION

100g banana shallots, sliced
200ml dry white wine
130g freshly shucked rock oysters
   (juice reserved)
150ml grapeseed oil
1 tablespoon crème fraîche

Put the shallots into a saucepan and pour over the white wine. Place on a medium to low heat and boil until all the wine has evaporated. Remove from the heat and allow to cool.

Tip the shallot mixture and oysters into a blender or food processor and blend until smooth. While blending, gradually add the oil to make a mayonnaise consistency. Add some of the reserved oyster juice to loosen the mixture. Stir in the crème fraîche. Keep the emulsion in the fridge until ready to serve.

## SHALLOT CRISPS

150g unsalted butter, diced
150g banana shallots, finely sliced
Maldon sea salt

Put the diced butter into a wide, flat-bottomed pan over a high heat. Stir the butter and cook until it starts to foam. Add the sliced shallots and cook, stirring, until they start to turn golden brown and the butter smells like toasted nuts.

Remove the pan from the heat and drain the shallots in a sieve. Spread out the shallot crisps on a tray lined with kitchen paper and season lightly with salt. Keep in a warm, dry place.

## BEEF TARTARE

250g 100-day-aged beef rump (or good-
   quality beef rump aged for a minimum
   of 28 days), trimmed and cut into 1cm dice
1 tablespoon Dijon mustard
1 tablespoon juice from Nasturtium Capers
   (see page 44)
2 teaspoons extra virgin olive oil
Maldon sea salt and freshly ground
   black pepper

Combine the beef, mustard and caper juice in a bowl and mix. Season to taste with salt and pepper. Finish with the olive oil.

## ASSEMBLY

25–30 'petals' of Sour Onions (see page 30)
Nasturtium Capers (see page 44)
nasturtium leaves, to garnish
bronze fennel or peppery leaves, to garnish

Spoon a teaspoon of the beef tartare into each onion petal and garnish with some oyster emulsion, nasturtium capers, the shallot crisps and leaves.

# LAMB TARTARE

Everyone associates tartare with beef or tuna, and the thought of a lamb tartare would freak most people out. But anything that can be served rare or medium-rare can usually be turned into a tartare by using salt and acid as an amazing alternative to heat for cooking. Before making the tartare we render the fat from our lamb, take off the fillets and brush them in the fat to coat the exterior, then age the meat for up to three weeks.

**serves 4–6**

## LAMB TARTARE

10g fennel seeds
100g rock salt
10g dried lemon zest (dry out in
   a dehydrator or a very low oven)
300g lamb fillet
1 tablespoon Dijon mustard
1 tablespoon capers, drained
1 tablespoon finely diced shallots
1 tablespoon Onion Treacle (see page 48)
a drizzle of olive oil
a pinch of Maldon sea salt

Toast the fennel seeds in a dry pan until they smell fragrant. Tip into a small blender or food processor, add the rock salt and lemon zest, and blend until finely ground.

Rub this mixture all over the meat, then set aside for 8 minutes. Rinse off the rub and pat the meat dry. Cut into 1cm dice.

Just before serving, season the tartare with the remaining ingredients.

## ASSEMBLY

100g Cabbage Ferment (see page 26)
1 tablespoon Dijon mustard
a drizzle of olive oil
slices of sourdough or other
   good-quality bread
lamb fat or olive oil
Maldon sea salt
flat-leaf parsley leaves
sorrel leaves
150ml Cultured Cream (see page 54)
a drizzle of Garlic Oil (see page 56)

Put the fermented cabbage, Dijon mustard and a drizzle of olive oil in a blender or food processor and blend to a pesto-like consistency. Toast the slices of bread under a grill, then spread with some lamb fat, or drizzle with olive oil, and sprinkle with salt. Run your knife through the parsley and sorrel leaves to create really thin strips.

Serve the lamb tartare topped with the herbs and spoon the fermented cabbage mixture on to the side of the plate. Put the cultured cream into a separate dish and drizzle with garlic oil. Serve the toast on the side and allow guests to help themselves at the table.

# ANCHOVY CRISPS

## LEMON AND SORREL

This is a really clever snack. The flavours remind me of those wonderful little skewers you find in San Sebastián in the Basque country – olives, anchovies in olive oil, pickled peppers – great to have with an aperitivo. These crispy anchovies are that and more, and you only need a couple per person. The lemon gel brings a welcome kick of freshness. We serve this with a bowl of fat green olives from Sicily called Nocellara del Belice and a glass of dry sherry, The Dairy's Americano, a negroni or a spritz.

**Makes 10**

### LEMON GEL

1 sheet/leaf of silver leaf gelatine
75g caster sugar
150ml fresh lemon juice

Soak the gelatine in cold water to soften it. Put the sugar and 50ml of the lemon juice in a pan and warm to just before boiling point to dissolve the sugar. Remove from the heat. Drain the gelatine, squeezing to remove excess water, and add to the pan, stirring until the gelatine has melted into the mixture. (If necessary, place the pan back over the heat to help melt the gelatine.) Add the remaining lemon juice. Leave to set in a covered container in the fridge until required.

### BATTER

100g rice flour
40g cornflour
50g potato flour
30g tapioca flour
1½ teaspoons baking powder
10g honey
195ml sparkling water

Put all the dry ingredients into a large bowl. Using a whisk, add the honey and then slowly whisk in the sparkling water. Whisk for a good 5 minutes to work the flours into the liquid.

### ASSEMBLY

vegetable oil, for deep-frying
10 best-quality canned anchovy fillets
3 sorrel leaves, torn into pieces

Blend the lemon gel in a blender or food processor to liquefy it, then decant it into a squeezy bottle.

Heat oil in a deep pan or deep-fat fryer to 180°C. Remove the anchovies from the can and pat dry. Dip them into the batter, then deep fry until golden and crisp. Drain on kitchen paper. Arrange the anchovies on your chosen plate, add a couple of dots of the lemon gel and garnish with the sorrel leaves.

# APPLEWOOD-SMOKED EEL

## GUINNESS SODA BREAD, HORSERADISH

This is one of the easiest and most satisfying bread recipes. The method is so simple yet the results are very pleasing. I bake this every Christmas and serve it with smoked salmon on the day, then the following days with jam and butter or a bowl of soup. It's a great recipe for involving the younger ones in the family as they can get their hands nice and dirty mixing the dough. Note to oneself, a pint of Guinness is not a bad partner.

serves 4–6

### GUINNESS SODA BREAD

**makes 1 loaf**

250g plain flour
200g wholemeal flour
15g bicarbonate of soda
¾ teaspoon fine table salt
150g jumbo oat flakes
1 tablespoon clear honey
1 tablespoon black treacle
250ml Guinness
250ml buttermilk

Preheat the oven to 200°C fan/220°C/Gas Mark 7. Line a large loaf tin (8 x 30 x 11cm) with baking parchment. Mix together all the dry ingredients in a large bowl and make a well in the centre. Add the remaining ingredients into the well and work the mixture with your hands to make a loose, smooth and wet dough.

Place the dough in the lined tin and score the top lengthways with a knife. Bake for 15 minutes, then turn down the oven to 175°C fan/195°C/Gas Mark 5–6 and bake for a further 20 minutes. Remove the bread from the tin and bake, directly on the oven rack, for a final 5 minutes or until the bread sounds hollow when tapped on the bottom. Remove from the oven and cool on a wire rack.

### HORSERADISH YOGHURT

100ml Greek yoghurt
2 teaspoons horseradish cream
5g fresh horseradish, grated
2–3 drops of Tabasco sauce
fresh lemon juice
Maldon sea salt

Mix together the yoghurt, horseradish cream, fresh horseradish and Tabasco sauce. Season with lemon juice and salt to taste.

### ASSEMBLY

1 shallot
200g applewood-smoked eel, cut into chunky dice
4 teaspoons capers, drained
dill fronds
borage flowers (if available)
grated fresh horseradish
Fennel Kimchi (see page 29)
Pickled Radishes (see page 45)

Cut the shallot into thin rings and plunge into iced water to crisp up. Slice the soda bread and build open sandwiches on the slices – start with the eel, then add horseradish yoghurt and garnish with the shallot rings, capers, dill, borage flowers, horseradish, kimchi and pickles.

# CRAB, NORI AND POTATO

Crab is one of my favourite foods. I have tried crab all over the world and I can say quite confidently that Cornish crab has to be the best and most flavourful. The white meat is delicate and sweet and the brown has an intensity of fresh sea flavours that you never forget. I was brought up on the south coast of Ireland, practically on the sea's edge, but it wasn't until I left that I appreciated how lucky I'd been to enjoy such seafood. So now, whenever we get a delivery of crabs, I'm the first to volunteer to take on the laborious job of 'picking'. The only problem is that the yield is never as good as it should be because I can't help myself from taking great big spoonfuls when nobody's looking.

**Makes about 12 'sandwiches'**

## BROWN CRAB MAYO

150g brown crab meat
50g egg yolks
155g Crab Oil (see page 55)
50g crème fraîche
1–2 drops of Tabasco sauce
juice of ½ lemon

Place the brown crab meat in a piece of muslin, gather into a pouch and gently squeeze out any excess liquid. Put the crab meat in a blender or food processor and add the egg yolks. Start blending at a medium speed, then slowly drizzle in the oil while blending (add a touch of cold water if the mix becomes too thick). Transfer to a mixing bowl and add the crème fraîche, Tabasco and lemon juice to taste. Mix together. Keep in the fridge until required.

## NORI MAYO

3 sheets of dried nori (3g each)
140ml warm water
20g wholegrain mustard
140ml grapeseed oil

Soak the nori in the warm water until softened. Transfer the nori and soaking water to a blender or food processor, add the mustard and blend on a medium speed. While blending, gradually drizzle in the oil until emulsified. Keep in the fridge until required.

## POTATO CRISPS

2 large Maris Piper or other best-quality chipping potatoes, washed well
vegetable oil, for deep-frying
Nori Powder (see page 60)
Maldon sea salt

Slice the potatoes very thinly on a mandoline (you need at least 24 slices). Heat oil in a deep pan or deep-fat fryer to 160°C. Deep-fry the potato slices, in batches, for about 5 minutes or until they are golden and crisp. Lift out and drain on kitchen paper. Season with salt and nori powder. Keep in a warm, dry area of your kitchen until ready to serve.

## ASSEMBLY

200g white crab meat
50g Pickled Wakame (see page 45)
Nori Powder (see page 60), for dusting

Gently mix the white crab meat with the brown crab mayo. Lay half of the crisps on a flat tray. Top each of these with a generous spoonful of the crab mixture, followed by the pickled wakame and, lastly, a spoonful of the nori mayo. Cover each one with another potato crisp to create a sandwich. Dust the top of each sandwich with nori powder.

# GARDEN

# FRESH PEAS

## ROOFTOP MINT AND FRIED BREAD

Everyone has food memories and most of us remember eating fresh peas from a pod. Sweet and juicy, the taste and bouncy texture alert you to summer just round the corner. As a chef, the last months of winter can be challenging, so fresh peas are a sign that soon the crates from the farm will be full and plentiful. In the morning, we work as a team to pick, pod, wash and trim. During the first hour or two we chat and plan what we are going to serve as we work our way through the vegetable preparation. As with most dishes that make a menu, it starts with a discussion and ideas based on what we have. This recipe was one of the first dishes created in this way, where we took one ingredient and discussed how best to treat it, then shared the labour to create a dish with the perfect balance of freshness, texture, acidity and surprise. This memory will always remind me to create collectively based on something perfect in its time and place.

serves 8–10

### PEA MOUSSE

1½ sheets/leaves of silver leaf gelatine
500g frozen peas
10g Sosa ProEspuma Cold

Soak the gelatine in cold water to soften it. Bring a suitable-sized pot of water to a rolling boil with a generous pinch of salt. Blanch the peas in the boiling water for 2 minutes, then drain. Tip into a blender or food processor and blend until smooth.

Drain the gelatine, then warm it in a small pan with a splash of water to melt it. Add to the pea purée along with the ProEspuma and blend to incorporate. Pass the mixture through a fine sieve on to a flat tray set over ice to cool the mixture as quickly as possible.

Decant the mixture into a siphon gun so that it is three-quarters full. Add two charges and give the siphon gun a violent shake. Keep refrigerated until required.

### LEMON GEL

½ sheet/leaf of silver leaf gelatine
35g caster sugar
75ml fresh lemon juice

Soak the gelatine in cold water to soften it. Dissolve the sugar in the lemon juice by warming it in a pan to just before it boils. Remove from the heat. Drain the gelatine, squeezing out excess water, and add to the pan. Stir until melted into the mixture. Allow to cool, then decant into a squeezy bottle or disposable piping bag and leave to set in the fridge until required.

### MINT GRANITA

2 bunches of mint (about 60g in total),
  leaves picked

Blanch the mint leaves in boiling salted water for 4 minutes. Drain, reserving the liquid, and refresh the mint in iced water. Drain the mint and squeeze out as much of the water as possible.

Blend the mint with a little of the reserved blanching liquid in a blender or food processor until smooth.

...continued on page 126

Pour into a metal tray or other freezerproof container to make a thin layer. Freeze until solid, then run a fork through to break it up and create a granita texture. Keep in the freezer until required.

## ASSEMBLY

500g podded fresh peas
1 head of celery
Nori Oil (see page 57)
fresh lemon juice
15g chives, chopped
100g Fried Bread (see page 59)
black mint leaves
Moroccan mint leaves
sorrel leaves
Maldon sea salt
marigold or chive flowers, to garnish
  (if available)

Separate the small, sweeter-tasting peas from the larger ones. Leave the small, sweet ones raw. Blanch the larger ones in boiling water for 30 seconds, then refresh in iced water. Keep all the peas in the fridge until required.

Peel the strings from the celery, then dice. Weigh the celery and calculate 1% salt to season.

Dress the peas and celery with a little nori oil, lemon juice and salt to taste. Stir through the chopped chives. Spoon this mixture around each plate. Pipe six or seven dots of lemon gel per plate. Sprinkle over the fried bread and add a generous mound of pea mousse. Scatter the mint and sorrel over the plates and finish with some of the granita. Garnish with flowers, if using.

# WILD GARLIC TAGLIATELLE
## TROMBETTA COURGETTE, SUNFLOWER SEED PESTO

You might think sunflower seeds are an unusual substitute for pine nuts, or that we use them just to be different. But when sunflower seeds are toasted to the extreme – borderline burnt – I think they have a better flavour than pine nuts at a fraction of the price. And they keep this dish nut-free. The pasta dough makes more than is required for the recipe but if you are going to the effort of making pasta then it is worth making a large batch. It can be dried and stored, or frozen. If made ahead of time and dried it will take about 4 minutes to cook.

*serves 4–6*

### TAGLIATELLE

2 tablespoons olive oil
4 eggs
2 egg yolks
480g type '00' flour
fine semolina, for dusting

The pasta dough can be made in a stand mixer fitted with a paddle attachment, or in a bowl or on the work surface by hand. Start by mixing together the olive oil, eggs, yolks and half of the flour until well worked. Add the remaining flour a handful at a time, mixing in well before adding the next handful. This should be a slow process – a little at a time really is best. Once the last of the flour has been incorporated, knead briefly in the mixer. If making by hand, knead the dough on the floured surface for at least 10 minutes or until the dough is firm, smooth and even in consistency. Wrap the dough in clingfilm and set aside to rest at room temperature for about 30 minutes.

Divide the dough into eight pieces. Flatten the pieces and dust lightly with flour. Work with one piece at a time. Feed through a pasta machine set on the widest setting, then fold the dough over and pass through this setting again. Repeat this process 3 times so that you have a rectangular shape and an even thickness. Continue to pass the dough through the pasta machine, changing the setting until you reach the second thinnest setting. Repeat with the remaining pieces of dough.

Dust the work surface with fine semolina. Roll up each sheet and cut across into 1cm wide ribbons using a sharp knife. Toss the ribbons with the semolina.

### TROMBETTA COURGETTES

2 Trombetta courgettes
2% brine (see page 20) (or the brine from jarred olives)

Put the whole courgettes in a container and cover with a 2% brine. Leave in the fridge for 6 hours. Remove the courgettes from the brine and slice lengthways into ribbons (the same width as the tagliatelle) using a mandoline or peeler.

*...continued on page 128*

## SUNFLOWER SEED PESTO

50g honey
250g sunflower seeds
100ml olive oil
25g Bread Miso (see page 65) or ready-
  made brown miso
a bunch of basil, leaves picked
3 sprigs of flat-leaf parsley, leaves picked
1 tablespoon golden marjoram leaves
50g aged Parmesan, finely grated
zest of 1 lemon

Put the honey in a small pan, bring to a gentle simmer and cook to
a nutty brown colour. Allow to cool.

Toast the sunflower seeds in the oil; remove from the heat. Put the miso,
honey and a third of the sunflower seeds and oil in a food processor and
pulse to mix. Add another third of the sunflower seeds and oil and pulse.
Finally, add the remaining seeds and oil and pulse to a pesto-like texture.

Roughly chop the herbs. Just before serving, fold them through the
sunflower seed paste along with the Parmesan and lemon zest.

## ASSEMBLY

100ml water
100ml whey
a drizzle of olive oil
a bunch of wild garlic leaves
fresh lemon juice
freshly grated Parmesan
golden marjoram (if available)
basil leaves
Maldon sea salt and freshly ground
  black pepper

Put the water, whey and olive oil into a large pan and season generously
with salt and pepper. Bring this emulsion to a simmer. Add about a third
of the pasta and simmer for 1–2 minutes so that it is still al dente. Drain
the pasta, reserving some of the cooking liquor, and tip into a bowl.

Add some of the reserved cooking liquor, the courgette ribbons, wild
garlic and a squeeze of lemon juice to the warm tagliatelle. Toss gently.
Divide the tagliatelle, wild garlic and courgette ribbon mixture among
the bowls. Garnish with the Parmesan, marjoram and basil. Serve the
pesto on the side.

# GARDEN COURGETTE

## SMOKED BUFFALO MILK CURD, ROOFTOP HONEY

For the curd here we use fresh buffalo milk, which is a little richer than cow's milk, but you could easily use any full-fat milk, even sheep milk. You'll notice that I use aged Parmesan to season and bring acidity to the courgette purée. I do this to keep the mix green. If you put an acid like lemon in the purée it would go brown. I like to use Parmesan as a seasoning in many purées, pulses and soups because I find it brings an incredible umami flavour that you sometimes can't achieve with just salt and lemon.

serves 4

### SMOKED BUFFALO CURD

500ml buffalo milk
25ml double cream
2 teaspoons buttermilk
a pinch of Maldon sea salt
zest of 1 lemon
a handful of dried hay
½ teaspoon liquid vegetable rennet

Preheat the oven to 180°C fan/200°C/Gas Mark 6. Combine all the ingredients, except the hay and rennet, in a large jug. Spread the hay in a deep baking tray and toast in the oven until it is an amber colour all over and has started to smoke. Carefully remove the tray of smoking hay from the oven and pour over the milk mixture. Leave to infuse for 30 minutes.

Strain the mixture through a fine sieve into a clean pot and add the rennet. Set over a low heat and heat to 36°C (the mix should be just warm on the fingertips). Transfer into a container and chill for at least 2 hours.

### COURGETTE AND BASIL PURÉE

2 courgettes
olive oil
1 garlic clove, crushed
a bunch of basil, leaves picked
20g aged Parmesan, finely grated

Cut the courgettes into quarters lengthways, then slice across into thin pieces. Set a medium-sized pan over a medium heat. Add a good drizzle of olive oil and the garlic and follow quickly with the sliced courgettes. Stir and add a spoonful of water. Cover with a lid to help create steam. After 2 minutes, add half of the basil leaves (reserve the best leaves for the assembly) and the Parmesan. Tip the mixture into a blender or food processor and blend until smooth. Transfer to a bowl placed over iced water to cool quickly so the bright green colour is retained.

### PUMPKIN SEED PRALINE DRESSING

125g pumpkin seeds
50ml vegetable oil
50ml honey
10g white miso
a pinch of Maldon sea salt

Toast the pumpkin seeds in the oil until really golden. In a separate pan, caramelise the honey to a dark golden colour. Put the seeds with their oil, the honey and miso into a blender or food processor and pulse until combined but still retaining a coarse texture. Season with salt to taste. Allow to cool to room temperature.

### ASSEMBLY

2 courgettes
fresh lemon juice
olive oil
5 Nocellara del Belice olives, stoned
smoked paprika, for dusting
sea salt and freshly ground black pepper

Slice the courgettes thinly lengthways using a mandoline or peeler. Season with salt, black pepper, lemon juice and olive oil to taste. Spoon the courgette and basil purée generously around each plate. Roll the courgette slices and place some on each plate. Slice the olives and add a few olive pieces and a spoonful of the smoked curd. Dust the curd with a little smoked paprika. Finish with the reserved basil leaves and dressing.

# HERITAGE TOMATOES

## CURED SARDINES, ROOFTOP HERBS

This is a theatrical dish, full of fun. I stole the idea from a supper club collaboration between Dean and Ben. In the restaurant we always have a mini milk bottle on each table full of flowers and herbs, mostly edible, from a local allotment. Rather than filling the bottles for this dish with water we used a smoky and aromatic dashi and a herb bouquet of entirely edible herbs and flowers. The trick is to place the bottles on the table just before the guests sit down. Serve the bowls of beautiful tomatoes and cured sardines, then snip the bouquets over the bowls and pour in the contents of the bottles. It's a great party trick of a dish.

*serves 4–6*

### ANCHOVY DRESSING

250ml olive brine (from jars of olives)
120g salted anchovies
50g capers, drained
180ml white wine vinegar
20g caster sugar
50ml extra virgin olive oil

Place all the ingredients, except the oil, in a blender or food processor. Blend on a high speed, then gradually add the oil while blending. The dressing can be stored in a sealed container in the fridge for up to 7 days.

### TOMATO DASHI

15g dried kombu
500ml water, boiled and cooled
   (or use filtered or still mineral water)
1 sheet of dried nori (3g)
10g bonito flakes
1 teaspoon white soy sauce
a pinch of Maldon sea salt
100g vine cherry tomatoes, sliced
   (vines reserved)
2–3 basil stalks
1 garlic clove, sliced

Add the kombu to the water in a pan and bring to a very gentle simmer (do not boil). Simmer for 1 hour. Strain the liquid through a fine sieve into a jug. Add the nori, bonito flakes, soy sauce, salt, tomatoes, tomato vines, basil stalks and garlic. Allow to infuse for 40 minutes.

Taste to check the seasoning – the dashi should have a strong savoury flavour – and adjust as required. Strain the dashi through the fine sieve.

### ASSEMBLY

800g mixed heritage tomatoes, chopped
4 fillets of Cured Sardines (see page 40),
   very finely chopped
1 fillet Smoked Mackerel (see page 41),
   chopped
wild rocket (both leaves and flowers)
tarragon leaves
bronze fennel
sorrel leaves
basil leaves

Dress the tomatoes with the anchovy dressing and the cured sardines. Spoon into bowls and top with the mackerel. Pour the tomato dashi into small glass bottles. Place a small bunch of rocket, tarragon, bronze fennel, sorrel and basil in the top of each bottle. At the table, use scissors to snip the herbs over the tomatoes and pour over the dashi. .

# BBQ SPRING CABBAGE

## FRESH RICOTTA, COPPA TRIM

We make our own charcuterie at the restaurant and over time we generate a substantial amount of trim from the ends of coppa and salami. As we try not to throw anything away, we have to find clever ways to use the trim in a dish. Any charcuterie trim would be delicious here – use what you have. The dish is kind of a play on bacon and cabbage. I love the shapes of vegetables so when plating the dish I like to arrange the cabbage back into its natural round shape.

serves 4–6

### DRESSING

50g honey
50ml grapeseed oil
1 teaspoon very finely diced peel from
    Preserved Amalfi Lemons (see page 30)
fresh lemon juice

Mix together the honey, oil and preserved lemon peel. Season with lemon juice to taste.

### BBQ CABBAGE

1 spring/Hispi cabbage
sheets of dried nori (3g each)
5% brine (see page 20), in a spray bottle

Remove the green outer leaves of the cabbage. Blanch them in a pan of boiling water for 1–2 minutes, then drain and squeeze out as much liquid as possible. Dry these leaves in a dehydrator, or in the oven at the lowest setting, for 3–6 hours or until completely dried out.

Preheat the oven to 150°C fan/170°C/Gas Mark 3–4. Weigh the dried cabbage leaves, then calculate 30% of this – this is the weight of nori you need. Toast the nori sheets on a baking tray in the oven for 10 minutes. Combine the toasted nori sheets and dehydrated cabbage leaves in a small blender or food processor and blend to a fine powder.

Separate the remaining cabbage leaves, then char on both sides on a barbecue, or a hot ridged grill pan. Spray them with the brine solution twice while they are on the barbecue or pan.

### ASSEMBLY

100g fresh ricotta
10g Parmesan, freshly grated
zest of ½ lemon
a drizzle of olive oil
a drizzle of vegetable oil
80–100g coppa trim, or Coppa (see page 35), diced
250g Cabbage Ferment (see page 26)
Maldon sea salt and freshly ground
    black pepper

Mix together the ricotta, Parmesan, lemon zest and olive oil. Season with salt and pepper to taste. Heat the vegetable oil in a pan over a low-medium heat, add the coppa trim and cook slowly until crispy.

Spread some of the ricotta mix on each plate, then pile up the BBQ cabbage leaves and fermented cabbage in alternate layers, scattering coppa and drizzling some of the dressing between each layer. (Note, for each portion you want about 70% fermented cabbage to 30% BBQ cabbage.) Dust cabbage-nori powder over the top of each dish.

# CORNISH CRAB

## FRIED CACKLEBEAN EGG AND COASTAL VEGETABLES

I love a good fried egg. It's a go-to late at night after work, on the rare occasion Sarah hasn't left me a plate of what she had earlier for dinner. A couple of slices of white bread, slapped with a lick of Kerrygold butter and topped with a fried egg seasoned with an unhealthy amount of salt and pepper does me right in under five minutes. This is a mega pimped-up version to make if you just happen to have freshly picked crab and brown crab mayo in the fridge. You probably don't but it's still worth the work as it's a fantastic combo.

serves 6

18 asparagus spears
300g fresh white crab meat
2 tablespoons Nori Powder (see page 60)
olive oil
50g sea purslane
100g samphire
18 radishes
50g Rock Samphire Pickle (see page 46)
juice of 1 lemon
50g unsalted butter, diced
6 eggs (we use CackleBean)
200g Brown Crab Mayo (see recipe for Crab, Nori and Potato on page 118)
Maldon sea salt and freshly ground black pepper

Remove the tough woody ends from the asparagus spears. Lay the asparagus on a flat tray, season with a pinch of salt and allow to sit for 10 minutes. Put a ridged grill pan on to heat up.

Meanwhile, season the white crab meat with a little of the nori powder, salt and olive oil to taste. Set aside.

Blanch the sea purslane and samphire together in a pan of boiling water for 10 seconds. Drain and refresh in iced water. Cut half of the radishes into quarters and the rest into thin round slices. Put the sea purslane, samphire and radishes into a mixing bowl with the pickled rock samphire. Season with a pinch of salt, the lemon juice and a little olive oil, and toss together gently.

Place the asparagus on the raging hot grill pan and scorch on all sides for 1–2 minutes or until the asparagus spears are blistered and blackened. Remove from the pan and cool slightly, then cut each spear in half lengthways and season with salt and pepper.

Place a couple of large non-stick frying pans over a medium heat. Add the butter and melt it. When it turns slightly golden, crack the eggs into the pans and season each with a pinch of salt and black pepper. Fry the eggs to your liking.

Place a generous spoonful of brown crab mayo in the centre of each plate. Top with a fried egg, placing it gently, and add a dollop of the white crab meat (don't cover the egg yolk). Scatter radishes, coastal vegetables and asparagus around. Finish by dusting the entire dish with the remaining nori powder.

# OUR FARM

My first exposure to a working farm occurred when I was quite young. My Auntie Emer lived in Mallow in West Cork with the charming and gentle Doctor Miles Frankel at Kilbrack farm. As a boy I used to go down and spend a couple of weeks there in the summer. I will never forget that mad kitchen in the old house. Stone floors, a big farmhouse table, old wood-burning stove heating the house and something delicious always bubbling away slowly on the stove.

My brother, Earl, was living and working there at the time, looking after the livestock and doing handyman stuff around the place. I remember the fresh bread he would bake and the hams he would cure. There were iron beams crossing all over the ceiling and he'd hang the hams and herbs from them. They had a parrot that used to parade from beam to beam above, barking orders. When we'd be sitting there, having tea or some soup, we'd have to cover our teacup or bowl to prevent unwanted parrot crap from plonking in. He had a good aim. His name was Apu. Funny that.

Patrick Frankel now runs Kilbrack and has turned it into one of the most respected organic farms in Cork. I was proud to see the Kilbrack branding on some beautiful vegetables ordered for Ballymaloe during the Litfest we took part in. The Allens at Ballymaloe have been pioneering growers for years, and if they hold events where they need to outsource a little, only the best will do.

The last time I visited Kilbrack was for my brother's wedding. The next day, my nephews and I went out to help Patrick get ready for the market. It was back-breaking work we did that day, with the attention to detail, careful trimming of the ingredients on our hands and knees. We were out there for hours and hours. Once it started to get dark, we came in, but not Patrick. He stayed on cutting things right into the night, to prepare for what would hopefully be a successful day at market.

When you think about the work that goes into farming at this level – on a certified organic farm with virtually no powered equipment – you have to appreciate the work that is done. Chefs win accolades, book and television deals, pats on the back and sponsorships of all types, basically taking credit for someone else's work, but farmers, working passionately in this way, are the unsung heroes.

Fast forward to 2017 and we have our own what I like to call 'guerilla urban farming' set up. Dean has claimed a space of unwanted ground near the restaurant and grows what he can there. We've had a garden on the rooftop of The Dairy since 2013 where we've been growing herbs and salads. But after we met Igor and Tom, who set up a company called Indie Ecology, what they have helped us to achieve is remarkable. They basically take our food waste and, using a Japanese method known as 'bokashi', they turn it into a rich, almost black compost. It's entirely organic, using a type of fermented molasses and naturally occurring micro-organisms to turn kitchen scraps into safe, nutrient-rich compost.

Igor and Tom have rented a farm in Sussex, which is divided among the ten restaurants that are involved. I have named The Dairy and Sorella part Our Farm. Each restaurant consults with Igor and Tom about what they would like to grow, then we buy the seeds and the rest is left to the guys and nature. We get deliveries twice a week and our menu works around what is produced.

We all get involved in the kitchen, preparing the vegetables covered in soil that were literally picked hours before. While we do this, we are brainstorming on how to incorporate what we have into the menu. We are now a step closer to the farmhouse kitchen by the sea. As Igor puts it: 'Forget field to fork; it's plate to farm and back to plate again.'

# SMOKED BEETROOT TARTARE

## CACKLEBEAN EGG YOLK, HAZELNUT

I've become slightly obsessed with smoking things. I started with the obvious, salmon, and moved on to meat like game, pigeon and venison, then to bone marrow (our smoked bone marrow butter became kind of legendary). We even started smoking ice creams. Playing around with smoking fruit and vegetables was exciting and opened up so many possibilities. Beetroot worked immediately. It's one of my favourite vegetables because of its versatility. I find the large ruby beetroot to be quite meaty so we thought up a play on a beef tartare. But not in the way of veggie burgers and vegan sausages. I hate that stuff! It is kind of fun to dress this tartare as you would imagine it being served in a Parisian brasserie.

**serves 6**

### HUNG YOGHURT

200g plain yoghurt

Line a large sieve with muslin and set it over a deep bowl. Put the yoghurt into the sieve, then gather up the edges of the cloth and secure them together. Leave in the fridge overnight to allow the liquid to drain out of the yoghurt (this liquid or whey can be reserved and used in ferments).

### SMOKED BEETROOT

500g raw beetroots
a drizzle of vegetable oil
rock salt
applewood chips for smoking

Preheat the oven to 190°C fan/210°C/Gas Mark 6–7. Drizzle each beetroot with oil, sprinkle with salt and wrap individually in foil. Bake for 1–1½ hours or until the core temperature reaches 90°C. Remove from the oven and allow to cool and steam in the foil for 15 minutes. Remove from the foil and rub off the skins.

Take a flat tray with a steam insert (such as a deep roasting tray that will hold a flat steaming rack) and spread the applewood chips over the bottom of the tray. Warm the tray over a medium heat until the chips start to smoke, then turn the heat down to low. Place the beetroot on the steam insert/steaming rack and set this over the smoking chips. Completely cover the top and sides tightly with oven-safe clingfilm so the smoke is sealed inside with the beetroot. Leave to lightly smoke for 7 minutes. Remove the beetroot from the tray and leave to cool.

### BRINED EGG YOLKS

500ml 7% brine (see page 20)
10 egg yolks (we use CackleBean) – this allows for a few breakages
a drizzle of vegetable oil

Pour the brine into a deep bowl. Gentle add the yolks using your hands or a slotted spoon. Cover the surface of the brine with the vegetable oil so that the yolks are held down in the brine. Allow the yolks to brine for 1 hour at room temperature. To serve, gently remove the yolks with your hands or a slotted spoon.

*...continued on page 144*

## ASSEMBLY

240g Fermented Beetroot (see page 24)
1 tablespoon Shallot Vinegar (see page 46)
2 tablespoons capers
a drizzle of Ember Oil (see page 56)
Maldon sea salt and cracked black pepper
handful fresh hazelnuts, finely sliced
bittercress or watercress to garnish

Mince the fermented and smoked beetroot through a mincer or chop finely with a knife. Season with the shallot vinegar, capers, ember oil and some salt and pepper. Using a small ring mould, make a disc of the beetroot mixture in the centre of each plate. Top with a layer of the hazelnut slices. Gently place a brined egg yolk to the side of each disc. Garnish with cracked black pepper and bittercress or watercress. Place a spoonful of the hung yoghurt to the side of each disc.

# CAULIFLOWER AND DATE

## RECIPE BY DEAN PARKER, HEAD CHEF OF THE MANOR

This is a classic Dean dish – working with flavours that bounce and burst around a similar flavour profile, yet tweaking all the senses with sweet, bitter and sour notes, leaving you with the best flavour possible from the humble yet complex cauliflower. A bit like Dean really...

serves 6

### HUNG KEFIR OR YOGHURT

500ml Kefir (see page 54) or plain yoghurt
Maldon sea salt

Line a large sieve with muslin and set it over a deep bowl. Put the kefir or yoghurt into the sieve, then gather up the edges of the cloth and secure them together. Leave in the fridge overnight to allow the liquid to drain out of the kefir/yoghurt (this liquid can be used in any of the recipes calling for whey).

Remove from the fridge and weigh the contents of the cloth. Calculate 1% salt and add this to the hung kefir to season.

### DATE PURÉE

2 black peppercorns
seeds from 1 cardamom pod
100g pitted dates
100ml water
½ teaspoon peeled and sliced root ginger
a small pinch of Maldon sea salt
⅓ vanilla pod, split lengthways
4 teaspoons fresh lemon juice

Grind the peppercorns and cardamom seeds to a powder in a mortar and pestle. Put all the ingredients except the lemon juice into a pot and bring to a simmer. Cover with a lid and simmer gently for 10 minutes, topping up with more water if the mixture gets too dry.

Remove the vanilla pod. Transfer the mixture to a blender or food processor and add the lemon juice. Blend until smooth, adding a little more water if the purée seems too thick.

### CAULIFLOWER MOUSSE

330g cauliflower florets (keep the cores/
  stems for other elements of the recipe)
125g unsalted butter, cut into small cubes
a large pinch of Maldon sea salt
½ sheet/leaf of silver leaf gelatine
330ml whey or whole milk
165g plain yoghurt
0.66g xanthan gum (Dean from The Manor
  uses the back of a teaspoon to pick up
  a small pinch)

Pulse the cauliflower florets in a blender or food processor into pieces about 5mm in size. Put the butter in a pan set over a high heat. When the butter starts to foam and turn a really golden colour, reduce the heat and add the floret pieces with the salt. Toast gently until the florets are golden and the bubbles have stopped (this means the moisture has evaporated). Soak the gelatine in cold water to soften it.

Drain the cauliflower well on kitchen paper, then tip into a pot and add the whey or milk. Bring to the boil. Drain the gelatine, squeezing out excess moisture, and add to the pot. Stir until the gelatine has melted into the mixture. Transfer the mixture to the blender or food processor, add the yoghurt and xanthan gum, and blend until smooth. Pass through a fine sieve into a bowl set over ice and leave to cool. Keep in the fridge.

*...continued on page 146*

## TOASTED GRUE DE CACAO

100g cacao nibs
50g unsalted butter

Combine the cacao nibs and butter in a pan set over a medium heat. As soon as the butter starts to turn golden and smell nutty, remove from the heat. Drain the nibs in a sieve.

## CAULIFLOWER CRUMB

florets from 1 medium cauliflower (keep the core/stems for other elements of the recipe)
375g unsalted butter, cut into small cubes

Grate the florets on a coarse grater into crumbs. Put the butter in a pan set over a high heat. When the butter starts to foam and turn a really golden colour, reduce the heat and add the floret crumbs. Gently fry until the bubbles stop (this means all the moisture has evaporated). Drain the crumbs in a fine sieve, pressing hard to remove all the liquid, then spread them over a clean J-cloth or tea towel to remove any excess fat. Season with salt.

## CAULIFLOWER STEMS

cores/stems from 2 cauliflowers
vegetable oil, for deep-frying

Slice the cores/stems thinly lengthways on a mandoline or grater. Blanch the slices in a pan of boiling salted water for 2 minutes, then refresh in iced water; drain. Dry in a dehydrator, or overnight in the oven set at the lowest temperature, until completely dried out.

Heat vegetable oil in a deep pan or deep-fat fryer to 170°C, then deep-fry the dried slices, in batches, until puffed and golden. Ensure that the oil returns to temperature between batches so that the cauliflower stems puff up as soon as they hit the oil. Drain on kitchen paper or a wire rack.

## BBQ CAULIFLOWER

½ medium cauliflower (without leaves)
a drizzle of vegetable oil
fresh lemon juice
Maldon sea salt and freshly ground black pepper

Portion the cauliflower into approximately 6cm florets with long stems of core. Toss with a drizzle of vegetable oil and seasoning of salt and pepper. Barbecue over a low fire, or grill on a hot ridged grill pan, until golden on all sides and cooked through – this should take about 8 minutes. Season the florets with lemon juice.

## FRIED FLORETS

½ medium cauliflower (without leaves)
vegetable oil, for deep-frying
Maldon sea salt

Cut the cauliflower into 1cm florets. Deep-fry, in batches, in vegetable oil at 190°C until golden. Drain on kitchen paper and season with salt.

## ASSEMBLY

Decant the cauliflower mousse into a siphon gun with one charge and shake well. Spread a brush of the date purée on each plate. Sprinkle over some of the toasted cacao nibs. Dot around some of the hung kefir/yoghurt. Arrange two BBQ florets, five fried florets and one slice of fried stem on each plate. Add two mounds of cauliflower mousse to each plate, one half the size of the other. Sprinkle the cauliflower crumb over the larger of the two mounds.

# ROAST AND FERMENTED ARTICHOKE

## PEAR, CHEESE TRIM MOUSSE

Never ever throw away the rinds and ends of cheese because they can make the most funky and amazing fondue or mousse. If you caramelise the cheese beforehand you can get an intense, nutty flavour. This idea came about at a lunch we cooked at the fabulous and inspiring Ballymaloe House. There was a lot of lovely cheese trim left on their trolley. We caramelised it and served it as a cold fondue, with a little herb roll of wild watercress and rocket from their beautiful gardens. It went down a storm. Cheese and pear are a natural match but the addition of artichokes elevates this dish into a stunner.

serves 4–6

### CHEESE TRIM MOUSSE

10g unsalted butter
300g edible cheese trim (we use the
    trimmings – white bloom/rind – of soft
    cheeses such as Baron Bigod)
400ml whole milk
5g Sosa Procrema Cold 100
    (ice cream stabiliser)
Maldon sea salt
Chardonnay vinegar

Melt the butter in a non-stick pan, add the cheese trim and stir the mixture over a low heat while scraping the bottom of the pan as the cheese will catch. Continue to cook, stirring, until the cheese caramelises and takes on a golden-brown colour. Add the milk and slowly bring to the boil, still stirring. Pour into a blender or food processor, add the Procrema and blend together – the mixture will resemble a loose custard. Season with salt and Chardonnay vinegar to taste. Set aside (in the fridge if making ahead).

### ROAST ARTICHOKES

a drizzle of vegetable oil
12 Jerusalem artichokes, washed
    and cut in half
50-100g unsalted butter
2 garlic cloves (skin on), lightly crushed
2 sprigs of thyme

Preheat the oven to 180°C fan/200°C/Gas Mark 6. Heat the vegetable oil in an ovenproof pan over a high heat. Add the artichokes and reduce the heat to medium. Add the butter. When it starts to foam, transfer the pan to the oven and roast the artichokes for about 10 minutes or until tender. Remove from the oven and add the garlic and thyme to the pan. Set aside to allow the garlic and thyme flavours to infuse the butter.

### ASSEMBLY

1–2 ripe pears, quartered, cored
    and thinly sliced
200g Fermented Artichoke (see page 22),
    thinly sliced on a mandoline
chervil leaves
fresh black truffle, thinly sliced

Warm the roast artichokes in the butter that they were roasted in, then spoon them on to the plates with some of the butter. Scatter the slices of pear and fermented artichoke around each plate but leave one large gap somewhere on the plate. Warm the cheese trim mousse over a gentle heat to no higher than 70°C, stirring constantly so that it does not catch. Decant into a siphon gun with one charge and shake well. Add some of the cheese trim mousse to the gap on each plate. Garnish with chervil and black truffle.

# FERMENTED BARLEY

## WILD MUSHROOM AND CHICKEN SKIN

The aroma of the fermentation process of the barley grains reminds me of a brewery. That's why in the restaurant we suggest drinking an ice-cold pale ale with this dish. It works a treat. We have added chicken skin for an extra depth of flavour but it is an excellent dish with just the wild mushrooms.

**serves 4**

### CRISPY CHICKEN SKIN

the skin from 1 chicken (about 150g)
Maldon sea salt

Preheat the oven to 175°C fan/195°C/Gas Mark 5–6. Trim any veins or bloody parts from the chicken skin, then lay it flat between two baking trays. Bake for 20–30 minutes or until crispy. Transfer the skin to kitchen paper to drain off the excess fat, then season with a pinch of salt and allow to cool. Once cool, chop with a knife to a coarse texture.

### ASSEMBLY

a batch of Fermented Barley (see page 24)
100g unsalted butter
a drizzle of sherry vinegar
300ml Brown Chicken Stock (see page 61)
20g crème fraîche
300g mixed wild mushrooms
juice of 1 lemon
Maldon sea salt and freshly ground
    black pepper
savory, to garnish

Drain the barley, reserving the liquid. Set a suitable-sized pan over a medium-high heat and add 75g of the butter. When it starts to foam, add the barley and cook out, scraping the bottom of the pan every couple of minutes as the barley starts to catch and caramelise, until it is dark and roasted in appearance with a nutty aroma (this could take up to 30 minutes).

Add the vinegar to deglaze the bottom of the pan, stirring and scraping well, then pour in half of the stock and season with a little salt. Turn down to a simmer and cook as you would a risotto: once the first addition of stock has been absorbed, gradually add the remaining stock and some of the reserved water from the barley, stirring the liquid into the grains until absorbed. It should take about 10 minutes for the barley grains to be cooked through and reach a risotto consistency. Adjust the seasoning and stir in the crème fraîche.

Set a frying pan over a high heat and add the remaining butter and the wild mushrooms. Cook for just a couple of minutes or until wilted. Finish with a pinch each of salt and pepper and lemon juice to taste.

Place a generous spoonful of barley in the bottom of each warm serving bowl. Top with the wild mushrooms and a sprinkle of crispy chicken skin. Garnish with savory.

# BBQ DUCK HEARTS

## WHITE POLENTA AND CORN

When sweetcorn is in season it's like one of those red-flag-to-a-bull type of things that lets us all know what time of year it is. Sweetcorn signifies the close of summer when the days are growing shorter and leaves are turning amber. It doesn't make me sad at all. Quite the opposite. There is such an abundance of things to cook with around the beginning of autumn, and dishes can become a little richer and more comforting. For me, this is the best way to cook white polenta – in the corn cooking liquid. It's such a natural combo: as you know, polenta is ground cornmeal. I think of starchy polenta as the northern Italian version of a great creamy mash. We had the honour of cooking this for the legend that is Alain Ducasse when he visited us at The Dairy. To say we were a little nervous is a huge understatement! He said that among the many dishes we cooked for him, this one stood out.

**serves 6**

4 fresh corn on the cob

50g unsalted butter

20 fresh cobnuts

1 white-skin onion, finely diced

80g white polenta

18 duck hearts

1 tablespoon Red Wine Shallot
   Gastrique (see page 46)

4 teaspoons Onion Treacle (see page 48)

2 sprigs of thyme, leaves picked

20g Parmesan, finely grated

fine table salt

Maldon sea salt and cracked black pepper

Remove the outer green leaf layers (the husk) from the corn. Pull off the golden hair-like fibres but reserve these. Melt the butter in a pan and bring to a simmer, then add the golden fibres and cook until the butter turns a dark golden colour and the fibres start to crisp. Strain the butter through a sieve into a bowl (the butter will now have the most amazing nutty sweetcorn aroma) and reserve. Tip the fibres on to kitchen paper and season them with a light pinch of fine salt. Set aside.

Put the corn on the cob in a suitable-sized pot, cover with water and add a good pinch of Maldon salt. Bring to the boil, then simmer for 12 minutes. Remove from the heat and allow the corn to cool in the cooking water.

Crack open the cobnuts and peel them, then cut each one in half.

For the polenta, put half of the reserved butter into a pan on a medium heat, add the diced onion and cook until soft. Add the polenta and cook, stirring, for 2 minutes. Pour in 200ml of the corn cooking water and simmer gently, stirring constantly with a whisk. Keep topping up with the corn cooking water, as you would when making a risotto, until the polenta is cooked and silky soft with only a slight bite – this can take 10–15 minutes. Remove from the heat and cover the surface of the polenta in the pan with greaseproof paper to prevent a crust from forming. Set aside. (If you are making the polenta in advance, remove from the heat and pour on to a flat tray; cover the top with greaseproof paper and leave to cool.)

Remove the corn from the pot (reserve any remaining cooking water). Using a sharp knife, cut the kernels from the cob on to a baking tray, trying to keep them attached together in randomly shaped pieces.

*...continued on page 154*

Reserve any loose kernels that fall away – put these into a pan with the cobnuts and a teaspoon of the sweetcorn-scented butter, ready to reheat for serving. Use a spoon to scrape off any tiny corn pieces that remain on the cob to be added to the polenta.

Meanwhile, fire up the barbecue or heat a ridged grill pan. Thread the duck hearts on to skewers. Barbecue, or cook on the hot pan, for 1–2 minutes, turning occasionally. Allow the hearts to rest for 2 minutes before removing them from the skewers. Cut each in half and put into a pan with the gastrique, a teaspoon of the sweetcorn-scented butter, the onion treacle, thyme leaves and a pinch each of Maldon sea salt and black pepper.

**ASSEMBLY**

thyme leaves, to garnish

Preheat the oven to 160°C fan/180°C/Gas Mark 4. Add the tiny pieces of scraped corn and some of the corn cooking water to the polenta and stir to mix – you want a loose risotto consistency. Heat through gently on the stove, then fold in the Parmesan. Place the larger corn kernel pieces on the baking tray in the oven and warm through for 3 minutes. Gently warm through the duck hearts as well as the cobnut and corn mixture.

Add a spoonful of polenta to each plate and top with the large corn pieces. Scatter over the duck hearts. Finish with the cobnut and corn mixture and garnish with the reserved corn fibres and some thyme leaves.

# SALT-BAKED CELERIAC

## NORI AND SUNFLOWER SEED PRALINE

serves 6

In my opinion, vegetables can be far more complex and exciting than most meat and fish. This quite technical dish is proof of that. It is Richie and Ben's dish and shows off their skill and respect for ingredients. The nori acts as a natural gelatine to hold the celeriac ballotine together. We have used the same technique with other ingredients, replacing the nori with wild mushrooms or game offal, and served the ballotine alongside venison as a very smart game combo – one to impress your foodie mates.

### ALMOND MILK

250g whole dried almonds
500ml water
about 2 tablespoons verjus
a pinch of Maldon sea salt, or to taste

Soak the almonds in the water for 24 hours. Tip it all into a blender or food processor and blend together for 2 minutes. Line a large sieve with muslin and set it over a deep bowl. Pour the blended almond mixture into the sieve. Gather up the edges of the cloth and secure. Place in the fridge and leave the almond milk to strain through.

Discard the contents of the muslin bag. Add the verjus and salt to the almond milk, to taste, and mix together with a spoon or whisk.

### SUNFLOWER SEED PRALINE

125g sunflower seeds
50ml rapeseed oil
50g honey
15g brown miso
a pinch of Maldon sea salt

Toast the sunflower seeds in the oil in a pan until they are quite dark brown. Tip on to kitchen paper.

Heat the honey in a small pan and caramelise to a dark golden colour. Put the honey, a third of the toasted seeds and the miso into a food processor and pulse to a coarse paste. Add another third of the sunflower seeds and pulse to incorporate. Finally, add the remaining seeds with a pinch of salt and pulse again for 1 second.

### SALT-BAKED CELERIAC

250g rock salt
250g plain flour
about 50ml cold water
1 celeriac (unpeeled)

Combine the salt and flour in a stand mixer fitted with a paddle attachment and mix on medium speed for 2 minutes. Gradually mix in enough cold water to make a dough-like consistency. Cover the bowl with clingfilm and rest in the fridge for 30 minutes.

Preheat the oven to 250°C fan/its highest temperature. Roll out the dough to approximately 3cm thickness in a shape large enough to wrap around the celeriac and completely enclose it. Wrap up the celeriac, smoothing out any air pockets in the dough. Place on a baking tray and bake for 15 minutes, then reduce the oven temperature to 160°C fan/180°C/Gas Mark 4 and bake for a further 30–40 minutes or until the core temperature reaches 80°C.

Carefully remove the top of the salt crust. Leave the celeriac to cool to room temperature before removing the remaining crust.

*...continued on page 156*

## CELERIAC BALLOTINE

1 Salt-Baked Celeriac (see page 155)
8 sheets of dried nori (about 3g each)

Peel the celeriac, then trim it into as large a cube as possible; reserve the trim. Using a mandoline, cut the cube into very thin square slices (you need 24 slices with some celeriac left over).

Lay out three layers of oven-safe clingfilm on a flat surface. Place the celeriac slices on the clingfilm in a rectangular shape, four slices across and three slices down. Lay the slices as close together as possible with no overlaps. Cover the rectangle with a layer of four nori sheets, leaving a 2cm border clear at the bottom. Using the clingfilm to help, roll up as you would a roulade or Swiss roll. Wrap the ballotine tightly in the clingfilm. Repeat the process to create a second ballotine. Reserve any leftover celeriac. Chill the ballotines for a minimum of 30 minutes to set.

## CELERIAC GLAZE

30g honey
400g peeled raw celeriac, chopped
reserved Salt-Baked Celeriac slices
    and trimmings from the ballotines
    (see above)
150g unsalted butter

Heat the honey in a small pan and caramelise to a dark golden colour.

Juice the raw celeriac – you want 100ml juice. Caramelise the reserved celeriac slices and trimmings in the butter to a nutty brown colour. Deglaze the pan with a little water, stirring well, then add the celeriac juice and top up with water to cover. Bring to a simmer and cook for 20 minutes. Remove from the heat, cover with clingfilm and allow to infuse for 10 minutes.

Strain through a fine sieve into a bowl, pressing down on the pulp to extract all the liquid; discard the pulp left in the sieve. Blend the strained liquid with some of the caramelised honey to taste in a blender or food processor – the amount of honey added to the glaze depends on the natural sweetness of the celeriac.

## ASSEMBLY

a drizzle of vegetable oil
a knob of unsalted butter
Lemon Gel (see recipe for Fresh Peas,
    Rooftop Mint and Fried Bread on
    page 124)

Preheat the oven to 175°C fan/195°C/Gas Mark 5–6. Trim the ends off the ballotines, then cut them, still wrapped in clingfilm, into six slices. Heat the oil in an ovenproof frying pan over a medium heat, add the ballotine slices, cut side down, and fry for 1 minute. Add the butter and transfer the pan to the oven to cook for 2 minutes. Flip the slices over and remove the clingfilm. Spoon the buttery juices over the slices. Remove from the oven and add the celeriac glaze. Allow it to warm in the residual heat of the pan.

Pour a pool of almond milk into the bottom of each bowl. Place a slice of ballotine in the middle, a quenelle of the sunflower praline to one side and a squeeze of lemon gel to the other side. Pour some of the glaze over the top of the ballotine.

# SEA

# JULIE GIRL SKATE

## WHITE ASPARAGUS, BREAD MISO

This is a deceptively simple dish that shows how we have grown and become quite confident in the kitchen. Rather than adding technique after technique, we let the ingredients do the talking. In the Larder section of this book, we've shown you how to make your own miso from stale bread, but this does take some time. A brown rice miso from a healthfood store would still do the trick.

serves 4–6

### SKATE

1 skate wing, weighing 600–700g
7% brine (see page 20)
300–400g unsalted butter, cut into
    small cubes
fresh lemon juice
Maldon sea salt

Brine the skate wing in a 7% brine for 3 hours. Remove, rinse and pat dry.

Preheat the oven to 60–80°C fan/80–100°C/Gas Mark low. Place the skate in a baking tray. Melt the butter in a pan set over a high heat and heat until the butter starts to foam and brown and gives off a nutty aroma. Remove from the heat immediately and cool quickly to stop the butter from burning (you can do this by setting the base of the pan in iced water).

Pour the brown butter over the skate to cover. Bake for 15–20 minutes or until the core temperature of the fish reaches 50°C. Lift the skate from the butter, take the flesh off the bone and portion into 4–6 pieces. Season with the poaching butter, lemon juice and salt to taste.

### ASPARAGUS

12 white asparagus spears
200ml Kombu Oil (see page 56)
fresh lemon juice

Remove the tough woody ends from the asparagus spears, then peel the stalks down their length. Put the asparagus in a pan and add the kombu oil and enough water just to cover the asparagus. Cover with a lid and simmer for 2–5 minutes or until the asparagus is just tender but retains a bite. Remove the asparagus from the cooking liquid and cut into pieces on an angle. Reserve the cooking liquid. Season with lemon juice.

### ASSEMBLY

4–6 tablespoons Bread Miso (see page 65)
    or ready-made brown miso
dill fronds
500ml White Onion Dashi (see page 66),
    warmed

Spread 1 tablespoon of miso in each bowl. Top with the asparagus. Add the skate to the side. Garnish with dill. Decant the warm dashi into a jug, and very gently stir through the reserved asparagus cooking liquid. The dashi should be poured over the dishes at the table.

# GALICIAN OCTOPUS

## SUMMER VEGETABLES AND NDUJA BRIOCHE

This is an absolute showstopper of a dish. I'm always amazed by the depth of flavour you get from octopus, one of the most bizarre and beautiful creatures of the sea. It always reminds me of the Med so that's why I've taken a very Mediterranean approach in this recipe and it fits quite well. The dish can be prepared in advance, then plonked down in the centre of the table family-style with a bottle of chilled sherry. In the Larder section of this book we have shown you how to make your own nduja, but it can be sourced from most good-quality Italian delicatessens.

**serves 6–8**

### NDUJA BRIOCHE

570g type '00' flour
40g caster sugar
10g fine table salt
15g fresh yeast
370ml whole milk
1 egg
310g unsalted butter, at room temperature
150g Nduja (see page 36, or use shop-bought)
beaten egg yolk to glaze

Put the flour, caster sugar, salt and yeast into a stand mixer fitted with the paddle attachment. Mix together, then mix in the milk and egg to form a dough. Mix in 60g of the butter, a little at a time, until combined and smooth. Cover the bowl and place in the fridge so the dough can slowly rise for 6–12 hours.

Place the remaining room-temperature butter between two sheets of greaseproof paper. Using a rolling pin, roll out the butter into a square about 2cm thick. Keep cool (in the fridge if necessary) while the dough finishes rising.

Remove the dough (and butter) from the fridge and place it on a lightly floured worktop. Shape the dough into a rough square about 2cm thick. Using a rolling pin, mark out another square in the centre of the dough by pressing into the dough with the length of the rolling pin (this square should be about the same size as the square of butter).

Roll out the dough from the sides of the marked square to create an even cross shape, leaving the thicker square area in the middle of the cross (this is what was the marked square). The 'arms' of the cross need to be about 5mm thick and large enough to fold over the square of butter.

At this point, the dough and butter should be the same texture to the touch. Place the square of butter in the middle of the cross, on the raised centre. Fold the right 'arm' over the butter so that it completely covers it. Repeat with the left 'arm', then the bottom one and, finally, the top. You will now have a square of dough completely encasing the butter.

Roll out the square away from you on the lightly floured worktop into a rectangle almost triple its original length and double the width. Fold the top third down and the bottom third up over this. Leave to rest at room temperature for 20 minutes.

Lift and turn the dough on the lightly floured worktop so that the folded edges are to the sides. Roll out the dough away from you into a rectangle

*...continued on page 164*

the same size as before. Fold into thirds as before, then lift and turn the dough so that the folded edges are to the sides again. Roll out and repeat the folding. Wrap the dough in clingfilm and chill.

Once the dough is chilled, roll out to a large rectangle roughly 30 x 50cm. Spread a layer of nduja about 5mm thick all over the surface of the dough. Roll up the dough from a long side to create a pinwheel effect. Wrap the roll in a floured cloth and chill until firm enough to slice.

Cut the roll across into 80g slices. Place the slices cut side down in an ovenproof greased saucepan, arranging them about 1cm apart so that when they rise and bake their sides will be touching. Brush the slices with a little egg yolk, then cover loosely with clingfilm and leave to rise in a warm part of the kitchen for about 30 minutes.

Preheat the oven to 180°C fan/200°C/Gas Mark 6. Place a pan of water in the bottom of the oven. Remove the clingfilm and bake the brioche for 15 minutes. Allow to cool on the baking tray.

## BRAISED OCTOPUS

1 bottle of white wine
30g fennel seeds
20g coriander seeds
2 tablespoons olive oil
15g dried chilli flakes
5 garlic cloves, sliced
3 bay leaves
10 black peppercorns
1 octopus, cleaned
1 bulb of fennel, cut in half
peel of 1 lemon (no pith)

Preheat the oven to 120°C fan/140°C/Gas Mark 1. Pour the wine into a pan and bring to the boil, then simmer for 2 minutes to evaporate some alcohol; set aside. Gently toast the fennel seeds and coriander seeds in the olive oil in a small pan for 3–5 minutes. Remove from the heat and stir in the chilli flakes, garlic, bay leaves and peppercorns. Allow to cool slightly, then rub this mixture all over the octopus.

Place the octopus in a large ovenproof pot. Add the fennel and lemon peel. Pour in the wine and top up with water to cover. Cover with a lid and place in the oven to braise for 2–3 hours or until the octopus is tender. Remove the fennel after 1 hour, cut it into wedges and reserve it. Once tender, drain the octopus, reserving the stock. Trim the octopus into portions. Strain the stock.

## BORLOTTI BEANS

100g podded fresh borlotti beans (if using dried borlotti beans , soak and cook according to the packet instructions)

Put the borlotti beans in a pan, cover with cold water and bring to the boil. Remove from the heat and drain. Return the beans to the pan and cover with a mixture of equal parts stock from the octopus and water. Simmer for about 40 minutes or until tender. Leave the beans to cool in the liquid before draining.

## ASSEMBLY

100g podded fresh broad beans
100g small tomatoes (Datterini or cherry)
1 Trombetta or normal courgette, sliced
50g Nduja (see page 36 or use shop-bought)
fresh lemon juice
olive oil
basil leaves

Blanch the broad beans in boiling water for 1 minute, then refresh in iced water and pop the bright green beans out of their thick skins by squeezing gently. Heat the remaining octopus stock in a pan, halve the tomatoes and add them to the pan along with the reserved fennel wedges, borlotti beans, broad beans, courgette, nduja and octopus to warm through. Season with lemon juice and a drizzle of olive oil. Ladle into bowls and garnish with basil. Serve the brioche on the side.

# APPLEWOOD-SMOKED EEL

## BROAD BEANS, PRESERVED LEMON, MINT

Applewood-smoked eel is one of the few ingredients that we buy in already prepared. This is because Corine and her family at the Dutch Eel Company in Lincolnshire have been producing it for centuries and it is one of the most amazing products I have ever come across. At first I had my reservations. I had once had an unpleasant jellied eel experience where all I could taste was vinegar, fish and jelly (it didn't help that I was quite hungover at the time). But when I tried this smoked eel I was hooked. Applewood-smoked eel is my go-to ingredient when cooking at events where I really want to impress. It is something that people are least excited about when reading the menu, but when they try it they fall in love. It's a surprise that captures you. I describe it as the smoked bacon of the sea as it has a sweet smoky flavour but is also very meaty.

*serves 4–6*

### SMOKED EEL CREAM

a drizzle of vegetable oil
50g skin and bones from smoked eel
100ml UHT double cream
2 teaspoons white soy sauce

Heat the vegetable oil in a pan and add the eel skin and bones. Sweat gently for about 10 minutes so that the flavour and fats from the eel are released. Add the cream and bring to the boil, then remove from the heat and allow to infuse for 20 minutes. Strain the cream and season it with the white soy sauce. Allow to cool to room temperature.

### BROAD BEAN AND PEA SALAD

100g podded fresh broad beans
100g podded fresh peas
½ lemon
10g Wild Garlic Pickle (see page 44) with
    a little of the pickling liquor
50ml olive oil
a little peel from Preserved Amalfi Lemons
    (see page 30), finely diced
1 fillet of Cured Sardines (see page 40),
    finely diced
garum sauce or fish sauce

Blanch the broad beans in boiling water for 1 minute, then refresh in iced water. Pop the bright green beans out of their thick skins by squeezing gently. If the peas are quite large, blanch them in boiling water for 30 seconds, then refresh in iced water; if they are small and sweet, leave them raw. Put the broad beans and peas in a metal sieve and place over a barbecue to warm through and smoke slightly (or you can warm them gently in a pan in a drizzle of olive oil).

Peel the lemon half and remove the segments, cutting them from the membrane. Cut the lemon flesh into very small pieces.

Mix together the pickled wild garlic, lemon, olive oil, preserved lemon peel, cured sardines and garum or fish sauce to taste to create a dressing. Toss through the warm broad beans and peas.

### ASSEMBLY

120g skinless applewood-smoked eel fillet,
    portioned into 4–6 pieces
mint leaves
sorrel leaves
wild rocket (leaves and flowers)
Bottarga (see page 38), optional

Place a heaped spoonful of the broad bean and pea salad down the centre of each plate. Put a piece of the eel to one side and a spoonful of smoked eel cream to the other. Garnish the salad with mint, sorrel and wild rocket. Grate over a little bottarga, if using.

# LOBSTER SALAD

## SQUASH MISO, SALAD FROM THE FARM

serves 4

I strongly recommend firing up the barbecue for this one. There is something so special about cooking lobster over wood and coals that after you do it for the first time you will not want to settle for anything else. The aroma from the smoke is just incredible. By rubbing the miso into the flesh of the lobster, the sugars will caramelise nicely. I have served greens and vegetables from our farm but a simple salad of any kind would work. It's all about the lobster!

### SQUASH MISO

50g cooked butternut squash
50g Miso (see page 64 or shop-bought)
50g lobster coral
½ garlic clove
1 teaspoon garum or fish sauce
140ml Lobster Oil (see page 57)

Put all the ingredients, except the oil, in a blender or food processor and blend until smooth. Drizzle in the lobster oil while blending to emulsify to a mayonnaise consistency. Let it down with a little water if it gets too thick.

### LOBSTER

2 live lobsters (about 600g each)

Bring a large pot of water to a rapid boil. As humanely as possible, kill the lobsters by placing the sharp tip of a knife into the spot on the lobster behind the eyes where a cross section of grooves appear on the shell. Place the lobsters in the pot and boil for 1 minute, then remove and refresh in an ice-water bath. Pull off the head and discard. Cut through the tail shell vertically to expose the tail meat – leave the meat in the shell but remove the digestive tract. Crack open the claws, remove the meat and pat dry. If you are going to finish cooking the lobsters on the barbecue, set it up to get the coals to the right temperature.

### VEGETABLES

50ml extra virgin olive oil
6 Tokyo turnips, cut in half
6 large spring onion bulbs, cut in half
50g unsalted butter
300g Siberian kale leaves
300g Cavolo Nero leaves
100g Cultured Cream (see page 54)
   or crème fraîche
juice of 2 lemons
Maldon sea salt and freshly ground
   black pepper

Preheat the oven to 190°C fan/210°C/Gas Mark 6–7. To cook the vegetables, place two large, wide-bottomed, ovenproof pans over a high heat. Add a drizzle of olive oil to one pan followed by the turnips, cut side down. Cook for 1 minute. Add the spring onions, also cut side down, to the same pan and cook for another minute. Add the butter and transfer the pan to the oven to cook for 5 minutes.

Meanwhile, add a generous drizzle of olive oil to the second pan and quickly add the kale and cabbage. Char the leaves until they take on a dark caramel colour, turning them with tongs. Season with salt and pepper, then remove from the heat. Add the cultured cream or crème fraîche and a squeeze of lemon juice; keep warm.

Remove the turnips and onions from the oven. Season with salt, pepper and a squeeze of lemon juice; keep warm.

...continued on page 170

## ASSEMBLY

extra virgin olive oil
3 sprigs of tarragon, leaves picked
100g miner's lettuce
lemon

To finish cooking the lobsters on the barbecue, brush the meat side of the tails (still in shell) and the claw meat with olive oil, then place on hot bars over the coals and cook for 1–2 minutes. Remove the lobster from the heat and brush over some of the squash miso. Return to the barbecue and cook for another minute to caramelise.

Alternatively, you can use a hot ridged grill pan set over a high heat to caramelise the lobster in exactly the same way. If necessary, place in the oven for a minute or two afterwards to be sure the lobster is warmed through.

Place the charred kale and cabbage in a serving bowl followed by the onions and turnips. Add a sprinkle of tarragon leaves and miner's lettuce.

Arrange the lobster on a serving plate with some tarragon leaves and a squeeze of lemon. Serve the miso on the side in a bowl. Serve family-style for everyone to help themselves at the table.

# SMOKED POLLOCK, POTATO MOUSSE

## RECIPE BY DEAN PARKER, HEAD CHEF OF THE MANOR

This was on Dean's first menu at The Manor and remains there to this day. It has all the components of a fish pie but, like Dean, it is clever, warm and exciting. That sounds a bit creepy, I know, but it is just a brilliant dish by a brilliant chef!

**serves 4–6**

### KOMBU DASHI

2 sheets of dried kombu (10g each)
2 litres filtered water
Maldon sea salt

Soak the kombu in the water in a pan for 2 hours. Then set on a low-medium heat and bring to a very gentle simmer. Simmer for 2 hours (do not boil). Measure the liquid and season with 1% salt. Clingfilm the top of the pot, leaving the kombu in to infuse, and set aside for 1 hour. Strain the liquid, reserving the kombu.

### SORREL EMULSION

a bunch of sorrel (about 60g)
60g Fermented Sorrel (see page 23)
100ml olive oil
100ml Kombu Dashi (see above)

Separate the stems from the leaves of the fresh sorrel. Put the stems in a blender or food processor and add the fermented sorrel (undrained), olive oil and dashi. Blend until smooth. Add the fresh sorrel leaves and pulse until smooth. Set aside at room temperature.

### POLLOCK

300g skinless pollock fillet
salt
applewood chips, for smoking

Cover the fish with salt and set aside for 5 minutes, then rinse well and pat dry. Place on a cloth-covered tray and leave in the fridge for 8 hours – change the cloth once during this time.

Take a flat tray with a steam insert (such as a deep roasting tray that will hold a flat steaming rack) and spread the applewood chips over the bottom of the tray. Warm it over a medium heat until the chips start to smoke. Remove from the heat. Place the fish on the steam insert/steaming rack and set this over the smoking chips. Completely cover the top and sides tightly with oven-safe clingfilm so the smoke is sealed inside with the fish. Leave to lightly smoke for 5 minutes. Once smoked, portion the pollock into 50g pieces.

### NORI BUTTER EMULSION

250g Nori Butter (see page 53)
1 litre Kombu Dashi (see above)
10g dried wakame
zest of 1 lemon
100ml Kefir (see page 54) or plain yoghurt
2g (about 2 small pinches) Gelespressa
fish sauce
bonito flakes

Put the nori butter, dashi, one sheet of the reserved kombu from the dashi, the wakame, lemon zest, kefir and Gelespressa in a pot and warm gently; do not boil. Season heavily with fish sauce and bonito flakes. Transfer the mixture to a blender or food processor and blend well.

...continued on page 172

## POTATO MOUSSE

500g Maris Piper potatoes (unpeeled),
    cut into 5cm dice
½ quantity Nori Butter Emulsion
    (see page 171)
lemon zest
fish sauce
1g (about a small pinch) Gelespressa
50g Smoked Butter (see page 53)
50g Cultured Cream (see page 54)
50g Bonito Butter (see page 52)

Simmer the potatoes in the nori butter emulsion until cooked. Blend the potatoes in a high-speed blender or food processor with enough of the emulsion to make a thick purée. Season to taste with lemon zest and fish sauce. While blending, gradually add the Gelespressa, smoked butter, cultured cream and bonito butter to emulsify. Pass through a fine sieve into another pan and allow to cool.

## CHERIE POTATOES

500g Cherie or other waxy new potatoes
    (unpeeled)
½ quantity Nori Butter Emulsion
    (see page 171)

Simmer the potatoes in the nori butter emulsion until tender. Drain but reserve the emulsion to warm the potatoes when serving.

## POTATO CRISPS

1 small Maris Piper potato (unpeeled)
vegetable oil, for deep frying
Nori Salt (see page 60)

Slice the potato very thinly on a mandoline. Heat vegetable oil in a deep pan or deep-fat fryer to 160°C, then deep-fry the potato slices for about 5 minutes or until they are golden and crisp. Drain on kitchen paper and season with nori salt. Hold the crisps in a warm, dry area of your kitchen.

## ASSEMBLY

30g Bonito Butter (see page 52)
1 sheet of kombu reserved from the Kombu
    Dashi (see 171)
3 spring onions
30g Nori Butter (see page 53)
chopped chives
fresh lemon juice
Maldon sea salt
sorrel leaves

Preheat the oven to 140°C fan/160°C/Gas Mark 3. Wrap the pollock with the bonito butter in the kombu sheet. Place on a baking tray in the oven to heat for 10 minutes.

Meanwhile, char the spring onions on a barbecue or hot ridged grill pan until blackened. Peel off the black outside layer and split each spring onion down the middle. Warm the halves in the nori butter.

Gently heat the potato mousse, stirring, to no higher than 70°C. Decant into a siphon gun with one charge and shake well.

Warm the Cherie potatoes in some of the reserved nori butter emulsion; drain them and add some chopped chives. Flake each portion of pollock into two pieces and season with lemon juice.

Spread the sorrel emulsion on the warmed plates. Place the Cherie potatoes, spring onions and pollock around each plate. Finish with potato mousse, off centre in the middle, topped with a potato crisp and a sorrel leaf.

# CHARRED MACKEREL

## CUCUMBER, DASHI, SEA PURSLANE

Generally speaking, mackerel must be at its absolute freshest – I detest mackerel once it has been more than two days out of the deep blue – so when buying your fish, make sure the flesh is firm, the gills are bright red and the eyes are bright and glistening. We use salt to season and firm up the fish, and I like to serve it medium-rare. This is a really fresh and vibrant dish to serve in late summer.

serves 4–6

### DILL-PICKLED CUCUMBER

2 small cucumbers or ½ regular-sized cucumber
75g ice
75g caster sugar
75ml Chardonnay vinegar
a bunch of dill, fronds picked
a large pinch of fine table salt

Peel the cucumbers and set aside; reserve the skin. Blend together the ice, caster sugar, vinegar, dill, the cucumber skin and salt in a blender or food processor. Strain through a fine sieve and pour this liquid over the peeled cucumbers. Leave to marinate for 1 hour.

### DILL OIL

150g picked dill fronds
150ml grapeseed oil

Blend together the dill and oil in a blender or food processor for 1 minute. Transfer to a pan, bring to the boil and boil rapidly for 2 minutes. Strain through a fine sieve into a bowl set over ice to cool.

### CHARRED MACKEREL

3 medium mackerel, filleted
fresh lemon juice

Blowtorch, barbecue or grill (on a hot ridged grill pan) the skin side of the mackerel fillets –you are just looking to scorch the skin and lightly cook the fish to medium-rare. Season the fillets with lemon juice and salt to taste.

### ASSEMBLY

4–6 teaspoons Roast Garlic Miso Purée (see page 65), at room temperature – 1 teaspoon per serving
purslane leaves
sea purslane, blanched for 30 seconds
Wild Garlic Capers (see page 44) with some of the pickling liquor
160–240ml Dashi (see page 66), warmed – 40ml per serving
Maldon sea salt

Drain the pickled cucumbers and slice into rounds. Spread a teaspoon of miso purée in each bowl, then add the mackerel. Top the fish with the cucumber slices (fanned). Place the fresh purslane, sea purslane and wild garlic capers to the side. Drizzle over some dill oil. In a jug, season the warm dashi with a little of the pickling liquor from the wild garlic capers. The dashi should be poured over each dish at the table.

# THE BEAN FAMILY

I first became aware of the Bean family when I was running Sauterelle in 2007. Dean was working at the time for a fellow manic-obsessive produce freak named Peter Weedon – I cannot talk about the Bean family and their company Kernowsashimi without giving a nod to Peter. In his normal excitable manner, Dean was jumping out of his seat describing the quality and freshness of the fish they were getting from Kernowsashimi for Paternoster Chop House. Peter was very kind and helpful, not to mention generous, in passing on this most valuable contact.

Chris Bean, his son Dylan and daughter-in-law Mutsuko, and their two amazing kids from St Martin in Cornwall are a family that has been very important to us since we first had the opportunity to start working with them all that time ago. Chris leads the fleet of about five day-boats on the Lady Hamilton, his first boat bought back in 1972. An estuary runs to a spot called Coverack, which is where at 5am most of the boats set off. They come ashore around 2pm with the landings. Dylan, Mutsuko and Michelle run things on the ground, coordinating where the stocks are sent.

I'm embarrassed to say that my first opportunity to go and see for myself how they work was to research for this book and for some photo ops. A good few of my team had already made the journey and came back somewhat changed in their way of thinking, inspired in a thoughtful way. I now know why. Ben and I hired a car to make the five-hour journey to the tip of Cornwall near to Lizard. On our arrival, we had quite a surreal moment, or at least it was surreal for me. Over ten years I had talked to Dylan almost every other day – he would explain and try to predict what would be caught so that we could arrange for a box of fish, which meant discussing tides, weather, boats and fish – and I considered it to be a very important relationship. When we finally met it felt like we had had a long-distance arranged marriage! Anyway, we quickly got over that weird moment, hugged it out, and he invited us into their home.

Mutsuko, if you hadn't guessed, is from Japan. She has done a pretty good job of holding on to her heritage and culture. When we met she had just arrived back from a trip to her home town and put together a feast full of rare treats like an indigenous rice, a particularly fresh yuzu only grown in her village, several types of what I would consider drinkable bottles of soy, fresh wasabi and shiso grown in her greenhouse. And naturally she had her pick of the finest catch of Cornwall's coast. Armed with bottles of Asahi beer and her favourite sake, we got stuck into smashing an array of spider crabs, cuttlefish sashimi, fried squid and a katsu-style pork with her own miso. We ate like kings. No pressure then when Ben and I in turn were to cook the following evening!

The next day we had hoped to get out on a boat but the weather was too rough. So we explored the coast for dinner inspirations and some more photo opportunities, pulling into half a dozen postcard-like coves and harbours. We were chasing the boats coming ashore and had hoped to capture an image of Lady Hamilton, but we missed it. So we raced back to the sorting bay, as I call it, at Dylan's house, to witness the sorting of the catch and where it is to be sent. Everything is weighed and recorded at a furious pace. In a human conveyor belt, the fish are carefully laid into the awaiting ice pack-pillowed boxes, which have the name of the restaurant scribbled on the side. I got to pack my own box and 20 minutes later a courier in a van arrived for collection. The Dairy received their fish six hours later. Quite often the fish we get is too fresh and needs to rest a day or two for the flesh to relax. I learned this the hard way by once trying to cook very fresh Dover sole on the bone. It was really tough and chewy, and a number of guests sent it back.

That afternoon Dylan and Mutsuko took us for Spingo ales at The Blue Anchor, and that night Ben and I cooked for the Bean family. The following day we returned home, inspired and a little wiser.

Many fishermen and women risk their lives and many are lost to deliver to us this most precious and controversial food source. To all the unsung heroes aboard Lady Hamilton, Lucy Mariana, Willy's, Julie Girl and many more that venture out to sea, we salute you.

# COD FEAST

Nose-to-tail cooking has been quite the fashionable way to cook over the last ten years, credited mostly to Fergus Henderson. This is a very good thing indeed, considering the way we eat today and the little time we have to cook at home. But what I have not seen, which is equally important, is the head-to-tail approach to fish. We have all heard the upsetting statistics regarding the fishing stocks worldwide and the massive fishing trawlers shovelling up the seabeds and coastline, landing up to 250 tonnes of fish a day. I believe we still don't do enough to cook and eat fish responsibly. Cod is probably the most popular yet controversial fish of the sea, and has been an important economic commodity in international markets for more than a thousand years. Here I show three techniques that use parts of the fish we usually don't see on any menus or that we cook at home. I have used cod here but the recipes could easily be transported to any fish. I have also included a couple of preservation recipes that could be made in bulk and kept in the store cupboard for months.

## MISO BBQ COD COLLARS

4 cod collars
7% brine (see page 20)
50g honey
2 teaspoons rice wine vinegar
20g brown miso
vegetable oil, for deep-frying
30g dried wakame
80g crème fraîche, seasoned with lemon
 juice and Maldon sea salt to taste
100g Pickled White Peaches (see page 45)
100g Fennel Kimchi (see page 29)
100g sorrel, leaves picked

Brine the cod collars in a 7% brine for 6 hours. Drain and rinse well.

Mix together the honey, vinegar and miso, and rub this paste into the collars. Cook over raging hot coals on a barbecue for 2 minutes on each side, then allow to rest for a minute. Alternatively, sear on a hot ridged griddle pan for 2 minutes each side, then rest.

Heat vegetable oil in a deep-fat fryer or a deep pan to 160°C and fry the dried wakame for 1 minute; drain on kitchen paper.

Serve all the components (cod, wakame, crème fraîche, pickled peaches and fennel kimchi) in separate bowls and allow guests to build their own 'tacos' at the table using the sorrel leaves as carriers.

## SMOKED COD'S ROE

80–100g Smoked Cod's Roe (see page 40)
20g Cultured Cream (see page 54)
a drizzle of Kombu Oil (see page 56)
Bottarga (see page 38), optional
a bunch of radishes

Gently warm the cod's roe with the cultured cream to 40°C. Carefully fold through the kombu oil. Decant into a ramekin and grate over the bottarga, if using. Serve with the radishes on the side.

## ASSEMBLY

Serve all dishes family-style in the centre of the table for guests to help themselves.

# LOCH DUART SALMON

## OYSTER EMULSION, FENNEL, FRIED WAKAME

The oyster emulsion here is an absolute winner. It's also amazing served as a dip with some oysters in tempura or with a beef tartare. The way the salmon is cooked is a trick I picked up from Raymond Blanc. I'll never forget tasting it for the first time. It simply blew my mind and taught me to understand the nature of cooking fish. You will often hear chefs say that it takes great skill to cook fish. I slightly disagree. I believe it just requires an understanding. Fish is delicate and in most cases should never be cooked at too high a temperature, otherwise the fish tenses up and an unpleasant white protein appears, which for me is an alarm bell screaming that I have overcooked the fish.

**serves 4**

### OYSTER EMULSION

100g banana shallots, sliced
200ml dry white wine
130g freshly shucked rock oysters (juice reserved)
150ml grapeseed oil
5 sorrel leaves
1 tablespoon crème fraîche

Put the shallots into a saucepan and pour over the white wine. Place on a medium to low heat and boil until all the wine has evaporated. Remove from the heat and allow to cool.

Tip the shallot mixture and oysters into a blender or food processor and blend until smooth. While blending, gradually add the oil to make a mayonnaise consistency. Add the sorrel leaves and blend through, then blend in some of the reserved oyster juice to loosen the mixture. Stir in the crème fraîche. Keep the emulsion in the fridge until ready to serve.

### FRIED WAKAME

200ml vegetable oil, for frying
50g dried wakame

Heat the oil in a deep pan to 160°C. Fry the wakame for 1½ minutes or until crisp. Remove and drain on kitchen paper.

### ASSEMBLY

250g Cured Salmon (see page 39)
8 slices Fennel Kimchi (see page 29)
dill fronds
fennel fronds

Portion the salmon into four pieces. Place a spoon of oyster emulsion on each plate and add a piece of salmon to the side. Arrange the fennel kimchi and fried wakame around the fish. Garnish with dill and fennel.

# CORNISH CRAB

## SALT-BAKED BEETROOT, COBNUTS

Crab meat has a natural sweetness so it makes sense to me that it would work with beetroot. Baking the beetroot in a salt dough is a clever way to keep the juices in the beetroot and intensify the flavour while helping to season the vegetable. If you can't be bothered to make the dough, just wrap the beetroot in foil. In the restaurant we use golden or white beetroot as it is a little sweeter, but any beetroot, or indeed any root vegetable, can be baked like this.

**serves 6**

### SALT-BAKED BEETROOT

500g rock salt
500g plain flour
about 100ml cold water
4 large raw beetroots (golden or white, if available)
applewood chips for smoking

Combine the salt and flour in a stand mixer fitted with a paddle attachment and mix on medium speed for 2 minutes. Gradually add enough cold water to bring together into a dough. Wrap in clingfilm and leave to rest in the fridge for 30 minutes before use.

Preheat the oven to 210°C fan/230°C/Gas Mark 8. Divide the dough into 4 portions. Roll out each to a round large enough to enclose a beetroot. Wrap the beetroots in the salt dough. Place on a baking tray and bake for 15 minutes. Lower the oven temperature to 150°C fan/170°C/Gas Mark 3–4 and bake for a further 20–30 minutes or until the beetroot has a core temperature of 85°C. Allow to cool before cracking off the salt dough crust (discard it). Rub the skin off the beetroots.

Take a flat tray with a steam insert (such as a deep roasting tray that will hold a flat steaming rack) and spread the applewood chips over the bottom of the tray. Warm it over a medium heat until the chips start to smoke. Remove from the heat. Place the beetroots on the steam insert/steaming rack and set this over the smoking chips. Completely cover the top and sides tightly with oven-safe clingfilm so the smoke is sealed inside with the beetroot. Return to a low heat so the wood chips smoke gently. Leave to lightly smoke the beetroots for 15 minutes.

Remove the beetroots from the tray. Slice them thinly on a mandoline.

### BROWN CRAB AND BEETROOT MAYO

25g egg yolks
75g brown crab meat (wrapped in muslin and squeezed to remove excess liquid)
50g Salt-Baked Beetroot (see above)
80ml Crab Oil (see page 55)
25g crème fraîche
1–2 drops of Tabasco sauce
juice of ¼ lemon or to taste

Put the egg yolks into a food processor with the brown crab meat and beetroot. Start blending at a medium speed, then slowly drizzle in the crab oil while blending (add a touch of cold water should the mix become too thick). Transfer the mixture to a mixing bowl and add the crème fraîche, Tabasco and lemon juice to taste. Keep in the fridge until required.

*...continued on page 186*

## ASSEMBLY

200g fresh cobnuts or hazelnuts
210g fresh white crab meat
Crab Oil (see page 55)
fresh lemon juice
Rock Samphire Pickle (see page 46)
Maldon sea salt

Crack open the cobnuts and peel, then cut each one in half.

Spoon a little of the crab and beetroot mayo into the bottom of each bowl. Season the white crab meat with a drizzle of crab oil, some lemon juice and a pinch of salt. Top the mayo with the white crab. Dress the remaining beetroot slices with some crab oil and a pinch of salt. Arrange the slices on top of the white crab. Garnish with the cobnuts and pickled rock samphire.

# RED MULLET

## CAULIFLOWER AND DULSE BUTTER

This dish is all about *mise en place*, timings and pan-cooking skill. With quite a bit happening all at once, the key here is to make the butter and purée in advance, and to be sure you have suitable pans for cooking the cauliflower and fish. I believe the cooking of the cauliflower is just as important as getting that beautiful crispy skin on the fish. Every second that both cauliflower and fish are not hitting nice heated plates, the more the dish deteriorates. Depending on the size of the cauliflower, the fish and cauliflower should only be a minute apart from cooking so use your instinct, get prepared and do your best!

### DULSE BUTTER

80g drained Fermented Dulse
   (see page 25), finely chopped
100g unsalted butter, at room temperature

Mix the dulse into the butter until well dispersed throughout.

*...continued on page 188*

## CAULIFLOWER PURÉE

½ cauliflower (use the outer part of
    the cauliflower, reserving the centre)
100g unsalted butter, cut into small cubes
1 teaspoon Maldon sea salt
150ml whole milk
50g Cultured Cream (see page 54)
a squeeze of fresh lemon juice

Grate the cauliflower through a coarse grater. Put the butter into a pan over a high heat and cook until the butter starts to foam, brown and take on a nutty aroma. Add the grated cauliflower and salt and cook over a high heat, stirring regularly, for up to 8 minutes or until the cauliflower is softened. Add the milk and bring to a simmer. Check that the cauliflower is cooked by tasting it.

Drain the cauliflower and tip into a blender or food processor. Add the cultured cream and lemon juice and blend until completely smooth. Taste and adjust the seasoning if necessary.

## RED MULLET AND CAULIFLOWER

80g sea purslane
handful of broccoli leaves (most leafy
    greens would work)
olive oil
reserved centre of cauliflower (see above),
    cut into 2 large flat slices
4 x 80g red mullet (skin on)
20g Nori Powder (see page 60)
30g capers
juice of 2 lemons

Preheat the oven to 185°C fan/205°C/Gas Mark 6. Pick the sea purslane, then blanch in a pan of boiling water for 30 seconds. Drain, refresh in iced water and set aside. Repeat with the broccoli leaves.

Set a large ovenproof pan over a high heat and add a good drizzle of olive oil, then place the cauliflower slices in the pan. Caramelise for 3–4 minutes or until the surface area is a nice even dark brown. Add half of the dulse butter. Transfer the pan to the oven to cook for 4 minutes.

When you start to caramelise the cauliflower, set another ovenproof non-stick frying pan over a medium heat and add a good splash of olive oil. Make sure the skin of the fish is dry, then place it skin side down in the pan. Turn the heat up – the fish will start to curl. Let it relax, when it will return to its natural shape. As the skin starts to crisp and the fat starts to spit, continue to cook, pressing down on areas that are not colouring. Once the skin is light golden brown, transfer the pan to the oven to cook for 1 minute.

Remove the fish from the oven and set the pan over a very high heat. Season the fish with nori powder and cook for 30 seconds to get the skin crispy again. Add the remaining dulse butter, turn the fish over and remove from the heat. Add the capers and half of the lemon juice. Remove the fish from the pan and keep warm. Reserve the pan juices.

Remove the cauliflower from the oven and reserve on a plate. Dust with the nori powder. In the same pan, add the purslane and cook over a high heat for 30 seconds, with a squeeze of lemon juice. Remove from the pan and reserve. Repeat with the blanched broccoli leaves and remaining lemon juice.

## ASSEMBLY

Put a heaped tablespoon of the purée on one side of each plate. Place the fish off centre on the other side and spoon over any pan juices. Add a couple of broccoli leaves to each plate. Place the cauliflower slices on a separate plate, and finish with another sprinkle of nori powder and top with the purslane. Put the cauliflower in the centre of the table for your guests to help themselves.

# LADY HAMILTON COD

## CHARRED LEEKS, LEEK MOLASSES

The method for cooking the leeks in this recipe is the most impressive part for me. Dean picked this up working with Tom Aikens, and it comes and goes on our menus in different guises, accompanying all sorts of things from cheese to beef and here with cod. This was on our very first menu. It was months before we removed it as we simply couldn't come up with a better-tasting dish. It's brilliant any time of the year so we revert back to it every now and again.

**serves 4–6**

### CHARRED LEEKS AND LEEK MOLASSES

3–4 medium leeks
vegetable oil, for roasting
80g demerara sugar
4 teaspoons rice wine vinegar
2 tablespoons olive oil
2 tablespoons water
fresh lemon juice
Maldon sea salt

Preheat the oven to 250°C fan/its highest temperature. Split the leeks down the middle and wash thoroughly, then blanch in boiling water for 5–7 minutes or until slightly softened. Drain the leeks and place on a rack in a baking tray, cut side up. Coat with vegetable oil and 50g of the demerara sugar. Roast for 12 minutes. Remove the very burnt ends from the leeks but reserve them for the molasses. Set the charred leeks aside.

For the leek molasses, melt the remaining 30g demerara sugar in a small pan and cook to a dark caramel. Stir in the rice wine vinegar to deglaze. Transfer the caramel mixture to a small blender or food processor and add the burnt ends of the leeks and the olive oil. Blitz to a purée. Emulsify the purée with the water. Season with lemon juice and salt to taste.

### COD

250g unsalted butter, cut into small cubes
350g skinless cod fillet

Turn the oven to 60–80°C fan/80–100°C/Gas Mark low.

Melt the butter in a pan set over a high heat and heat until the butter starts to foam and brown and gives off a nutty aroma. Remove from the heat immediately and cool quickly to stop the butter from burning (you can do this by setting the base of the pan in iced water). Place the cod in a baking tray and cover with the brown butter. Poach in the oven for 15–20 minutes or until the core temperature of the cod reaches 50°C.

### ASSEMBLY

chopped chives
fresh lemon juice
olive oil
150g Smoked Cod's Roe Emulsion (see page 67)
100g Fried Bread (see page 59)
sorrel leaves, torn
Maldon sea salt

Spoon some of the leek molasses into the centre of each plate and spread it with the back of a spoon. Gently pull apart the charred leeks and season them with chopped chives, lemon juice, olive oil and salt. Scatter them over each plate. Flake the cod around the plates and pipe around a few dots of smoked cod's roe emulsion. Scatter fried bread and sorrel leaves over the top.

# APPLEWOOD-SMOKED EEL

## FERMENTED CHARD, SHALLOT CRISPS, WHITE SOY

The technique of blending the egg yolk emulsion long enough to reach a mayonnaise consistency is a great trick to learn. You can basically give the emulsion any flavour you want by simply browning and infusing the butter – here shallots make it slightly sweet. Chard was one of the first vegetables we fermented that made it on to our menu.

serves 6

### SHALLOT CRISPS

200g unsalted butter, diced
4 banana shallots, thinly sliced
   on a mandoline
fine table salt

Put the butter into a pan and melt, then bring to a simmer over a high heat. Add the shallots and cook, stirring constantly, for 5–10 minutes or until the butter turns a nutty brown and the shallots are crisp. Drain the shallots immediately through a sieve set in a bowl to reserve the butter. Press the shallots to drain out all the butter, then tip them on to kitchen paper to drain. Season the shallot crisps with a pinch of salt.

The butter reserved in the bowl will now taste of caramelised shallot – it will be the base for the miso and egg yolk emulsion.

### MISO AND EGG YOLK EMULSION

50g egg yolks
20g brown rice miso
2–3 tablespoons white soy sauce
2 tablespoons rice wine vinegar
100ml shallot-flavoured butter (see above)

Put the egg yolks into a blender with the miso, white soy and vinegar. While blending, drizzle in the shallot-flavoured butter, as you would when adding oil for a mayonnaise. Blend to a mayonnaise consistency, adding a touch of water if the emulsion thickens too much. Adjust the seasoning to your liking with more soy, miso and vinegar.

### ASSEMBLY

240g applewood-smoked eel, divided into
   6 portions
200g Swiss Chard Ferment (see page 27),
   drained, stalks diced and leaves
   kept whole
50g Cultured Cream (see page 54)

Preheat the oven to 170°C fan/190°C/Gas Mark 5. Warm the eel on a baking tray in the oven for 5 minutes. Warm the diced Swiss chard stalks in the remaining shallot-flavoured butter in a small pan. In a separate pan, warm the chard leaves with the cultured cream.

Place a spoonful of the egg yolk emulsion to the side of each plate and sprinkle over a few shallot crisps. Arrange a piece of eel to the other side of the plates and add some diced chard stalks, covering them with the chard leaves.

# LAND

# MERGUEZ

## FENNEL KIMCHI

At one time I had only ever had merguez bought from a butcher or a supplier. It was always perfectly nice but nothing to write home about. But then I tried a recipe brought to us by Joe. My first taste kind of slapped me in the tastebud chops! Toasting your own spices and barbecuing the peppers makes such a difference. There are obviously Middle Eastern flavours in the merguez so it made sense to pair it with fennel kimchi. One of the guys in the kitchen said upon tasting: 'It's the perfect kebab!' Not sure I was happy with that but actually he may have had a point.

serves 4–6

### MERGUEZ SAUSAGES

5–6 red peppers
15g paprika
15g sweet smoked paprika
5g ground cinnamon
10g ground cumin
4 cloves
2.25kg lamb mince (ask your butcher for a mince that contains at least 25% fat)
40g fine table salt
10g light brown sugar
20g garlic, finely chopped
50ml red wine (cold)
300g hog casing

Char the red peppers on a barbecue or under the grill. Remove the peppers from the heat and immediately place them in a bowl. Cover with clingfilm and allow to cool slightly, then remove the skins and seeds. Weigh out 175g of red pepper flesh and blend in a blender or food processor to a paste.

Toast all the spices in a dry pan, then grind together to a powder. Mix with the red pepper paste, lamb, salt, sugar, garlic and wine.

Stuff the mixture into the hog casing, using a sausage stuffer or mincing attachment on a stand mixer, or pipe, to make sausages approximately 150–200g in weight; tie the ends. (The sausages can be kept in the fridge for a couple of days before cooking, or they can be frozen for 3 months.)

### SAUCE

50g Merguez Sausages (see above)
a drizzle of sherry vinegar
Lamb Sauce (see page 62)

Chop up 50g of the sausages and place in a pan over a medium heat. Allow the fat to render out of the sausages. As soon as they start to catch, stir in the sherry vinegar to deglaze the pan. Strain the juices from the sausages into a saucepan (discard the sausage). Weigh these juices and top up with an equal weight of lamb sauce. Set aside.

### ASSEMBLY

350g Merguez Sausages (see above)
180g Fennel Kimchi (see page 29)
100g Cultured Cream (see page 54)
a drizzle of Herb Oil (see page 56)
bronze fennel, to garnish

Fire up the barbecue or heat a ridged grill pan. Cook the sausages on the barbecue or in the hot grill pan until browned all over and the core temperature reaches 60°C.

Put the fennel kimchi and cultured cream into a pan and warm through. Drizzle in some herb oil and stir so that it just marbles through but does not fully mix in.

Warm through the sauce. Slice the barbecued sausages into pieces. Place the fennel on one half of each plate, spooning over the cultured cream/herb oil. Garnish with bronze fennel. Place the sausages on the other side of the plates and drizzle over the sauce.

# LAMB FEAST

## SLOW-COOKED LAMB SHOULDER, BBQ CABBAGE, RICOTTA

This is the ultimate in big feast dining. What is great about the dish is that most of
the work can be done in advance so you get to enjoy the lucky company you've invited
round. You pretty much can't go wrong with the lamb shoulder by cooking it low and
slow. It's a showstopper. I love the accompaniments spread out all over the table too.
Invite only your nearest and dearest for this one.

**serves 8**

### LAMB

1 lamb shoulder

7% brine (see page 20)

2.5–3 litres Brown Chicken Stock
(see page 61)

2 carrots, finely diced

1 onion, finely diced

Brine the lamb shoulder in a 7% brine for 12 hours. Drain.

Preheat the oven to 140°C fan/160°C/Gas Mark 3. Place the lamb in
a deep roasting tray and almost cover it with the chicken stock (top up
with water if needed). Add the carrots, onion, celery, leek, bay leaf and
bulb of garlic. Cover the tray with foil and place in the oven. Cook for
about 4 hours or until the meat is tender.

3 celery sticks, finely diced

1 leek, finely diced

1 bay leaf

1 garlic bulb, cut in half horizontally

45g Onion Treacle (see page 48)

3 tablespoons Lamb Sauce (see page 62)

60g lamb fat (trimmed from the shoulder)
  – add unsalted butter if you don't have
  enough fat

20g black mustard seeds

20g fennel seeds

50ml vegetable oil

1 garlic clove (peeled)

Maldon sea salt

chive and rosemary flowers, to garnish

To make the glaze, gently melt together the onion treacle, lamb sauce and lamb fat in a saucepan until combined.

Remove the lamb shoulder from the stock and place on a clean roasting tray. Lower the oven temperature to 100°C fan/120°C/Gas Mark ½. Brush an even coating of the glaze over the meat using a pastry brush. Place back in the oven to roast for 40 minutes, brushing with the glaze every 10 minutes during this time.

To make the spice mix, warm the mustard seeds in a dry pan over a gentle heat, shaking the pan constantly. The seeds will eventually puff slightly and crack. Once they reach this stage, remove from the heat and grind in a pestle and mortar. Tip back into the warm pan off the heat. Add the fennel seeds and allow them to warm in the residual heat of the pan. In a separate pan, warm the oil slightly with the garlic clove. Add the spices to the oil (off the heat).

Spoon the spice mix over the lamb just before serving, season with Maldon salt and garnish with chive and rosemary flowers.

## BRINED AND CHARRED CABBAGE WITH RICOTTA

1 spring/Hispi cabbage

2% brine (see page 20)

olive oil

100g ricotta

10g Parmesan, freshly grated

zest of ½ lemon

Maldon sea salt and freshly ground
  black pepper

Brine the cabbage in a 2% brine for 1 hour. Drain but reserve some of the brine – decant this into a spray bottle and add a drizzle of olive oil.

Fire up the barbecue, or heat a ridged grill pan.

Cut the brined cabbage in half and place it cut side down on the barbecue or really hot grill pan. Cook for about 10 minutes, turning the cabbage halves occasionally, until they are softened slightly and charred. Keep spraying the cabbage with the brine mixture as it cooks.

Season the ricotta with the Parmesan, lemon zest, and salt and black pepper to taste. Drizzle over some olive oil.

Serve the cabbage on a plate and the ricotta in a bowl alongside.

## FRESH MINT SAUCE

a bunch of mint (about 30g), leaves picked

150ml boiling water

1 sheet/leaf of silver leaf gelatine

75g caster sugar

100ml fresh lemon juice

black mint leaves, to garnish

Moroccan mint leaves, to garnish

Blanch the mint in the boiling water for 1–2 minutes or until soft. Drain in a sieve set in a bowl, pushing down on the mint so that the flavourful juice passes through. Reserve 50ml of the blanching liquid in the bowl.

Soak the gelatine in cold water to soften it. Dissolve the sugar in 50ml of the lemon juice by warming them in a pan to just before boiling point. Drain the gelatine and stir through the lemon mixture until melted. Add the remaining lemon juice and the reserved 50ml mint blanching water. Leave to set in a suitable container in the fridge. Just before serving, top with the black mint and Moroccan mint leaves.

## ASSEMBLY

Serve the dishes family-style so that guests can help themselves.

# ROAST WOOD PIGEON

## CHICORY, RHUBARB

serves 4

Game is around at a time of year when the rest of nature has little to offer. My first experience with game was also my first experience in one of the most exciting kitchens there has ever been, the Oak Room Marco Pierre White. I was literally fresh off the boat from Dublin. Robert Reid was running the kitchen and to this day he has been one of the biggest influences on the way I cook.

Rob was going off-road on the menu, knocking up something special. It was game season and as he stormed through each section of the kitchen, commanding caramelised ceps here, roast foie gras there, I looked up to see him stuffing the cavity of a grouse with juniper, bay and a bunch of thyme; after rolling the bird in nutty foaming butter, he popped it into the oven. We had 4 minutes to respond to all his requests perfectly or... We were, of course, ready and waiting. It was 2 minutes for the bird to rest before he smashed the heart and liver into the warm pan, added a dash of sherry vinegar and proceeded to carve.

As we dressed the plate, he rolled a bunch of watercress through the warm pan with the bird's offal, before delicately placing the breasts and legs on the plate and scattering the watercress. That's when he did it... It's a moment that will live with me, something that made me forget about the long hours, terrible money and unforgiving girlfriend. None of that mattered! He took the bloody carcass in his hands, and with brute force he squeezed. The blood and innards trickled between his fingers and on to the plate.

I took all the chefs out one night for dinner about two years ago and Rob Reid's technique came up. After many a bottle of wine, we all decided we would do it table-side at The Dairy. We would carry the bird through the dining room over to the table on a roasting-hot pan, hay and heather smoking away. We'd plonk the plated dish in front of the guests and politely request they pull up their white, starched napkins as we performed our pigeon press by hand. It is a shocking showstopper of a dish – not for the faint-hearted, but one for the adventurous foodie.

### GRILLED RHUBARB

10g Maldon sea salt

50g caster sugar

2 stalks forced rhubarb, cut into strips

Mix together the salt, sugar and rhubarb in a mixing bowl. Leave to marinate for 1 hour, then drain off the excess liquid. Char the rhubarb on a very hot ridged grill pan for 2 minutes, to scorch on all sides, until it is just tender. Remove and keep warm.

### BRAISED CHICORY

2 heads red chicory

50g soft unsalted butter

5g Maldon sea salt

20g caster sugar

500ml water

juice of 1 lemon

Cut the chicory in half lengthways. Put all the remaining ingredients into a pan and bring to the boil. Whisk together, then place the chicory in the liquid. Simmer on a low heat for 10–15 minutes or until the chicory is tender on the stem. Allow to cool in the liquid. Warm through for serving.

...continued on page 204

## ROAST WOOD PIGEON AND SAUCE

a bunch of thyme

10 juniper berries, crushed

4 wood pigeons, plucked and trussed (ask your butcher to clean the carcass but to give you the livers and hearts separately for your sauce)

a drizzle of vegetable oil

a knob of butter

50ml Brown Chicken Stock (see page 61)

200g muscat grapes or black seedless grapes (removed from the stem)

1 teaspoon sweet sherry vinegar

Preheat the oven to 150°C fan/170°C/Gas Mark 3–4. Stuff the thyme and juniper into the cavities of the birds. Set a large pan over a high heat, add a little vegetable oil and colour the birds all over. Transfer them to a roasting tray and roast for 12–15 minutes. Allow the birds to rest for 5 minutes.

Meanwhile, finely chop the hearts and livers. Add the butter to the pan you used to brown the birds, followed by the chopped hearts and livers, the stock and grapes. Cook for 2 minutes. Add the vinegar to taste and keep warm.

Remove the breasts and legs from the wood pigeon carcasses and keep warm in the roasting tray.

## ASSEMBLY

Arrange the drained chicory and rhubarb on each plate, followed by the pigeon breasts and legs, and the heart and liver sauce. Take the bloody carcasses to the table and hand-squeeze over the entire dish. It's bound to cause a stir!

# RABBIT FEAST

Serves 4–6

Simon Woodrow, who worked with us for three and a half years, across all sites, deserves all the credit for the raves that this dish so deservedly gets. I love it as it represents so many great things: it is nose-to-tail at its best and gets loved ones around the table without costing a fortune. The dish was inspired by one of our late-night Bloodshot supper clubs. There was a crazy recipe created by Dean and Ben called 'reservoir hogs' – all you need to know is that it was a gory, Tarantino-esque dish where whole hogs' heads were served with pig's blood syringes and surgical gloves as cutlery. Anyway, in a strange way that was the inspiration for Simon and me to come up with a less intimidating but equally impressive beast feast.

It's not surprising that rabbit was Simon's choice of meat. He had come across 400 of them a month during his time with Anthony Demetre at Arbutus, where rabbit has been celebrated on the menu since day one. This is not a 20-minute, midweek one-pan wonder; it requires time to prepare. The first thing you must do is speak to your favourite local butcher and order the rabbit; it may take a week. Then you need to ask the butcher to bone it for you. I'm suggesting that you do all the component parts for one cracking spring lunch, but they could easily be broken down into many variations as they are versatile. For example, the rabbit could easily be replaced with chicken, guinea fowl or hare. Any pickle would be a welcome addition to this dish although the Artichoke Piccalilli (see page 47) works particularly well.

...continued on page 206

## RABBIT SADDLE

1 saddle of rabbit, with the liver
(if unavailable, substitute 150g
chicken livers)
a drizzle of vegetable oil
12 slices of Pancetta (see page 37 or
shop-bought)
10g Preserved Amalfi Lemons
(see page 30), finely chopped
4 sprigs of tarragon
300g caul fat, soaked in cold water
and cleaned well
Maldon sea salt and freshly ground black
pepper

Bone the saddle of rabbit (or have the butcher do this for you); reserve
the bones for the gravy.

Heat a frying pan on a high heat until smoking hot. Drizzle a little
vegetable oil over the rabbit liver (or chicken livers), add to the smoking
pan and sear all over. Remove and allow to cool.

Lay out three layers of clingfilm on a flat surface. Cover with the
pancetta slices, placed side by side. Place the rabbit, skinned side
down, on the pancetta layer and open the breasts out, exposing a gap
in the centre between the fillets. Add the livers, preserved lemon and
tarragon to the gap and season with salt and pepper. With the help of
the clingfilm, roll the pancetta around the rabbit to create a sausage-like
shape, then remove the clingfilm.

Spread out the caul fat on the work surface and cut so the caul is
a rectangular shape just big enough to wrap around the rabbit. Place
the rabbit at one long side of the caul fat and roll it up around the rabbit,
folding in the sides. Secure the caul fat by tying butcher's twine around
the roll. Keep in the fridge until required.

## RABBIT GRAVY

50g plain flour
2 tablespoons vegetable oil
8 chicken wings, chopped
rabbit bones from the saddle, chopped
80g unsalted butter
4 garlic cloves, crushed
2 shallots, sliced
100ml white wine
800ml water
a sprig of lemon thyme
zest of 1 lemon

Preheat the oven to 200°C fan/220°C/Gas Mark 7. Toast the flour on
a baking tray in the oven for 15 minutes.

Set a wide-bottomed pan over a high heat and add the vegetable oil,
chicken wings and rabbit bones. Once they start to caramelise, add
the butter and continue cooking until the bones take on a golden-brown
colour. Add the garlic and shallots and cook until they are translucent.
Using a slotted spoon, remove the contents from the pot to a bowl;
drain off the fat from the pan but reserve it. Deglaze the pan with the
white wine, stirring well, and reduce by half. Pour into a bowl and
reserve. Clean the bottom of the pan, then add half of the reserved fat
and the toasted flour and stir until the flour absorbs the fat. Add the
bones mixture and water and bring to the boil. Skim and simmer for
45 minutes.

Remove from the heat and add the thyme, lemon zest and reduced white
wine. Allow to infuse for 15 minutes. Strain into a clean pan and reduce
to a gravy consistency.

## RABBIT TURNOVERS

600g duck fat
4 rabbit shoulders
2 bay leaves
3 garlic cloves, crushed
1 carrot, peeled and diced
3 celery sticks, diced
1 white-skin onion, diced
100ml Rabbit Gravy (see page 206)
1 tablespoon Dijon mustard
1 sheet of puff pastry (see page 253
    for homemade)
1 egg, beaten
Maldon sea salt and freshly ground
    black pepper

Preheat the oven to 140°C fan/160°C/Gas Mark 3. Put 500g of the duck fat into a cassoulet pot or other flameproof casserole. Season the rabbit shoulders generously with salt and pepper, then add to the pot with the bay leaves and garlic. Bring to a simmer. Transfer to the oven to cook for 1½ hours or until the meat is falling away from the bone.

Meanwhile, put each type of diced vegetable into a small pan with some of the remaining duck fat and cook until tender. Allow to cool.

Remove the rabbit shoulders from the pot (the fat could be reused). While the rabbit is still warm, pick the meat off the bones.

Reduce the gravy by a third – it should be quite thick. Add the meat, vegetables and mustard to the gravy. Allow the mixture to cool.

Turn the oven back on to 180°C fan/200°C/Gas Mark 6. Cut the pastry into four to six triangles, depending on how many people you want to serve. Place a spoonful of the rabbit mixture into one corner of each triangle. Roll the pastry over the mixture and crimp the edges. Place on a baking tray and brush with beaten egg. Bake for about 15 minutes or until golden and crisp.

## VEGETABLES

50g unsalted butter
200ml water
a generous pinch of Maldon sea salt
a bunch of breakfast radishes
2 Baby Gem lettuces, quartered
    lengthways
1 head of red chicory, quartered lengthways
40g capers
a small bunch of flat-leaf parsley, chopped

Make an emulsion with the butter, water and salt in a pan by bringing to the boil, whisking. Add the radishes, lettuces and chicory and cook until the lettuce starts to wilt. Drain, then add the capers and parsley and toss together.

## ASSEMBLY

Artichoke Piccalilli (see page 47)

Preheat the oven to 210°C fan/230°C/Gas Mark 8. Take a suitable-sized ovenproof pan, set it over a medium-high heat and sear the rabbit saddle until golden brown all over. Transfer to the oven to roast for 5 minutes. Turn the saddle over and roast for another 5 minutes. Allow to rest for 12 minutes before removing the twine and carving. Heat the remaining gravy and decant into a jug.

Serve the saddle, turnovers, vegetables and gravy family-style, with the piccalilli, for guests to help themselves.

# BELTED GALLOWAY ONGLET

## PIATONE BEANS, YOUNG GARLIC, HAY

It's all about the smoke here. The hay butter is a revelation – a Canadian chap named Joe showed us this trick. Its sweet, smoky flavour is amazing. Make a big batch and try frying an egg in the hay butter with some wild mushrooms. Delicious! I like to use onglet as it has a great depth of flavour and is cheap as chips. You must serve it rare with a nice pinch of Maldon sea salt.

serves 4–6

### HAY EMULSION

250ml Brown Chicken Stock (see page 61)
125g hay
250g unsalted butter

Boil the stock to reduce to 125ml. In another pan, combine the hay and butter. Set over a high heat and cook until the butter starts to foam, turns a nut-brown colour and has a nutty aroma. Pass the butter through a fine sieve and whisk it into the stock to create an emulsion. Set aside in the pan.

### BEANS

250g piatone or white runner beans
1 teaspoon Maldon sea salt
250g fine green beans

Toss the piatone beans with the salt and allow to soften in the fridge for 3 hours. Char the beans on a barbecue or hot ridged grill pan.

Blanch the fine green beans in boiling salted water for 2–3 minutes or until tender. Drain and refresh in cold water, then split each bean down the middle.

### NEW SEASON'S WHITE GARLIC PURÉE

2 bulbs of new season's garlic, cloves
  separated and peeled
1 bay leaf
whole milk
2 egg yolks
50ml olive oil
crème fraîche
fresh lemon juice

Blanch the garlic cloves in boiling salted water for 1 minute. Drain and refresh in cold water, then repeat the blanching. Put the blanched cloves back in the empty pan with the bay leaf and a pinch each of salt and black pepper, and cover with milk. Gently simmer until the garlic has softened. Drain but reserve the milk.

Put the garlic cloves and egg yolks into a food processor. Blend together and, while blending, drizzle in the olive oil until emulsified. If the mixture thickens too much, let it down with a little of the reserved milk. Stir in the crème fraîche and salt, pepper and lemon juice to taste.

### ONGLET

400–500g onglet steak
a drizzle of vegetable oil (if pan-cooking)
a knob of unsalted butter (if pan-cooking)

Ensure that the meat has come up to room temperature. Season well on both sides with salt and pepper. Barbecue the steak until medium-rare. Alternatively, heat the vegetable oil in a pan over a high heat, add the steak with the butter and cook for 2 minutes on each side while basting with the foaming butter.

Allow the steak to rest for 5 minutes before serving; reserve any pan/resting juices.

...continued on page 212

## ASSEMBLY

1 shallot
fresh lemon juice
tarragon leaves
chervil leaves
wild rocket leaves
Maldon sea salt and freshly ground
    black pepper

Slice the shallot into thin rings, then crisp up in a bowl of iced water. Add the piatone beans, the fine green beans and the drained shallot rings to the hay emulsion in a pan and warm through. Season with lemon juice and black pepper to taste.

Slice the steak. Spread some of the garlic purée on each plate. Scatter around the beans, shallots and the slices of steak. Drizzle over some of the pan/resting juices from the steak. Finish with a scattering of herbs.

# SUCKLING PIG BELLY

## BAO, KIMCHI

Aahhhh, pig belly... crispy, succulent pig belly. I sound like a dribbling Homer Simpson! But that's what this dish turns me into. A soft, white, steamed rice bun and hot-as-hell kimchi... I'm literally dribbling as I type. Our Sichuan mayonnaise is a welcome addition. Try our Ginger Beer (see page 82) recipe with this and you will be a very happy camper indeed.

**serves 6**

### SUCKLING PIG BELLY

15g curry powder
14 black peppercorns
5g ground cumin
5g ground five spice
5g ground coriander
50ml vegetable oil
3 garlic cloves, crushed
2 red chillies, roughly chopped
a good pinch of Maldon sea salt
1.5kg boned suckling pig belly (skin on)
500ml water

Preheat the oven to 150°C fan/170°C/Gas Mark 3–4. Put all the spices and the vegetable oil in a pan and toast the spices over a medium heat for 2–3 minutes. Remove from the heat and tip the spice mix into a food processor (or a mortar). Add the garlic, chillies and salt, and blend (or crush) into a paste.

Rub the paste into the meat. Place the belly in a deep roasting tray with the water, cover with foil and cook in the oven for 1½ hours. Allow the meat to cool in the liquid.

Once cool, drain off the liquid, then weigh down the pork by covering with another tray and setting something heavy on this (e.g. cans of food). Leave in the fridge to press for 6–8 hours.

### BAO

1 tablespoon fresh yeast
350ml tepid water
600g rice flour
75g caster sugar
3 tablespoons milk powder
1 tablespoon fine table salt
½ teaspoon bicarbonate of soda
½ teaspoon baking powder
2½ tablespoons duck fat

Put all the ingredients into the bowl of a stand mixer fitted with the paddle attachment. Mix on the slowest speed for about 20 minutes or until you have an elastic dough. Cover the dough with a tea towel and leave to rise at room temperature for an hour. The dough will puff up. Knock back the dough, then divide into 12 balls. Leave to rise again for 30 minutes at room temperature.

On a surface dusted lightly with rice flour, flatten each ball into an oval, then fold over to create the bao shape (an elongated half-moon). Leave to prove at room temperature until the bao puff up to at least double in size.

Steam the buns in a bamboo or regular steamer lined with greaseproof paper over a high heat for 11 minutes. (The bao should be eaten straight away but can be warmed gently in the oven if made ahead.)

### ASSEMBLY

Tokyo turnips or any radishes
a drizzle of vegetable oil
300g Kimchi (see page 28)
coriander
Sichuan Mayonnaise (see page 67)
lime wedges

Thinly slice the turnips, then soak in iced water for an hour; drain.

Preheat the oven to 220°C fan/240°C/Gas Mark 9. Remove the pork from the fridge and score the skin. Heat the vegetable oil in a large ovenproof pan on a high heat. Add the pork, skin-side down, and lower the heat to medium. Cook for 10 minutes or until the skin is golden and crisp. Put the pan in the oven and cook for 5 minutes to heat the pork through.

Meanwhile, place the kimchi in a bowl and garnish with coriander. Slice the pork. Serve all the elements – pork, bao, kimchi, mayonnaise, turnips and lime wedges – separately for guests to build their own buns.

# MARY
# HOLBROOK

In restaurant kitchens in London, and I imagine
in most places, there are so many reps and
middlemen trying to sell you something. The meat
industry has had some pretty horrific press over
the years, and as a chef I find it quite hard to trust
or believe some jerk in a suit trying to sell me some
meat from a price list offering beef/lamb/chicken/
hippo from who knows where. They always come in
unannounced (for any reps reading this, it is a pet
hate for me) and their photos always show a kind-
eyed, weather-beaten farmer hugging a cow that
looks as though it just stepped out of a salon! Then
you come across someone like Mary Holbrook.

Mary is famous for making cheese. At one
time, we were hosting monthly events at Paradise
Garage to highlight our favourite suppliers. Neal's
Yard Dairy is one of these, a well-known company
that does a rare thing for these times, which is to
celebrate and support the smaller, more passionate
folk who dedicate their lives to producing something
special. Simon, who was designing the menu, had
a tough task in planning a meal based on a cheese
supplier. But he picked a favourite cheese, which was
Tymsboro, produced in Bath on Sleight Farm, and he
thought that goat would be the obvious choice
of meat. But then he found something else.

Mary was producing a massive excess of whey
from her cheese production but didn't know what to
do with it. So she bought a couple of Lop pigs and fed
them the whey. This natural cycle has been a huge
success – her cheese production has grown a bit as
the pig population has also grown. The pigs roam
free and happy over ten acres of rich ground.

We shared a pig with Simon for his event and
now we take a whole pig every second week. We use
every scrap, paying the utmost respect to the pig in
our charcuterie programme. Mary delivers them
herself, and no rep or middleman is involved in our
relationship. It's built on trust, passion and friendship.
She turns business and expansion away – she is hard
working but content and we are very lucky to work
with her.

# SMOKED BONE MARROW AGNOLOTTI

## WILD MUSHROOMS

This has become kind of a cult classic on our menu. It's an idea brought to life by Richie. The clever so-and-so wanted to create a burst of liquid with the bone marrow filling inside the agnolotti. People go nuts for the dish, often asking for a second serving, which can make a chef cry as it's not the easiest of dishes to do. The hard work is worth it, though. Just be prepared for your guests to want more.

serves 4–6

### PASTA

2 tablespoons olive oil
4 eggs
2 egg yolks
480g type '00' flour
fine semolina, for dusting

The pasta dough can be made in a stand mixer fitted with a paddle attachment, or by hand in a bowl or on the work surface. Start by mixing together the olive oil, eggs, yolks and half of the flour until well worked. Add the remaining flour a handful at a time, mixing in well before adding the next handful. This should be a slow process – a little at a time really is best. Once the last of the flour has been incorporated, knead briefly in the mixer. If making by hand, knead the dough on the floured surface for at least 10 minutes or until firm, smooth and even in consistency. Wrap the dough in clingfilm and set aside to rest at room temperature for about 30 minutes.

Divide the dough into eight pieces. Flatten the pieces and lightly dust with flour. Work with one piece at a time. Feed through a pasta machine set on the widest setting, then fold the dough over and pass through this setting again. Repeat this process three times so that you have a rectangular shape and an even thickness. Continue to pass the dough through the pasta machine, changing the setting until you reach the second thinnest setting. Repeat with the remaining pieces of dough.

Lay out the sheets of pasta dough on the semolina-dusted work surface.

### SMOKED BONE MARROW FILLING

50ml Worcestershire sauce
200ml Brown Chicken Stock (see page 61)
65g egg yolks
135g Smoked Bone Marrow (see page 37), melted but not hot
Cabernet Sauvignon vinegar
black truffle oil
Mushroom Powder (see page 60)
Maldon sea salt

Boil the Worcestershire sauce in a small pan until reduced by half to 25ml. In another pan, boil the stock until reduced to 100ml. Allow both to cool.

Pour the reduced stock into a blender or food processor and add the egg yolks. Blend, then transfer to a clean non-stick pan. Cook over a gentle heat, stirring constantly, until the mixture reaches 79°C. Once it has reached this temperature, pour it back into the blender. While blending, gradually add the bone marrow so that the mixture emulsifies. Season to taste with a few drops of vinegar, Worcestershire sauce and truffle oil, plus mushroom powder and salt. Allow the mixture to cool, then spoon into a disposable piping bag and keep in the fridge until needed.

...continued on page 222

### AGNOLOTTI

Pasta dough (see page 220)
Smoked Bone Marrow Filling
 (see page 220)
fine semolina, for dusting

Pipe a line of the filling along the length of one sheet of pasta, near one long edge and leaving enough pasta uncovered to fold over. Fold the pasta over the filling and press firmly to seal. Using a pastry wheel, cut the filled tube of pasta away from the rest of the sheet but leave a border of the sealed section attached.

Pinch the filled tube of pasta into uniform sections, creating a seal between the pockets of filling. Use the pastry wheel to separate the sections. Repeat with the remaining pasta and filling. Keep the agnolotti in the fridge, on a tray sprinkled with semolina, until required.

### GIROLLES AND PEAS

a knob of unsalted butter
300g girolles, cleaned, trimmed
200g podded fresh peas
100ml Brown Chicken Stock (see page 61)

Melt the butter in a large pan and add the girolles, halved if large, followed by the peas. Whisk in the chicken stock and cook, stirring, for 2 minutes.

### ASSEMBLY

200g podded broad beans
a bunch of wild garlic leaves, chopped
fresh lemon juice
Mushroom Powder (see page 60)
shaved fresh black truffle
Maldon sea salt

Blanch the beans in boiling water for 1 minute. Drain and refresh in iced water, then pop the bright green beans out of their thick skins by squeezing gently.

Bring a large pan of water to the boil. Add salt (3% of the volume of water in the pan) followed by the pasta and simmer for 1–2 minutes or until the pasta rises to the surface. Use a slotted spoon to remove the pasta from the water and add to the pan with the girolles and peas. Add the wild garlic leaves and broad beans and season with lemon juice. Warm through. Transfer to plates and garnish with mushroom powder and fresh black truffle.

# CHICKEN SKIN

## LEEK AND CAVOLO NERO STALK

This was our dish for Dan Barber's WastED takeover on Selfridges rooftop. Each dish had to use ingredients that normally would go to waste. In our case it was leek trimmings, chicken skin and cheese trim. Even the stock from the leeks didn't go to waste and was added back into the cheese trim sauce to give an almost cheese and onion flavour. As it was made for a crowd, this recipe is slightly on the large size but it could certainly be scaled down as required.

serves 7–10

### CHICKEN SKIN TERRINE

1.5kg chicken skin
Maldon sea salt
cracked black pepper

Preheat the oven to 130°C fan/150°C/Gas Mark 2. Line a large terrine mould with oven-safe clingfilm. Layer the chicken skin in the mould, sprinkling each layer lightly with salt and every third layer with cracked black pepper. Cover the top of the layered chicken skin with a piece of folded foil, then cover the top of the terrine with oven-safe clingfilm. Set the terrine mould in a bain marie (or roasting tin/tray of water) and bake for 8–10 hours or overnight.

Remove the mould from the bain marie and place it in an empty roasting tray. Peel off the clingfilm from the top and press down on the terrine (foil still on top) – any stock that overflows will be caught in the tray (reserve this stock). Place a weight on the top of the terrine and allow it to cool, then chill.

### CAVOLO NERO AND LEEK TOPS BALLOTINE

stock reserved from the terrine (see above)
Brown Chicken Stock (see page 61)
leek top trimmings from 10 leeks
10 Fermented Cavolo Nero Stalks
  (see page 24), drained
6 sheets of dried nori (3g each)

Measure the stock from the terrine and top it up with brown chicken stock so that you have 750ml in total. Bring the stock to the boil in a pan. Braise the leek trimmings and cavolo nero stalks in the stock until the leeks are soft. Remove the vegetables from the pan with a slotted spoon; reserve the stock.

Lay out a sheet of nori on a piece of clingfilm. Spoon some of the vegetables down the centre. With the help of the clingfilm, roll up the nori so that the vegetables are encased inside to create a ballotine. Repeat this process to make two more ballotines, then remove the clingfilm from each. Spread out a large piece of oven-safe clingfilm and lay the three ballotines on it side by side. Use the clingfilm to roll up the three ballotines together so you have one large ballotine. Tie off the ends. Repeat with the remaining nori and vegetables to make three more large ballotines. Leave to set in the fridge for 2–3 hours.

*...continued on page 224*

## CHEESE TRIM SAUCE

10g unsalted butter

300g edible cheese trim (we use the
  trimmings – white bloom/rind – of soft
  cheeses such as Baron Bigod)

300ml whole milk

5g Sosa Procrema Cold 100 (ice cream
  stabiliser)

200ml buttermilk

stock reserved from braising the leeks and
  cavolo nero stalks (see page 223)

Maldon sea salt

Chardonnay vinegar

Melt the butter in a non-stick pan over a low heat. Add the cheese trim and stir the mixture as it heats, scraping the bottom of the pan because the cheese will catch. Continue to cook, stirring, until the cheese caramelises and takes on a golden-brown colour. Add the milk and slowly bring to the boil, still stirring. Remove from the heat and blend with the Procrema and buttermilk using a stick blender. Blend in some of the stock both for flavour and to loosen the consistency. Season with salt and Chardonnay vinegar to taste. Set aside in the pan.

## ASSEMBLY

a drizzle of vegetable oil

chives (with flowers, if available)

Preheat the oven to 180°C fan/200°C/Gas Mark 6. Remove the mould from the fridge and turn out the terrine. Cut into 1.5cm slices (you want 7–10 slices). Heat a drizzle of oil in a large ovenproof pan over a medium to high heat. Add the slices of terrine and brown slightly on both sides. Transfer the pan to the oven and bake for 8 minutes. Turn the terrine slices over and bake for a further 6 minutes. The slices should be crispy and golden on the outside and soft in the centre.

Slice the ballotines into 1.5cm pieces, leaving the clingfilm on. Place them on a roasting tray and warm through in the oven for 4–5 minutes. Remove the clingfilm.

Gently warm through the sauce, stirring constantly so that it does not catch. Spread some of the sauce on one side of each plate and top with the terrine. Add a piece of ballotine to the other side of the plate. Wilt the chives and chive flowers in a dry pan over a medium heat and use them to garnish each plate.

# LAMB'S TONGUE HOTPOT

This dish came about when I was cooking in the City of London. I was running a beautiful little restaurant in The Royal Exchange called Sauterelle, overlooking Bulgari, Tiffany's, Boodle's and Cartier. It was my first real head chef position. Before this I had been working in two and three Michelin star kitchens, exposed to the best and most expensive ingredients. Then three months after I took my position as head chef came the big financial crisis in 2008. Suddenly I was faced with the massive challenge of cooking great food but with more humble ingredients to keep our prices down. This is where I really started to explore nose-to-tail cooking. I found lamb's tongue to be one of the tastiest and leanest parts of the animal – also bloody cheap. I thought that nobody would order it so I hid it in a hotpot with layers of onion and potato and a great stock, and baked it to perfection. Everyone who ordered it loved it. They just didn't realise they were eating tongue. Well, they never asked!

*serves 4–6*

## HOTPOT

500g lamb's tongues

2 litres 7% brine (see page 20)

500ml white wine

1.5 litres Lamb Stock (see page 61)

1 bulb of garlic, cut in half horizontally

10 black peppercorns

3 fresh bay leaves

1.5kg small baking/frying-type potatoes
such as King Edwards

2 large white-skin onions, thinly sliced

a bunch of lemon thyme, leaves picked

soft unsalted butter, to glaze

Maldon sea salt and freshly cracked
black pepper

Place the lamb's tongues in the brine in a bowl and leave in the fridge for 8 hours. Boil the wine until reduced by half, then set aside.

Preheat the oven to 130°C fan/150°C/Gas Mark 2. Drain the tongues and place in a cassoulet pot or other heavy casserole with the reduced wine, stock, garlic, peppercorns and bay leaves. Lay a sheet of greaseproof paper over the top followed by a lid. Place in the oven to cook for 3–4 hours or until the tongues are tender but still retain their shape and are still very slightly firm. Allow the tongues to cool in the liquid.

Once cool enough to handle, drain the tongues in a fine sieve set in a bowl so you can retain the stock (discard the garlic, peppercorns and bay leaves). While the tongues are still warm, peel away the membrane that covers the outside using a paring knife – it is like peeling an egg. Once the membrane is removed, slice the tongues lengthways as thinly as possible. Set aside.

Peel the potatoes, then slice very thinly on a mandoline – slices about 1.5mm thick.

Clean the cassoulet pot, then build the hotpot in it. Start with potato, placing slices neatly and evenly over the bottom, overlapping them like a fan from the outside in and filling any gaps. Scatter over an even layer of sliced onion and season with a pinch of salt, some cracked black pepper and a pinch of lemon thyme leaves. Add an even layer of tongue slices and press flat, then add a ladleful of the strained stock. Repeat the layers all the way to the top, using up all the ingredients and saving the best-looking sliced potatoes for the top layer.

*...continued on page 228*

Brush a little softened butter over the top potato layer, then cover with a sheet of greaseproof paper and a lid. Bake for 1 hour and 20 minutes – check if the hotpot is ready by piercing through to the bottom with a cake tester or long thin knife: it should meet no resistance.

Remove the lid and paper. Increase the oven temperature to 220°C fan/240°C/Gas Mark 9 and bake the hotpot for about 5 minutes or until the potato layer on top is beautifully golden brown and the edges have started to crisp up.

### LAMB GLAZE

35ml Lamb Sauce (see page 62)
35g unsalted butter, at room temperature
35ml Onion Treacle (see page 48)

Towards the end of the hotpot cooking time, whisk all the ingredients for the glaze together until combined.

### ASSEMBLY

Maldon sea salt
lemon thyme leaves and flowers (if they
    are in season)

Brush the top layer of the hotpot with the lamb glaze and season with a pinch of salt and a pinch of lemon thyme leaves (and flowers if using). Serve with a loaf of crusty bread and a pot of mint sauce.

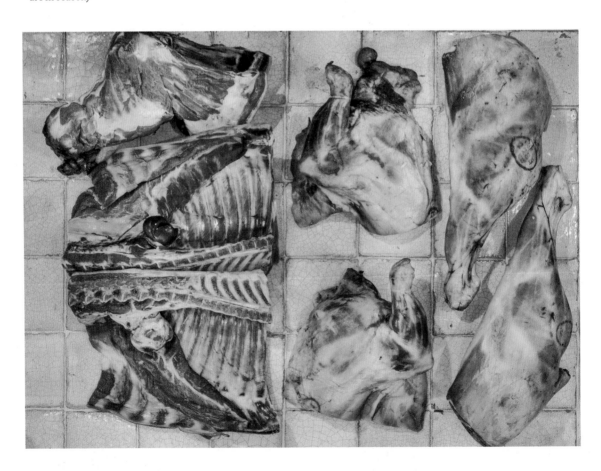

# GAME FAGGOTS

## CELERIAC, TOASTED HAZELNUTS

This is a really comforting dish that is also versatile. The quantities here are a guideline only, and the game could easily be replaced with lamb, beef or pork. The celeriac purée adds a richness and the pickle helps to cut through that richness. I add fresh shavings of truffle at our restaurant, which bring a bit of luxury to what really is a peasant dish made from leftovers.

**serves 8**

### FAGGOTS

3 juniper berries
50g skinless boneless chicken
   breast, diced
75ml double cream
75g duck liver, minced or finely chopped
75g duck hearts, finely chopped or minced
100g minced venison (could even be
   minced haunch)
3 black peppercorns, freshly cracked
a pinch of ground mace
a pinch of freshly grated nutmeg
a sprig of thyme, leaves picked
5g Mushroom Powder (see page 60)
1 teaspoon Cognac
150g caul fat, soaked and cleaned well
Maldon sea salt

Toast the juniper berries in a small dry pan until they smell fragrant, then crush them coarsely with a mortar and pestle. Blend the chicken in a food processor with a pinch of salt until smooth. Add the cream and blend it in. Scrape down the sides of the processor bowl and blend again until the cream is evenly incorporated. Transfer the mixture to a mixing bowl set over ice to keep it cold.

Stir in all the remaining ingredients (with the crushed juniper), except the caul fat, and season with 1 teaspoon salt. Mix well. Chill for 30 minutes, then fry off a little spoon of the mixture to taste for seasoning and adjust accordingly.

Divide the mixture into eight portions and roll each into a sausage shape. Wrap the sausages individually in two layers of caul fat. They can be kept in the fridge in an airtight container for 1 or 2 days or can be frozen for up to 2 months.

### CELERIAC PURÉE

25g unsalted butter
¼ celeriac, diced into small pieces
fresh lemon juice
100ml whole milk
25g crème fraîche
fine table salt and freshly ground
   black pepper

Add the butter to a hot pan. When the butter starts to foam and turns brown, with a nutty aroma, add the celeriac and a pinch of salt. Cook for 10 minutes, stirring regularly. Add a squeeze of lemon juice and the milk. Turn the heat down to a simmer and cook for 5 minutes or until the celeriac is softened (check the largest piece).

Transfer to a blender and add the crème fraîche. Blend to a smooth purée. Taste and adjust the seasoning, then keep warm.

...continued on page 230

## ASSEMBLY

a knob of unsalted butter
a drizzle of vegetable oil
24 slices Celeriac Pickle (see page 43)
100g toasted hazelnuts, crushed lightly
black truffle (optional)

Preheat the oven to 190°C fan/210°C/Gas Mark 6–7. Heat the butter and oil in a suitable-sized ovenproof frying pan over a medium heat. Add the faggots and sear all over to get a little colour. Transfer the pan to the oven and cook for 6–7 minutes. Remove from the oven and leave to rest in the hot pan while you gently warm the pickled celeriac in another pan with a little of its pickling liquid.

Place a spoonful of celeriac purée on each plate, followed by the faggots together with a spoonful of the oil and juices from the pan. Finish with the celeriac pickle and hazelnuts. Shave over the black truffle, if using.

# GAME TERRINE

On our last day of shooting photographs for this book, I knew there would be a late addition, namely this terrine. It came about after a Halloween Blood and Guts-themed supper club was hosted at The Dairy. Richie and Patrick Powell, a dear friend of ours, concocted an off-the-wall menu. It began with a welcome drink, a Negroni with duck heart and sour cherry, served in a goblet made from grouse carcasses. This was no mean feat – we had to order in an extra 30 birds just for the carcasses! So we were left with all the breasts. We needed to turn them into something special as grouse is a pretty special (and bloody expensive) game bird. This idea came out of the bag and I just had to add it to the book in the last minute. Note: You don't need all the foie gras for the terrine, but I would prepare the whole lobe and keep what you don't use to have on toast.

Makes 1 terrine
– 10 generous slices

## FOIE GRAS

1kg foie gras (de-veined)
2 teaspoons fine table salt
½ teaspoon pink curing salt
1 teaspoon caster sugar
a pinch of freshly ground black pepper
a drizzle of Armagnac

Season the foie gras with the salts, sugar, pepper and Armagnac. Cover and leave in the fridge overnight.

## MUSHROOM DUXELLES

100g chestnut mushrooms
100g trompette mushrooms
½ teaspoon Spiced Salt (see page 60)
20g unsalted butter
10g black truffle
a drizzle of truffle oil

Put the mushrooms and spiced salt in a blender or food processor and blend to a coarse paste. Melt the butter in a pan, add the mushroom mixture and gently sweat over a low heat until any liquid has evaporated. Remove from the heat and grate in the truffle. Mix in the truffle oil. Allow to cool completely.

## CHICKEN MOUSSE

200g skinless, boneless chicken
  breast, diced
½ teaspoon Spiced Salt (see page 60)
250ml cold double cream

Season the chicken with the spiced salt, then chill in the fridge or freezer for a few minutes so it is really cold. Blend the chicken in a blender or food processor until it forms a tight ball. Push down so it is flat and blend again while drizzling in the cream. Scrape down the sides of the container occasionally so that the chicken mousse is evenly blended. Decant into a bowl set over ice.

## GROUSE

9 skinless, boneless grouse breasts
Spiced Salt (see page 60)

Weigh the breasts (all together) and calculate 1.5% – this is the weight of spiced salt to use to season the breasts. Rub the salt all over the breasts, then set aside until needed.

...continued on page 234

## ASSEMBLY

8 large cabbage leaves (outer leaves)
20 slices lardo
seasonal leaves and pickles, to serve

Preheat the oven to 110°C fan/130°C/Gas Mark ½–1. Line a 1-litre terrine mould (35.5 x 11cm and 12cm deep) with oven-safe clingfilm.

Blanch the cabbage leaves in boiling water for 20 seconds. Drain and refresh in iced water, then remove the stalks and central rib/stem.

Shape 200g of the foie gras into a rectangle roughly the size of the terrine mould and 1cm thick. Fold the mushroom duxelles into the chicken mousse.

Line the terrine mould with slices of lardo so there is a slight overhang, then do the same with the cabbage leaves. Make a layer of three of the grouse breasts, slightly overlapping, on the bottom of the mould so there are no gaps. Add a layer of chicken and mushroom mousse (about a quarter of it) about 1cm thick. Place the foie gras rectangle on this and top with another layer of chicken and mushroom mousse. Add three more grouse breasts, then a layer of mousse followed by the remaining grouse breasts and the remaining mousse. Fold the overhang of cabbage leaves over the top, followed by the overhang of lardo. Cover the top of the mould with oven-safe clingfilm.

Set the terrine mould in a bain marie and place in the oven to cook for 45 minutes to 1 hour or until the core temperature reaches 55°C (use a temperature probe to check). Remove from the oven and weigh down the top of the terrine with a mould of a similar size.  Once cooled, leave in the fridge overnight to set.

To serve, remove the terrine from the mould, cut into slices and peel off the clingfilm. Serve with a seasonal leaf and your pickle of choice.

# CHART FARM VENISON

## BROGDALE PEAR, ARTICHOKE AND TRUFFLE

I always think of bitter chocolate and fruit when it comes to cooking venison. To my mind (or tastebuds), the Jerusalem artichokes here have the same malt-like flavour you get from chocolate. Pickled pears bring a welcome sharpness to the dish, which can help cut through the richness of the venison. An elegant dish that will go down a storm!

**serves 4**

### ARTICHOKES CONFIT

500g duck fat
3 sprigs of thyme
½ bulb of garlic (cut horizontally),
    cut in half vertically
500g Jerusalem artichokes, scrubbed
    clean with a brush

Preheat the oven to 90°C fan/110°C/Gas Mark ¼. Put the duck fat in an ovenproof pot and heat to 90°C. Add the thyme, garlic and artichokes. Cover the pot with a lid and place in the oven. Cook for up to 3 hours until the artichokes are softened (the cooking time can vary dramatically, so checking regularly is advised). Remove the artichokes from the pot and cut each in half or into smaller wedges, depending on how large they are.

*...continued on page 236*

## PEARS IN PEAR PICKLE

50g caster sugar
200ml cider vinegar
250ml fresh pear juice (pressed from
   about 6 pears)
2 sweet, ripe pears, cored and quartered

Warm the sugar in the cider vinegar until just dissolved. Add the fresh pear juice and pears. Remove from the heat and leave to pickle at room temperature for 2 hours.

## JERUSALEM ARTICHOKE CRISPS

300ml vegetable oil
1 Jerusalem artichoke, scrubbed clean
   with a brush
Mushroom Powder (see page 60)

Heat the vegetable oil in a deep pan or deep-fat fryer to 170°C. Using a mandoline, cut the artichoke into thin slices, cutting down the widest part. Deep-fry in batches (about 10 slices at a time) until golden brown. As each batch is fried, drain on kitchen paper and season while hot with mushroom powder. Keep in a warm, dry spot until required.

## VENISON AND MARINADE

1 venison loin, trimmed (about 300g)
a drizzle of vegetable oil
a knob of unsalted butter
2 garlic cloves, lightly crushed
2 sprigs of thyme

### MARINADE
300g beetroots, peeled and
   roughly chopped
200g rock salt
100g caster sugar
100ml vegetable oil
zest of 1 orange
15 black peppercorns
20 juniper berries

Turn the oven back on to 90°C fan/110°C/Gas Mark ¼. Put all the ingredients for the marinade into a food processor and blend to a paste. Cover the venison with the paste, then marinate for 8 minutes only. Rinse well and pat dry with kitchen paper.

Set a flameproof roasting tray over a medium to high heat, add the oil and brown the venison on all sides. Add the butter, garlic and thyme sprigs. Transfer the tray to the oven and roast the venison for about 12 minutes, turning over halfway through, or until the core temperature reaches 50°C. Remove from the oven and leave to rest.

## ASSEMBLY

a knob of unsalted butter
a sprig of lemon thyme, leaves picked
100ml Venison Sauce (see page 63)
5g black truffle, finely chopped
black truffle shavings, to garnish

While the venison is resting, strain some of the juice from the pickled pears into a pan, add the butter and whisk over a medium heat to emulsify. Add the artichokes confit, drained pears and lemon thyme leaves and warm through. Warm the venison sauce in a separate pan, stirring in the finely chopped truffle and any pan juices from the venison.

Carve the venison into four pieces. Arrange them on plates with the pears and artichokes. Finish with the venison sauce, artichoke crisps and shavings of black truffle.

# ONGLET TARTARE

## LEA & PERRINS, SMOKED BONE MARROW AND MUSHROOM

I use onglet here as I love the flavour but sirloin, fillet or bavette are all good substitutes. Just ask your butcher for the longest-aged piece of beef he has as it will be the most tender and tasty. The mushroom and bone marrow purée is so easy. Serving it with a roast scallop would be a winning combo too.

serves 4–6

### PARIS MUSHROOM PURÉE

125g Paris or chestnut mushrooms, roughly chopped
50ml water
½ teaspoon sherry vinegar
a sprig of tarragon
50g Smoked Bone Marrow (see page 37), melted but not hot
fresh lemon juice

Put the mushrooms, water, vinegar and tarragon into a food processor and blend together. While blending, drizzle in the bone marrow until smoothly emulsified. Season with lemon juice and salt to taste.

### ONGLET TARTARE

250g onglet steak
100ml Worcestershire sauce
100ml red wine vinegar
60ml olive oil
1 shallot, finely diced
3–4 sprigs of tarragon, leaves picked and chopped
½ bunch of chives, chopped
2–3 sprigs of flat-leaf parsley, leaves picked and chopped
Maldon sea salt

Sprinkle the meat with 1¼ teaspoons sea salt, then leave in the fridge for 1 hour.

Boil the Worcestershire sauce and vinegar (in separate pans) to reduce to 2 tablespoons each; cool. Mix together the reduced sauce and vinegar with the olive oil.

Pat the steak dry with kitchen paper, then chop into 1cm dice. Season with the oil mixture and with the remaining ingredients to taste.

### ASSEMBLY

1 shallot
200g chestnut mushrooms
wild rocket
land cress
tarragon leaves
finely grated fresh horseradish

Thinly slice the shallot into rings, then immerse in iced water to crisp up. Shave the raw mushrooms into thin pieces.

Spread some of the mushroom purée on each plate. Top with the tartare and garnish with the shallot rings, shaved mushrooms, wild rocket, land cress, tarragon and horseradish.

# SWEET

# CULTURED CREAM

## SORREL, COBNUTS

Sorrel is something most people would use with fish – the famous Trosgrois salmon
and sorrel combo has been replicated thousands of times by thousands of cooks. But
when we had a heap growing on our rooftop garden, we thought the sharpness would
be a perfect palate-cleanser to set you up for a final sweet dish. It's an ideal pre-dessert.

serves 4–6

### SORREL GRANITA

100g sorrel
100ml fresh apple juice
a pinch of citric acid

Blend together the sorrel, apple juice and citric acid in a blender
or food processor until as smooth as possible. Strain through a fine
sieve. Freeze until solid, then break up by scraping with a fork to create
a granita texture.

### ASSEMBLY

about 24 fresh cobnuts
60g Cultured Cream (see page 54)
honey for drizzling
fresh sorrel leaves

Crack open the cobnuts, peel them and cut each in half. Spread a small
amount of cultured cream on the bottom of each plate. Top with a
spoonful of the sorrel granita. Garnish with a couple of cobnuts, a drizzle
of honey and sorrel leaves.

# MILK, HONEY, BLUEBERRIES
## BREAD CRISPS

Milk and honey is one of those classic combos, like tomato and basil, almost meant
to be. We are lucky enough to have our own beehives above The Dairy so we can take
credit for all of the bees' hard work. The bread crisps are a clever and easy way
to transform leftover bread into something elegant.

serves 6–8

### YOGHURT PANNA COTTA

2 sheets/leaves of silver leaf gelatine
125ml whole milk
35g honey
250g plain yoghurt

Soak the gelatine in cold water to soften it. Warm the milk with
the honey in a pan to just short of boiling point. Drain the gelatine,
squeezing out excess water, add to the pan and stir until melted. Strain
the mixture through a fine sieve on to the yoghurt in a bowl and fold
together. Pour into a container and leave to set in the fridge.

### YOGHURT SORBET

100ml whole milk
60g liquid glucose
45g trimoline
20g glycerine
5g Maldon sea salt
1 tablespoon fresh lemon juice
500g plain yoghurt

Put all the ingredients, except the yoghurt, in a pan and heat, stirring,
until evenly combined. Allow the mixture to cool slightly, then blend
with the yoghurt in a blender or food processor. Churn in an ice cream
machine according to the manufacturer's instructions. Store in the
freezer until required.

### BREAD CRISPS

frozen, slightly stale sourdough bread
icing sugar, for dusting

Preheat the oven to 180°C fan/200°C/Gas Mark 6. Allow the bread
to thaw slightly, then cut into very thin slices using a serrated knife (you
want to have 20 slices). Lay them on a baking tray. Toast the slices in the
oven until golden on both sides. Remove from the oven and dust with
icing sugar while still hot, then leave to cool.

### ASSEMBLY

240g blueberries
a drizzle of olive oil
a pinch of Maldon sea salt
50g comb honey, chopped into small pieces

Season the blueberries with the olive oil and salt.

Put a spoonful of panna cotta in the bottom of each bowl and make
a well in it. Fill the well with some blueberries and comb honey. Top with
a scoop of sorbet and some bread crisps (broken into shards).

# SUSSEX ALEXANDER

## APPLE, SUNFLOWER SEEDS, CRÈME FRAÎCHE SORBET

A lovely young chap named Dan, who worked with us, would always take the train to Brighton to see his girl (or his 'babe' as he used to call her) on his days off. On his return he would bring gifts of all sorts of weird and wonderful foraged things in bags, such as alexanders, which have a stunning, light, liquorish type of flavour. It's thanks to him that this dish came about. He now runs the wonderful Silo in Brighton.

serves 6–8

### SUNFLOWER SEED PURÉE

125g sunflower seeds
100ml cold water
30g maple syrup
2½ teaspoons fresh lemon juice
a pinch of Maldon sea salt

Simmer the sunflower seeds in a pan of boiling water for 15 minutes or until slightly softened. Drain the seeds and tip into a blender or food processor. Add the remaining ingredients and blend to a smooth purée.

### MERINGUE

125g egg whites
250g caster sugar
30g alexanders flowers (picked
   from stems)

Whisk the egg whites in a stand mixer fitted with the balloon whisk attachment until they will hold stiff peaks. Meanwhile, put the sugar and a splash of water into a pan and set over a low-medium heat to melt the sugar. Bring the sugar syrup to a simmer. When it reaches 116°C, pour it in a thin, steady stream on to the egg whites while whisking. Continue to whisk until the meringue mixture is cold, stiff and shiny.

Spread the meringue thinly on trays lined with greaseproof paper. Sprinkle over the flowers. Dry out in a dehydrator, or overnight in the oven at its lowest setting, until completely dry. Allow the meringue to cool before breaking into large pieces.

### CRÈME FRAÎCHE SORBET

300ml whole milk
60g liquid glucose
40g trimoline
15g glycerine
5g Maldon sea salt
1 tablespoon fresh lemon juice
30g Sosa Procrema Cold 100
   (ice cream stabiliser)
1 teaspoon Stab 2000 (ice cream stabiliser)
300g crème fraîche

Put all the ingredients, except the crème fraîche, in a pan and gently heat until they all melt together. Remove from the heat and allow to cool, then fold in the crème fraîche. Churn in an ice cream machine according to the manufacturer's instructions. Store in the freezer until required.

...continued on page 248

### ALEXANDERS PICKLE

50g alexanders leaves
50ml apple juice
a pinch of citric acid
2 Granny Smith apples, peeled, cored
    and cut into 1cm dice

Blend the alexanders leaves, apple juice and citric acid together in a blender or food processor for about 1 minute or until smooth. Strain through a fine sieve. Pour over the diced apples in a bowl. Cover and leave in the fridge for about 1 hour.

### ASSEMBLY

a drizzle of olive oil

Spread some of the sunflower seed purée in the bottom of each bowl. Top with a scoop of sorbet. Make a well in the sorbet and fill it with some diced apple and pickling liquor from the alexanders pickle plus a drizzle of olive oil. Top each plate with one of the meringue pieces.

# CHOCOLATE, WILD FENNEL

## RECIPE BY DEAN PARKER, HEAD CHEF OF THE MANOR

This dish has become a staple of the restaurant, changed through the seasons. Anise flavours are sourced from our farm or with the help of Sarah's nearby allotment – in spring it is wild fennel; in summer, anise hyssop; and in winter, wild alexanders. Dean has created one of those dishes that you dare not remove from the menu as he guides it through the seasons like a pro!

serves 10

### CHOCOLATE MOUSSE

60g egg yolks
90g whole eggs
60g caster sugar
90g egg whites
10g Maldon sea salt
15g molasses
270g 70% dark chocolate buttons
    (or chopped dark chocolate)
375ml double cream

Whisk together the egg yolks, whole eggs and half of the sugar in a bain marie (or heatproof bowl set over a pan of simmering water) until light and fluffy. Remove from the heat, but keep the bowl over hot water.

Put the egg whites into a stand mixer fitted with the balloon whisk attachment and whisk to stiff peaks. Whisk in the salt. Meanwhile, melt the remaining sugar with a splash of water in a pan, then bring to a simmer. Continue to simmer until the syrup reaches 116°C; as soon as it reaches this temperature, pour it in a thin, steady stream on to the egg whites while whisking. Continue to whisk until the mixture is cold, stiff and shiny.

Bring the molasses and 90ml of water to the boil in another pan. Pour over the chocolate in a large bowl and leave to the side for the chocolate to melt. Whip the cream until it will form soft peaks.

Fold the egg yolk mixture into the melted chocolate mixture. Fold in the meringue. Lastly, fold in the cream. Leave to set in the fridge.

### WILD FENNEL ICE CREAM

10g liquorice root, ground to a powder
2 round seeds from a star anise
25g glycerine
150g caster sugar
500ml whole milk
4 sprigs of chervil, leaves picked
20g dill fronds
2 mint leaves
20g wild fennel fronds
80g Sosa Procrema Cold 100
    (ice cream stabiliser)
480ml buttermilk

In a dry pan, gently toast the liquorice powder and star anise seeds until fragrant. Add the glycerine, sugar and milk and heat, stirring, until the sugar has dissolved. Bring to the boil, then add the chervil, dill, mint and wild fennel. Simmer for 1 minute. Transfer this mixture to a blender or food processor and blend with the Procrema until very smooth. Pour into a bowl set over ice to cool.

Once cold, stir in the buttermilk. Churn in an ice cream machine according to the manufacturer's instructions. Store in the freezer.

...continued on page 250

## CRYSTALLISED CHOCOLATE

185g caster sugar
70ml water
85g 70% dark chocolate buttons
  (or chopped dark chocolate)
2g (about 2 pinches picked up on the back
  of a teaspoon) bicarbonate of soda

Put the sugar and water in a pan over a medium heat. Once the sugar has dissolved, bring the mixture up to 120°C. Add the chocolate and stir vigorously until it has crystallised – pale, grainy and crunchy. Stir in the bicarbonate of soda, remove from the heat and allow to cool.

## SALTED LIQUORICE CARAMEL

200g caster sugar
25g honey
75g molasses
300ml double cream
100g white chocolate buttons
  (or chopped white chocolate)
75g unsalted butter, cut into small cubes
10g liquorice root, ground to powder
Maldon sea salt

Melt the sugar in a pan, then cook to a golden caramel. Add the honey and molasses and caramelise further to 110–115°C.

Add the cream, stir in and bring to the boil. Pour this mixture over the chocolate in a bowl and allow to melt.

In a separate small pan, melt the butter over a high heat and cook until it starts to foam, brown and take on a nutty aroma. Immediately remove from the heat and cool slightly, then stir into the caramel mixture along with the liquorice. Season with salt to taste.

## WHITE CHOCOLATE TRUFFLES

200ml double cream
500g white chocolate buttons
  (or chopped white chocolate)
50g unsalted butter
50g cacao butter
70g cacao nibs

Heat the cream until it just starts to simmer, then pour it over the chocolate in a bowl. Leave aside to melt. In a separate small pan, melt the butter over a high heat and cook until it starts to foam, brown and take on a nutty aroma. Immediately remove from the heat, add the cacao butter and stir until melted.

Stir the two mixtures together, then place in the fridge to cool.

Pour the cooled mixture into a stand mixer fitted with a balloon whisk attachment and whisk until pale and fluffy. (The mixture may appear split when first mixed. Keep the mixer going until it warms up. It will eventually become pale and fluffy.) Fold in the cacao nibs.

Using a teaspoon, spoon small rounds on to a tray lined with greaseproof paper (these truffles can be quite random in shape; they do not need to be uniform). Store in the freezer.

## ASSEMBLY

Drizzle some of the caramel on to each plate. Using a tablespoon, spoon two rounds of chocolate mousse on to each plate. Scatter some of the crystallised chocolate around. Place two truffles on each plate and finish with a rocher or quenelle (or scoop) of ice cream.

# GARIGUETTE STRAWBERRY MILLE-FEUILLE

## CACAO BUTTER ICE CREAM

serves 6–8

When making mille-feuille, you can of course use a good-quality shop-bought puff pastry but making your own is a real achievement. There are a few notes to keep in mind. Throughout the process, take care when rolling out, being as even as possible. Do not press hard into the pastry as you may merge the delicate layers of butter. Try to maintain square corners and straight edges, especially when folding so that the folds are as even as possible. Be aware of temperature when making the pastry: too warm and the butter will become too soft and melt into the dough; too cold and the butter will crack within the pastry, forming rips and gaps between layers. You can make the mille-feuille whatever size you like. In fact, you could even make one large one that could be cut into slices at the table. Any excess pastry dough stores well in the freezer to be used in other recipes.

## CACAO BUTTER ICE CREAM

500ml whole milk
100ml double cream
65g liquid glucose
40g trimoline
15g glycerine
30g Sosa Procrema Cold 100
   (ice cream stabiliser)
1 teaspoon Stab 2000 (ice cream stabiliser)
100g cacao butter

Put the milk, cream, glucose, trimoline, glycerine, Procrema and Stab 2000 into a pot and gently warm through, stirring occasionally. In a separate small pan, gently melt the cacao butter.

Pour the milk mixture into a food processor. While blending, drizzle in the cacao butter to emulsify. Allow the mixture to cool to room temperature, whisking occasionally so that the cacao butter does not solidify.

Churn in an ice cream machine according to the manufacturer's guidelines. Store in the freezer.

## PUFF PASTRY

550g plain flour
50g unsalted butter, melted
210ml water
25ml white wine vinegar
400g unsalted butter, at room temperature

Put the flour into the bowl of a stand mixer fitted with the paddle attachment. While mixing on a low speed, add the melted butter, water and vinegar. Continue to mix at a low speed until a dough forms. Turn up the speed slightly and mix until the dough is smooth and even to the touch. (Alternatively you can mix/knead the dough by hand.) Knead the dough a little on a floured worktop before forming into a ball. Wrap in clingfilm and leave to rest in the fridge for 1 hour.

Place the slab of room-temperature butter between two sheets of greaseproof paper. Using a rolling pin, roll out the butter into a square about 2cm thick.

Remove the dough from the fridge and shape it into a rough square on the floured worktop. Using a rolling pin, mark out another square on top of the dough by pressing into the centre with the length of the rolling pin (this square should be about the same size as the square of butter).

Roll out the dough from the sides of the marked square to create an even cross shape, leaving the thicker square area in the middle of the cross (the marked square). The 'arms' or flaps of the cross need to be about 5mm thick and large enough to fold over the square of butter.

At this point the square of butter and the dough should be the same texture to touch. Place the square of butter in the middle of the cross, on the raised centre square. Fold the right flap over the butter so that it completely covers it. Repeat with the left flap, then the bottom flap and, finally, the top flap. You will now have a square of dough with the butter completely encased within.

Roll out the square away from you on the lightly floured worktop into a rectangle almost triple its original length and double the width. Fold the top third down and the bottom third up over this. Wrap in clingfilm and rest in the fridge for 20 minutes.

Place the dough on the lightly floured worktop so the folded edges are to the sides. Roll out away from you into a rectangle the same size as

*...continued on page 254*

before. Fold as before, then turn the dough so that the folded edges are to the sides and roll out again. Repeat the folding (making a total of three folds up to this point). Wrap in clingfilm and rest in the fridge for 20 minutes.

Repeat the previous rolling and folding process so that the dough will have five folds in total. Rest the pastry in the fridge again before rolling out for use.

Preheat the oven to 200°C fan/220°C/Gas Mark 7. Roll out the pastry dough to a 5mm thickness and cut into 8 x 30cm strips. Place the strips on baking trays lined with greaseproof paper. Bake for 10 minutes, then lower the oven to 180°C fan/200°C/Gas Mark 6 and bake for a further 30 minutes. Drop the temperature to 160°C fan/180°C/Gas Mark 4 for 10 minutes of baking, then to 150°C fan/170°C/Gas Mark 3–4 for another 10 minutes and finally to 140°C fan/160°C/Gas Mark 3 for the last 10 minutes. The oven door must remain closed during the entire baking process.

Remove the pastry from the oven and allow to cool on a wire rack. Portion to desired size rectangles (you need three for each mille-feuille).

## STRAWBERRY JAM

300g strawberries, hulled and cut in half
200g caster sugar
½ vanilla pod, split open in half

Put the strawberries and sugar into a pot with a splash of water and scrape in the seeds from the vanilla pod. Cook, stirring, until the sugar has dissolved and the fruit begins to break down. Bring the mixture to 105°C, then remove from the heat. Allow to cool.

## HONEY CREMEAUX

25g egg yolks
½ sheet/leaf of silver leaf gelatine
65ml UHT double cream
65ml whole milk
25g honey
100g white chocolate buttons
   (or chopped white chocolate)
about 300ml double cream

Put the egg yolks into a large bowl. Soak the gelatine in cold water to soften it. Bring the UHT cream and milk to the boil in a pan. Drain the gelatine, squeezing out excess water, add to the pan and stir until melted. Pour this mixture over the honey in a bowl, stirring. Gradually add the honey mixture to the yolks, stirring constantly to prevent scrambling. Add the chocolate and whisk until fully emulsified. Pour into a container and leave to set in the fridge.

Weigh the honey mixture and add an equal weight of double cream. Whisk together until the mixture is light and will hold form.

## ASSEMBLY

2 punnets of Gariguette strawberries,
   hulled and sliced
sherbet (see page 272)

To assemble each mille-feuille, lay one rectangle of pastry on the worktop. Spoon over some cremeaux, then jam and add some sliced strawberries. Place a second pastry layer on top and gently press down. Spoon over some cremeaux, then jam and add some sliced strawberries. Place a final layer of pastry on top and press down gently. Repeat for each mille-feuille. Dust the tops with sherbet and serve each one with ice cream on the side.

# WHITE PEACH

## ALMOND SKIN ICE CREAM, ELDERFLOWER JELLY

This dish shows off seasonality and nature's gifts. After producing it just once, it went straight on the menu – one of the rare times this has happened. The skins of fresh almonds are normally discarded as they are too tough and fibrous to eat, but we use them to infuse the milk and cream for our ice cream. It is a light, fresh-tasting ice cream, with its own unique flavour. The dessert has a short life on the menu as fresh almond season runs only from April to early June – an exclusive 6 weeks. White peaches and elderflower have the same short season – it's as if it was meant to be!

**serves 6–8**

### ALMOND SKIN ICE CREAM

800g–1kg fresh almonds
500ml semi-skimmed milk
200ml double cream
100g caster sugar
10g liquid glucose
90g pasteurised egg yolks

Peel the green outer shells from the almonds and discard. Peel off the orange skin or flesh closest to the nuts – you want 100g of these skins for the ice cream. Set the fresh almonds aside for serving.

In a suitable-sized pan, combine the milk, cream and almond skins and set over a medium heat. Bring to a simmer, then remove from the heat. Once cooled, refrigerate overnight to allow the flavour from the skins to infuse the milk/cream.

The next day, pour the milk infusion into a pan and bring to a simmer. Meanwhile, whisk the sugar with the glucose and egg yolks until pale and creamy. Strain the milk infusion through a fine sieve, then pour half of it on to the egg yolk mixture and whisk to combine. Pour this back into the saucepan with the rest of the strained milk infusion. Cook over a gentle heat, stirring all the time, until the mixture thickens enough to coat the back of the spoon (it should reach 84°C). Remove from the heat and pass through a fine sieve into a flat tray set over ice to cool it down quickly. Once cool, transfer to an ice cream machine and churn according to the manufacturer's instructions. Freeze until required.

### ELDERFLOWER JELLY

2 sheets/leaves of silver leaf gelatine
juice of 2 lemons
320ml Elderflower Cordial (see page 73)

Soak the gelatine in cold water to soften, then drain, squeezing out excess water. Mix the lemon juice with the cordial. Warm 80ml of this liquid and melt the gelatine in it. Add this to the rest of the liquid and mix together. Pour into a suitable container and leave to set in the fridge.

### ASSEMBLY

4 white peaches
elderflower pulp (from making cordial)
  or fresh elderflowers (if available)

Before serving, put the ice cream in the fridge to soften slightly. Slice the fresh white peaches and divide among the plates. Using a teaspoon, add 3–4 scoops of elderflower jelly to each plate. Scatter the reserved fresh almonds around the plates and finish each with a scoop of ice cream and some elderflower pulp or fresh elderflowers, if using.

# SALTED CARAMEL

## CACAO, MALT ICE CREAM

One of the first dishes to be created at The Dairy, this recipe has been improved and enhanced by the quality of the chocolate we now use and the addition of a special malt we buy from a local brewery. A well-known chef said this about the dessert: 'I would run completely naked across the Common just to have that again.' If you are left with any excess truffles, they can be stored in the freezer and served as petits fours.

**serves 6–8**

### CHOCOLATE TRUFFLES

50g unsalted butter, cut into small cubes
100ml double cream
250g 72% dark chocolate buttons
    (or chopped dark chocolate)
40g cacao nibs
a pinch of Maldon sea salt
cocoa powder, for dusting

Put the butter in a pan over a high heat and cook until it starts to foam and brown and has a nutty aroma. Stir in the cream, then bring just to the boil.

Pour this mixture over the chocolate in the bowl of a stand mixer fitted with the balloon whisk attachment. Whisk on a low speed until the chocolate has fully melted. Turn up the mixer speed gradually until the mixture begins to whip. When it is light and aerated, add the cacao nibs and salt, and mix on a high speed briefly to incorporate.

Transfer the mixture to a disposable piping bag and snip off the end. Pipe into lengths (1.5cm in diameter) on greaseproof paper. Freeze before roughly cutting into pieces (about 1.5cm long). Dust with cocoa powder. Keep in the freezer until required.

### CHOCOLATE SOIL

250g ground almonds
150g demerara sugar
150g buckwheat flour
80g cocoa powder
1 teaspoon Maldon sea salt
140g unsalted butter, melted

Preheat the oven to 160°C fan/180°C/Gas Mark 4. Mix together all the dry ingredients in a stand mixer fitted with the paddle attachment. Add the melted butter and mix to combine.

Spread the mixture on a baking tray. Bake for 30 minutes, stirring the mixture every 10 minutes. Allow to cool, then store in an airtight container in a cool, dry place.

### SALTED CARAMEL

300g caster sugar
7.5g trimoline
75g unsalted butter, diced
300ml double cream
100g 66% dark chocolate buttons (or
    chopped dark chocolate)
1 teaspoon Maldon sea salt

Place the sugar and trimoline in a pan. Add a little water to make a 'wet sand' consistency. Set over a high heat to melt the sugar, then boil until the syrup reaches a dark caramel stage (165–175°C). Remove from the heat and whisk in the butter a third at a time. Continue whisking until smooth.

In a separate pan, warm the cream until it just reaches boiling point. Pour over the chocolate in a bowl and whisk until smooth and glossy.

*...continued on page 260*

Pour the cream/chocolate mixture into the butter caramel and whisk together until smooth. Add the Maldon salt and mix through.

## CHOCOLATE TUILE

50g liquid glucose
50ml double cream
125g unsalted butter
155g caster sugar
¾ teaspoon pectin powder
175g cacao nibs

Put the glucose, cream, butter and 150g of the sugar in a pan and melt together. Mix the pectin with the remaining sugar and add to the pan. Boil the mixture until it reaches 107°C. Remove from the heat and allow the mixture to cool down to at least 45°C before folding through the cacao nibs.

Roll out the mixture between sheets of greaseproof paper as thinly as possible. Freeze and keep in the freezer until ready to bake.

Preheat the oven to 160°C fan/180°C/Gas Mark 4. Place the frozen tuile sheet (still with greaseproof paper top and bottom) on a large baking tray and set a large wire rack over the top to hold down the edges of the greaseproof paper. Bake for about 15 minutes or until the tuile is set and doesn't appear to be liquid when the tray is gently knocked. Allow to cool before breaking into shards. Store in an airtight container.

## MALT ICE CREAM

375ml double cream
375ml whole milk
35g milk powder
25g trimoline
1 teaspoon Stab 2000 (ice cream stabiliser)
75g malt extract
90g pasteurised egg yolks
65g caster sugar

Put the cream, milk, milk powder, trimoline, Stab and malt extract in a pan. Whisk together and bring to the boil. In a large bowl, mix together the yolks and sugar. Pour a third of the hot mixture over the yolks and sugar and whisk together. Add this to the rest of the hot mixture in the pan and whisk in. Heat until the temperature of the mixture is 85°C.

Pass through a chinois or very fine sieve into a deep tray set over ice to cool the mixture quickly. Once cool, churn in an ice cream machine according to the manufacturer's instructions. Store in the freezer.

## ASSEMBLY

Spoon some of the salted caramel over the bottom of each plate. Sprinkle with a few truffles and scatter over chocolate soil. Add a couple of quenelles of ice cream to each plate and finish with a few tuile shards.

# JERUSALEM ARTICHOKE

## CRÈME FRAÎCHE, POACHED QUINCE

serves 8–10

Kira Ghidoni helped put The Manor on the map. We received a five-star review from the late, great A.A. Gill (not a relative unfortunately) in which he called Kira 'a tweezer-twirling pâtissier: unequivocally the best pudding in London'. Thanks A.A., and well done Kira. This is still one of my favourite puddings ever.

### JERUSALEM ARTICHOKE ICE CREAM

200g Jerusalem artichokes, scrubbed clean and grated
100g unsalted butter
300ml whole milk
100ml double cream
15g milk powder
25g trimoline
25g caster sugar
80g egg yolks

Put the Jerusalem artichokes into a pan with the butter and cook until the butter turns golden brown. Drain off the butter. In another pan, bring the milk, cream, milk powder, trimoline and caster sugar to the boil. Blend this hot liquid with the artichokes in a blender or food processor until smooth, then pass through a fine sieve into a clean pan.

Add the egg yolks and cook the mixture over a very gentle heat, stirring constantly (as you would a crème anglaise) until it thickens enough to coat the back of the spoon. Pass through a fine sieve again, then allow to cool. Churn in an ice cream machine according to the manufacturer's instructions. Store in the freezer until required.

### POACHED QUINCES

seeds from 5 cardamom pods
3 quinces
1 lemon, cut in half
400ml fresh apple juice
40ml cider vinegar
30g caster sugar
5g fine table salt

Preheat the oven to 120°C fan/140°C/Gas Mark 1. Toast the cardamom seeds in a small dry pan until fragrant, then lightly crush them.

Peel the quinces and cut in half. As each is prepared, drop it into a bowl of lemon water (water with squeezed lemon halves) to prevent browning.

Combine the apple juice, vinegar, sugar, salt and cardamom in an ovenproof pot and bring to the boil. Add the quince halves. Cover with a lid and transfer to the oven to cook for 3 hours.

Allow the quinces to cool in the poaching liquid, then lift them out (reserve the liquid). Remove the cores and cut the quince flesh into a uniform dice, reserving the trimmings for the gel.

### QUINCE GEL

125g quince trimmings (if there are not enough trimmings, use some of the diced quince to make the 125g)
50ml fresh apple juice
½ teaspoon agar agar

Put the quince trimmings and apple juice in a blender or food processor with 50ml of the quince poaching liquid. Blend until smooth, then pass through a fine sieve into a pan. Add the agar agar and simmer, stirring, for 2 minutes. Pour into a jug or bowl. Leave in the fridge until set, then blend again before decanting into a squeezy bottle. Store in the fridge until required.

*...continued on page 262*

### FROZEN CRÈME FRAÎCHE

150ml whole milk
110g crème fraîche
20g Sosa Procrema Cold 100
   (ice cream stabiliser)
10g dextrose
35g caster sugar
juice of ¼ lemon

Put all the ingredients into a blender or food processor and blend until thoroughly mixed. Decant into a siphon gun with one charge. Shake vigorously, then express the mixture into a freezerproof container. Cover with a lid and freeze.

### ARTICHOKE CRISPS

2 Jerusalem artichokes, scrubbed clean
vegetable oil for deep frying
Maldon sea salt

Thinly slice the artichokes on a mandoline. Heat oil in a deep pan or deep-fat fryer to 170°C. Fry the artichoke slices a few at a time in the hot oil until golden and crisp. Drain on kitchen paper and season with a little salt. The crisps can be stored in an airtight container for up to 2 days before using.

### ASSEMBLY

Scrape the frozen crème fraîche with a fork to make a granita texture. Place a spoonful of the artichoke ice cream in the centre of each plate. Scatter poached quince around the ice cream and dot gel around the plate. Scatter frozen crème fraîche and artichoke crisps over the top.

# TOASTED WHITE CHOCOLATE

## PANNA COTTA, FORCED RHUBARB

This is a little showstopper, rich with white chocolate but with sharp flavours of rhubarb cutting through nicely. The hint of salt on the vanilla biscuit is very much welcome. Did you know that forced rhubarb is actually grown in barns in complete darkness and harvested in candlelight to avoid photosynthesis, which would otherwise turn the rhubarb green and tough? Wow!

serves 4–6

### VANILLA SABLÉ

120g unsalted butter, at room temperature
100g caster sugar
1 egg yolk
2 vanilla pods, split open in half
150g plain flour
½ teaspoon fine table salt
5g baking powder

Put the butter and sugar in a stand mixer fitted with the whisk attachment and whisk together until light and fluffy. Mix in the egg yolk and the seeds scraped from the vanilla pods. Add the flour, salt and baking powder and bring together with your hands into a dough.

Divide the dough into two pieces. Roll out each piece of dough on a lightly floured surface into a rectangle about 2mm thick and place on a baking tray lined with greaseproof paper. Chill for 30 minutes.

Preheat the oven to 175°C fan/195°C/Gas Mark 5–6. Bake the sablé sheets for 10 minutes or until golden. Cool on the trays, then break into random shards.

### TOASTED WHITE PANNA COTTA

125g white chocolate chips (or white chocolate broken into pieces)
1 sheet/leaf of silver leaf gelatine
250ml double cream

Preheat the oven to 160°C fan/180°C/Gas Mark 4. Spread out the chocolate on a baking tray lined with greaseproof paper. Bake for 8–12 minutes or until caramelised to a golden colour. Remove from the oven and allow to cool slightly.

Soak the gelatine in cold water to soften it. Bring 125ml of the cream to the boil in a pan. Remove from the heat. Drain the gelatine, squeezing out excess water, and add to the cream along with the chocolate. Whisk until the gelatine has melted and the mixture is smooth. Pour into a bowl and chill for 3–4 hours to set.

Whip the remaining double cream to soft peaks. Whisk the white chocolate mixture with the whipped cream. Keep in the fridge until required.

### MARINATED RHUBARB

200g forced rhubarb, cut into 5mm dice
½ teaspoon fine salt
juice of ½ lemon
1 teaspoon caster sugar

In a bowl, mix the rhubarb with the salt, lemon juice and sugar. Cover tightly with clingfilm and leave in the fridge for 8 hours.

...continued on page 266

## RHUBARB COMPOTE

250g caster sugar
125ml water
500g forced rhubarb, roughly diced into
   1cm pieces
a squeeze of lemon juice

Put the sugar and water into a pan and bring to the boil, stirring to dissolve the sugar. Boil until the syrup reaches 120°C. Add the rhubarb and cook over a high heat, stirring, until the rhubarb breaks down. Remove from the heat and stir in the lemon juice. Allow to cool to room temperature.

## RHUBARB SNOW

100g caster sugar
100ml water
250g forced rhubarb (rhubarb trimmings
   can be used here), roughly chopped
20ml lemon juice or citric acid

Dissolve the sugar in the water in a pan. Add the rhubarb and lemon juice or citric acid and bring to a simmer. Cook until the liquid has taken on a strong pink colour and the rhubarb has broken down. Strain through a fine sieve, gently pressing on the rhubarb so as much flavour passes through as possible. Allow the liquid to cool, then pour into a freezerproof container and freeze until solid. Break it up by scraping with a fork to create a granita texture.

## ASSEMBLY

Spoon a generous mound of panna cotta on to the centre of each plate. Make a well in the centre of it and fill it with all the rhubarb elements. Serve the sablé biscuits on the side.

# IVY HOUSE MILK TART

## SOUR APPLE SORBET

This is one of those challenging dishes that takes some skill and a lot of patience to perfect. We've had a few grown men close to tears trying to make it, not to mention some near punch-ups over oven space! When it's done well, there is nothing but pure satisfaction in its seemingly simple beauty. It caresses all the senses. We make it every day and it must be all sold on the day. There are fights over the remaining spoonful once last orders hit the kitchen.

**serves 8**

### SOUR APPLE SORBET

2 sheets/leaves of silver leaf gelatine
590ml Fermented Apple Juice
  (see page 22)
150g caster sugar
20ml fresh lemon juice
60g liquid glucose
1 heaped teaspoon citric acid

Soak the gelatine in cold water to soften it, then drain and put into a pan with all the other ingredients. Heat to melt the gelatine, then simmer gently until the sugar and glucose have dissolved. Allow to cool.

Churn in an ice cream machine as per the manufacturer's instructions. Store in the freezer until ready to use.

### TART BASE

165g Weetabix
170g unsalted butter, cut into small cubes
170g Campaillou bread flour
30g cornflour
2 whole eggs
20g egg yolks
240g caster sugar
egg wash

Preheat the oven to 175°C fan/195°C/Gas Mark 5–6. Crush the Weetabix finely in a blender or food processor, then tip on to a baking tray and toast in the oven until golden.

Melt the butter in a pan over a high heat and cook until it starts to foam, brown and take on a nutty aroma. Immediately remove from the heat and cool quickly (set the base of the pan in cold water) to stop the butter from burning. Whisk during cooling so the milk solids are spread evenly through the butter as it sets.

Put the toasted Weetabix back in the food processor and add the flour and cornflour. With the machine running, gradually add the cooled brown butter through the feed tube to make a breadcrumb consistency.

Whisk the eggs and egg yolks with the sugar until light and fluffy. Add the flour and butter mixture and fold through thoroughly. Wrap this pastry in clingfilm and leave to rest in the fridge for 30 minutes.

Preheat the oven to 160°C fan/180°C/Gas Mark 4. Roll out the pastry into a large rectangle on a lightly floured surface, about a 4mm thickness. Place on a large baking tray. Now take a 30cm square bottomless tin

*...continued on page 268*

(with the bottom removed) and press into the pastry, cutting through the pastry but keeping it on the tray. Cover the pastry within the square tin with greaseproof paper and weigh down with baking beans. Blind bake for 15 minutes. Remove the beans and paper from the internal square, lower the oven to 150°C fan/170°C/Gas Mark 3–4 and bake for a further 10 minutes. Reduce the oven to 140°C fan/160°C/Gas Mark 3 and bake for a final 10 minutes.

When you take the pastry out of the oven, remove the trimmings/edge of the pastry (i.e. the pastry outside of the square) from the tray, allow to cool and crumble into a crumb. Meanwhile, brush the bottom of the square pastry case with egg wash and allow to cool.

## BURNT APPLE PURÉE

100g demerara sugar
4 Granny Smith apples, diced
50g malt extract
50ml apple juice
½ teaspoon fresh lemon juice

Preheat the oven to 190°C fan/210°C/Gas Mark 6–7. Mix the sugar with the apples and spread out on a baking tray. Bake for about 20 minutes or until the apples are a deep, dark brown colour. Tip into a food processor, add the remaining ingredients and blend to a smooth purée. Pass through a fine sieve.

Turn the oven down to 90°C fan/110°C/Gas Mark ¼. Spread a thin layer of the purée over the bottom of the tart case and bake for 10 minutes to set the purée. Leave to cool.

## CUSTARD

200g egg yolks
110g caster sugar
350ml double cream (we use Ivy House)
330ml UHT cream

Whisk the egg yolks and sugar together until the sugar has dissolved.

Pour the two types of cream into a pan and bring to a simmer. Remove from the heat and allow to cool until a skin forms across the top. Remove the skin. Repeat this three more times, removing the skin each time. Finally, bring the cream to a simmer, then slowly stir it into the egg yolk mixture.

Preheat the oven to 90°C fan/110°C/Gas Mark ¼. Pour the custard into the pastry case. Bake the tart for about 1 hour or until it takes on a panna cotta wobble. Allow to cool to room temperature.

## ASSEMBLY

Slice the tart and place a slice on each plate. Add a spoon of the reserved pastry crumb and top with a quenelle of sour apple sorbet to each plate.

# BLACKBERRY LEAF PANNA COTTA
## BLACK PEPPER SABLÉ

In late summer it's such a nice idea to flavour a cream or panna cotta with blackberry leaves, which have a wonderful herbaceous green-tea-like flavour. We sometimes use fig or citrus leaves as an alternative.

**serves 10**

### BLACK PEPPER SABLÉ

120g unsalted butter, at room temperature
100g caster sugar
1 egg yolk
2 vanilla pods, split open in half
150g plain flour
½ teaspoon fine table salt
5g baking powder
½ teaspoon freshly cracked black pepper

Put the butter and sugar in a stand mixer and whisk together until light and fluffy. Mix in the egg yolk and the seeds scraped from the vanilla pods. Add the flour, salt, baking powder and black pepper and bring together with your hands into a dough.

Divide the dough into two pieces. Roll out each piece of dough on a lightly floured surface into a rectangle about 2mm thick and place on a baking tray lined with greaseproof paper. Chill for 30 minutes.

Preheat the oven to 175°C fan/195°C/Gas Mark 5–6. Bake the sablé sheets for 10 minutes or until golden. Cool on the trays, then break into random shards.

### PANNA COTTA

4 sheets/leaves of silver leaf gelatine
500ml double cream
250ml whole milk
75g caster sugar
10g Blackberry Leaf Powder (see page 60)

Soak the gelatine in cold water to soften it. Drain and squeeze out excess water, then put into a pan with all the remaining ingredients. Bring to the boil, stirring occasionally. Remove from the heat and strain through a fine sieve into a bowl. Cover and chill the mixture to set.

### BLACKBERRY LEAF OIL

50g fresh unsprayed blackberry leaves, rinsed well in a colander
50ml olive oil

Blend the leaves and oil together in a blender or food processor until as smooth as possible. Pour into a pan and bring quickly to the boil over a high heat. As soon as the mixture reaches the boil, remove from the heat and strain through a fine sieve into a bowl set over ice (this will cool the oil quickly and help it retain its bright green colour).

### BLACKBERRY LIQUOR

150g very ripe blackberries
75g dextrose
a pinch of citric acid

Put all the ingredients in a pan, bring to a simmer and simmer for 8 minutes or until the fruit has completely broken down. Pass through a fine sieve, pushing down on the fruit so that all the juice passes through. Cool.

### ASSEMBLY

fresh blackberries
an aromatic herb such as sorrel or lemon balm

Whip the panna cotta mixture just to loosen it, then decant into a piping bag. Pipe a round of panna cotta in the bottom of each bowl. Drizzle a little blackberry leaf oil and blackberry liquor into the bottom of the bowl. Garnish with fresh blackberries and whatever herb you have chosen. Serve the sablé biscuits on the side.

# OLD-FASHIONED ICE CREAM SANDWICHES

Ice cream 'sambos' take me back to where I was brought up. I lived a stone's throw from the infamous Teddy's Ice Cream in Sandycove, where many a summer's day was spent rummaging through my father's jingles (loose change) or reaching down the side of the couch to raise enough pennies for another ice cream sandwich! This dessert uses the flavours of an Old-Fashioned cocktail. In the process of making our cocktail, Kerry G Old-Fashioned (see page 80), we fat-wash the whiskey with butter. It's this butter that we use to make the parfait for this dessert.

Makes 8–10

## WHISKEY BUTTER PARFAIT

1½ sheets/leaves of silver leaf gelatine
125g butter that has been used for
   Fat-washed Whiskey (see page 74)
485ml double cream
150g egg yolks
190g caster sugar

Soak the gelatine in cold water to soften it. Melt the butter in a pan, add 50ml of the cream and bring just to the boil. Drain the gelatine, squeezing out excess water, and stir into the cream mixture until melted. Remove from the heat and allow to cool.

Whisk the egg yolks in a stand mixer until pale and fluffy. Meanwhile, melt 100g of the sugar in a pan with a little water, then boil until it reaches 116°C. Gradually pour the hot sugar syrup down the side of the mixer bowl while whisking to incorporate it into the egg yolks. Continue to whisk at a high speed until the mixture begins to stiffen.

Put the remaining sugar and cream into a bowl and whip to soft peaks. Gently fold the butter/gelatine mixture into the egg yolk mixture, then fold in the whipped cream. Pour the mixture into a freezerproof container or tray in a layer about 4cm thick. Freeze.

## PÂTE DE BRICK 'WAFERS'

6 sheets of feuille de brick pastry
50g unsalted butter, melted
icing sugar, for dusting

Preheat the oven to 160°C fan/180°C/Gas Mark 4. Brush a sheet of the pastry with butter and dust with icing sugar. Top with another sheet of pastry, brush this with butter and dust with icing sugar. Top with a third sheet of pastry. You'll now have three sheets of pastry stuck together. Repeat with the remaining three sheets of pastry.

Cut out 4 x 9cm rectangles. Place them on a baking tray lined with greaseproof paper. Lay another sheet of greaseproof paper on top and weigh down with a second baking tray. Bake for 12 minutes or until golden brown. Allow to cool before storing in an airtight tin.

## SHERBET

60g icing sugar, sifted
½ teaspoon citric acid

Mix the icing sugar with the citric acid.

## ASSEMBLY

100g Blood Orange Marmalade (see page 49)

Portion the parfait into 4 x 9cm rectangles. Set each rectangle on one of the wafers and drizzle with some of the marmalade, then top with another wafer to create a sandwich. Dust the sandwiches with the sherbet.

# HIBISCUS DOUGHNUTS

These mini doughnuts make a wonderful snack or petits fours at the end of a meal. It is worth serving them with something creamy on the side such as Ben's Beeswax Cream (see page 55), crème fraîche or yoghurt.

Makes about 30
bite-sized doughnuts

### HIBISCUS SHERBET

100g caster sugar
5g dried hibiscus flowers
5g citric acid

Blend all the ingredients together in a blender or food processor to a powder.

### DOUGHNUTS

500g plain flour
25g caster sugar
a good pinch of fine table salt
5 eggs
125ml water
25ml vegetable oil
zest of ½ orange
zest of ½ lemon
10g fresh yeast
115g unsalted butter, softened
vegetable oil, for deep-frying

In a stand mixer fitted with the paddle attachment, mix together the flour, caster sugar and salt for a minute. Add the eggs, water, oil, zests and yeast and mix for 2 minutes. Add the butter and mix for another 2 minutes to make a dough. Spoon the dough into disposable piping bags, filling each only by a third; do not tie closed. Keep in the fridge until required.

About an hour before you want to serve the doughnuts, place the dough (in the piping bags) in an ambient area – about 25°C – and allow to rise.

Heat oil in a deep pan or deep-fat fryer to 200°C. Have a small bowl of water nearby so you can dip your fingers. Pipe a little of the dough into the hot oil, squeezing the top of the bag with one hand and using the wet fingertips of your other hand to separate the dough into round balls as it is piped out. Fry the doughnuts – in batches – for about 1 minute or until golden all over. Drain well on kitchen paper.

### ASSEMBLY

Ben's Beeswax Cream (see page 55)

Once drained, roll the doughnuts in hibiscus sherbet and serve immediately with the beeswax cream on the side.

# SALTED LEMON AND SUNFLOWER SEED NOUGAT

When making nougat at home, you can add so many different flavours. There are just a few things to keep in mind. Have all the equipment and ingredients ready before you start as you won't have time for any preparation once the sugars are hot. Do not take the sugar and honey any higher than the temperatures specified in the recipe. If adding a praline or nut paste, stir it in at the end of the process but while the stand mixer is still whisking.

**Makes 1 tray
(about 30 x 24cm)**

20g peel from Preserved Amalfi Lemons (see page 30), very finely diced
300g sunflower seeds
435g caster sugar
90g liquid glucose
125ml water
250g honey
50g egg whites

**TO DUST**
cornflour
icing sugar

Preheat the oven to 140°C fan/160°C/Gas Mark 3. Spread the preserved lemon peel on a small baking tray and slightly dry out in the oven for 5–10 minutes. In another baking tray, toast the sunflower seeds in the oven for 8–10 minutes or until golden brown. Keep them warm.

Put 415g of the sugar, the glucose and water in a pan and heat to dissolve the sugar. Put the honey in a separate pan and heat. While the honey and sugar syrup are heating up, put the egg whites and remaining sugar in the bowl of a stand mixer fitted with a balloon whisk attachment and whisk to stiff peaks.

Once the honey has reached 125°C, gradually pour it into the egg whites while whisking. Continue to whisk at a high speed while the sugar syrup carries on boiling. When it reaches 145°C, slowly pour it into the egg white mixture, whisking constantly. Then whisk at full speed for a further 1 minute. Remove the bowl from the mixer and, using a large metal spoon, fold in the warm seeds and the preserved lemon.

Spoon on to a tray (about 30 x 24cm) lined with greaseproof paper. Spread out the mixture as much as possible before placing another sheet of greaseproof on top and using the back of the spoon or a dough scraper to spread the nougat evenly. Allow it to set at room temperature before portioning into 2cm squares. Dust each piece with a mixture of equal parts cornflour and icing sugar.

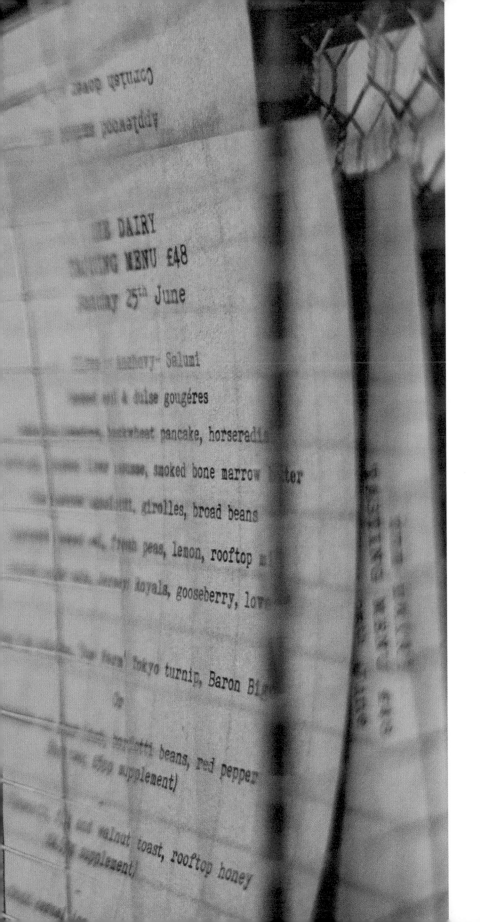

# A

alexanders 246
**almonds**
   ice cream 256
   milk 155
**anchovies**
   crisps 114
   dressing 132
**apple juice** fermented 22
**apples**
   burnt purée 268
   and fennel Hendricks 79
   fermented 22
   purée 73
   sour sorbet 267
**Applewood-Smoked Eel** 116
   broad beans, preserved lemon,
      mint 166
   chard, shallot crisps, soy 192
**apricots**
   gel 96
   and lemon thyme jam 48
Arsenal FC 14
**artichoke**
   confit 235
   fermented 22
   piccalilli 47
   roast and fermented 148
   *see also* Jerusalem artichoke
**asparagus** Julie Girl skate 160

# B

**barley**
   fermented 24
   fermented, wild mushroom and
      chicken skin 150
   puffed 59
BBQ Duck Hearts, White Polenta
   and Corn 152
BBQ Spring Cabbage, Ricotta
   and Coppa 134
Bean family 176
beans 210
**beef**
   bressola 34
   Galloway onglet 210
   onglet tartare 238
   tartare 109
**beer**
   ginger 82
   pickled onions 43
   pumpkin 83
**beeswax** cream 55
**beetroot**
   fermented 24

gin 75, 79
   salt-baked 182
   smoked tartare 142
Belted Galloway Onglet 210
Ben's Beeswax Cream 55
**black pepper** sablé 270
**blackberries**
   brandy 75, 81
   leaf panna cotta 270
   leaf powder 60
   and lemon verbena jam 50
   syrup 72
Blanc, Raymond 14
Blood Orange Marmalade 49
**blueberries** with milk and honey 244
**bone marrow**
   smoked 37
   smoked butter 53
   smoked with agnolotti 220
Bonito Butter 52
Bottarga 38
brandy 75
Brasserie Na Mara 12
Brawn 98
**bread** 88
   bao 213
   crisps 244
   fermented potato flatbread 86
   fig and walnut 90, 92
   fried 59
   Guinness soda 116
   hibiscus doughnuts 274
   miso 65, 160
   nduja brioche 162
Bressola 34
brines 20–1
Bring That Beet Back 79
**broad beans** and pea salad 166
**brown sugar** syrup 72
**buckwheat** pancakes 89
**butters** 51
   bonito 52
   chicken and savory 52
   dulse 187
   nori 53
   smoked 53
   smoked bone marrow 53
   whiskey cultured 53

# C

**cabbage**
   BBQ charred 198
   BBQ spring 134
   ferment 26
   January King ferment 25

**cacao butter** ice cream 253
cacao nibs 146
**capers**
   nasturtium 44, 109
   wild garlic 44
**caraway** and carrot pickle 43
Carrot and Caraway Pickle 43
**cauliflower**
   and date 145
   red mullet, dulse butter 187
**cavolo nero**
   fermented 24
   and leek ballotine 223
**celeriac**
   pickle 43
   purée 229
   salt-baked 155
**charcuterie** 31–2
   bressola 34
   coppa 35
   fennel salami 33
   goose ham 33
   lomo 36
   nduja 36
   pancetta 37
   wild garlic and sunflower
      salami 38
**chard** fermented 27, 192
Charred Mackerel 174
Chart Farm Venison 235
**cheese**
   Mornay sauce 102
   ricotta 134
   ricotta with cabbage 199
   trim mousse 148
   truffle Baron Bigod 92
**chicken**
   brown stock 61
   crispy skin 150
   and savory butter 52
   skin terrine 223
Chicken Liver Parfait 95
**chicory** braised 202
**chillies** Sichuan oil 57
**chocolate**
   mousse 249
   truffles 258
   tuile 260
   *see also* white chocolate
Cider with Rosie 77
**cocktails**
   Apple and Fennel Hendricks 79
   Bring that Beet Back 79
   Cider with Rosie 77
   Dairy Americano 81
   Dairy-Quiri 77

Dill or Die 76
Kerry G Old-Fashioned 80
Panic! at the Pisco 78
Pea and Mint Sour 78
Ramble in the Bramble 81
Rosie and Gin 80
Sorrel Bellini 78
Thyme for Another 80
Vodka and Coffee Affogato 81
**cod**
feast 180
Lady Hamilton 190
salt cod brandade 104
**cod's roe**
bottarga 38
smoked 40, 180
smoked emulsion 67
**coffee** vodka affogato 81
Coppa 35, 134
**cordials** elderflower 73
Cornish Crab, Fried Egg and
Coastal Vegetables 136
Cornish Crab, Salt-Baked Beetroot,
Cobnuts 184
**courgettes**
garden 130
Trombetta 127
**crab**
Cornish with egg and
vegetables 136
Cornish with salt-baked
beetroot, cobnuts 182
and nori and potato 118
oil 55
**crackers** seaweed 58
**cream**
Ben's beeswax 55
cultured 54
cultured, sorrel, cobnuts 242
**crème fraîche** sorbet 246
**crisps**
artichoke 262
bread 244
Jerusalem artichoke 236
levain 59
potato 118
shallot 110, 192
**cucumber** dill-pickled 174
**Cultured Cream** 54
sorrel, cobnuts 242
**curd** 54
smoked buffalo 130
Cured Salmon 39
Cured Sardines 40
custard 268

**D**
Dairy, The 16, 138
Dairy Americano, The 81
Dairy-Quiri 77
**dashi** 66
tomato 132
**dates** and cauliflower 145
Dean's Green Tea Kombucha 74
dehydration 58
**desserts**
blackberry leaf panna cotta 270
chocolate, wild fennel 249
cultured cream, sorrel, cobnuts 242
ice cream sandwiches 272
Jerusalem artichoke, crème
fraîche, poached quince 261
milk, honey, blueberries 244
milk tart 267
salted caramel, cacao, malt ice
cream 258
strawberry mille-feuille 252
Sussex Alexander 246
white chocolate panna cotta 264
white peach 256
Diamond Club, The 14
**dill**
cocktail 76
pickled cucumber 174
syrup 72
Don Alfonso 1890 12, 14
**doughnuts** hibiscus 274
**dressings**
anchovy 132
pumpkin seed praline 130
squid ink 104
**drinks**
elderflower cordial 73
fermented apple juice 22
green tea kombucha 74
kefir 54
see also beer; brandy; cocktails;
gin; whiskey
**duck** hearts 152
**dulse**
butter 187
fermented 25

**E**
**eel**
applewood-smoked 116
applewood-smoked with broad
beans, lemon, mint 166
smoked, fermented chard, shallot
crisps, soy 192
**eggs**

brined yolks 142
custard 268
fried with Cornish crab 136
**elderberries** pickled 45
**elderflower**
cordial 73
jelly 256
vinegar 66
Ember Oil 56
equipment 21

**F**
farming 138
Fat-Washed Whiskey 74
**fennel**
and apple Hendricks 79
ice cream 249
kimchi 29, 196
salami 33
**fermentation** 20–1
apples 22
artichoke 22
barley 24
beetroot 24
cabbage 26
cavolo nero stalks 24
dulse 25
January King 25
kale 25
nettle 23
potato 23
salsify 27
sloe 27
sorrel 23
Swiss chard 27
see also kimchi; miso
Fermented Barley, Wild Mushroom
and Chicken Skin 150
Fermented Potato Flatbread 86
**figs** and walnut bread 90, 92
**fish**
bonito butter 52
cured sardines 40
Julie Girl skate 160
red mullet, cauliflower, dulse
butter 187
see also anchovies; cod; cod's
roe; eel; mackerel; pollock;
salmon; seafood
foie gras 232
Forced Rhubarb, Hibiscus
and Ginger Jam 49
Frankel, Patrick 138
Fresh Curd 54
Fresh Peas 124

Fried Bread 59
**fruit**
blood orange marmalade 49
blueberries with milk
and honey 244
date and cauliflower 145
fermentation 20–1
fig and walnut bread 90, 92
pickled elderberries 45
poached quince 261
sloe ferment 27
*see also* apples; apricots;
blackberries; lemons;
peaches; pears; rhubarb;
strawberries

# G

Galician Octopus 162
**game**
faggots 229
rabbit feast 205
roast wood pigeon 202
terrine 232
*see also* venison
Garden Courgette 130
Gariguette Strawberry Mille-
Feuille 252
**garlic**
oil 56
purée 210
roast miso purée 65
*see also* wild garlic
**gin** 75
apple and fennel Hendricks 79
Rosie and Gin 80
**ginger**
beer 82
rhubarb and hibiscus jam 49
Goose Ham 33
**green tea** kombucha 74

# H

**herbs**
lovage seed pickle 44
miso 65
oil 56
*see also* dill; mint; rosemary;
sorrel; thyme
Heritage Tomatoes, Cured
Sardines, Rooftop Herbs 132
**hibiscus**
doughnuts 274
rhubarb and ginger jam 49
Holbrook, Mary 216
**honey**

cremeaux 254
with milk and blueberries 244
**horseradish** yoghurt 116

# I

**ice cream**
almond 256
cacao butter 253
Jerusalem artichoke 261
malt 258
sandwiches 272
wild fennel 249
Ivy House Milk Tart 267

# J

**jams** 42
apricot and lemon thyme 48
forced rhubarb, hibiscus and
ginger 49
onion treacle 48
sour tomato 50
strawberry 254
wild blackberry and lemon
verbena 50
*see also* marmalade
January King Ferment 25
jars 21
**jellies** elderflower 256
**Jerusalem artichoke**
crisps 236
ice cream 261
Julie Girl Skate 160

# K

**kale** ferment 25
Kefir 54
Kernowsashimi 176
Kerry G Old-Fashioned 80
Kilbrack farm 138
**kimchi** 28
fennel 29, 196
Koji 64
Kombu Oil 56

# L

Lady Hamilton Cod 190
**lamb**
feast 198
Merguez 196
sauce 62
stock 61
tartare 112
Lamb's Tongue Hotpot 226
Lancaster, John 20
**leeks**

and cavolo nero ballotine 223
charred and molasses 190
**lemon verbena** blackberry jam 50
**lemons**
gel 114, 124
preserved Amalfi 30
and sunflower seed nougat 276
Levain Crisps 59
**lobster**
oil 57
salad 168
Loch Duart Salmon 182
Lomo 36
Lovage Seed Pickle 44

# M

McNerney, Paul 8, 12
**mackerel**
charred 174
smoked 41
Manoir aux Quat' Saisons, Le 14
**marmalade** blood orange 49
**mayonnaise** 67
brown crab 118
brown crab and beetroot 182
**meat** dry-curing 31–2; *see also*
beef; bone marrow; charcuterie;
game; lamb; offal; pork
Merguez 196
**milk**
almond 155
with honey and blueberries 244
kefir 54
smoked buffalo curd 130
tart 267
**mint**
granita 124
sauce 199
**miso** 64–5
bread 160
and egg yolk emulsion 192
squash 168
**mousses**
cauliflower 145
cheese trim 148
chicken 232
chocolate 249
pea 124
potato 171
**mushrooms**
duxelles 232
fermented barley 150
powder 58, 60
purée 238
wild 220

## N

Naples 12
Nasturtium Capers 44, 109
Nduja 36
Nettle Ferment 23
**nori**
    butter 53
    butter emulsion 171
    and crab and potato 118
    oil 57
    powder 60
    salt 60
    salt-baked celeriac 155
**nougat** lemon and sunflower
    seed 276
nuts *see* almonds; walnuts

## O

Oak Room Marco Pierre White 12
**octopus** Galician 162
**offal**
    chicken liver parfait 95
    lamb's tongue hotpot 226
**oils** 51
    blackberry leaf 270
    crab 55
    dill 174
    ember 56
    garlic 56
    herb 56
    kombu 56
    lobster 57
    nori 57
    Sichuan 57
Old Fashioned Ice Cream
    Sandwiches 272
Onglet Tartare 238
**onions**
    beer-pickled 43
    miso 65
    sour 30, 109
    treacle 48
    white dashi 66
    *see also* shallots
**oranges** blood marmalade 49
Orlando, Matt 14, 16
**oysters** 109
    emulsion 110, 182

## P

pancakes 89
Pancetta 37
Panic! at the Pisco 78
**pasta**
    smoked bone marrow

agnolotti 220
    wild garlic tagliatelle 127
**pastry (savoury)** pâté en
    croûte 106
**pastry (sweet)**
    pâte de brick 'wafers' 272
    strawberry mille-feuille 252
Pâté en Croûte 106
**peaches**
    pickled white 45
    white peach, almond ice cream,
        elderflower jelly 256
**pears** 148
    in pear pickle 236
**peas**
    and broad bean salad 166
    gin 75, 78
    mousse 124
Piccalilli 47
**pickles** 42
    artichoke piccalilli 47
    beer-pickled onions 43
    carrot and caraway 43
    celeriac 43
    dill cucumber 174
    elderberries 45
    lovage seed 44
    nasturtium capers 44
    radish 45
    rock samphire 46
    wakame 45
    white peaches 45
    wild garlic 44
    wild garlic capers 44
**pollock**
    smoked, potato mousse 171
    spiced gougères 101
**pork**
    brawn 98
    coppa 35
    fennel salami 33
    lomo 36
    nduja 36
    pancetta 37
    pâté en croûte 106
    suckling pig belly 213
    wild garlic and sunflower
        salami 38
**potatoes**
    and crab and nori 118
    fermented 23
    fermented flatbread 86
    mousse 171
**poultry**
    duck hearts 152
    goose ham 33

    *see also* chicken
**powders** 58
    blackberry leaf 60
    mushroom 60
    nori 60
Preserved Amalfi Lemons 30
Puffed Barley 59
**pumpkin**
    beer 83
    seed praline dressing 130
**purées**
    apple 73
    burnt apple 268
    celeriac 229
    date 145
    mushroom 238
    rhubarb 73
    roast garlic miso 65
    sunflower seed 246

## Q

**quince** poached 261

## R

Rabbit Feast 205
**radish** pickled 45
Ramble in the Bramble 81
Red Mullet, Cauliflower and Dulse
    Butter 187
Reid, Robert 12, 14
**rhubarb**
    compote 266
    grilled 202
    hibiscus and ginger jam 49
    liqueur 75
    marinated 264
    purée 73
**rice** koji 64
Roast and Fermented
    Artichoke 148
Roast Garlic Miso Purée 65
Roast Wood Pigeon 202
Rock Samphire Pickle 46
**rosemary**
    cider brandy 75, 77
    gin 75
Rosie and Gin 80

## S

**salads**
    broad bean and pea 166
    lobster 168
**salami**
    fennel 33
    wild garlic and sunflower 38

**salmon**
  cured 39
  Loch Duart 182
Salsify Ferment 27
**salt** 20–1, 32
  nori 60
  solution 72
  spiced 60
Salt-Baked Celeriac 155
Salt Cod Brandade 104
Salted Caramel, Cacao, Malt
  Ice Cream 258
Salted Lemon and Sunflower Seed
  Nougat 276
salted liquorice caramel 250
**samphire** pickle 46
**sardines** cured 40, 132
**sauces**
  lamb 62
  mint 199
  Mornay 102
  red wine shallot gastrique 46
  venison 63
  white wine shallot gastique 46
**sausages** Merguez 196
**savory** and chicken butter 52
**seafood**
  octopus, summer vegetables,
    nduja brioche 162
  squid ink dressing 104
  *see also* crab; lobster; oysters
**seaweed**
  crackers 58
  dashi 66
  kombu oil 56
  *see also* dulse; nori; wakame
**shallots**
  crisps 110, 192
  red wine gastrique 46
  vinegar 46
  white wine gastrique 46
Sichuan Mayonnaise 67
Sichuan Oil 57
**skate** Julie Girl 160
Sloe Ferment 27
Smoked Beetroot Tartare 142
Smoked Bone Marrow 37
Smoked Bone Marrow Agnolotti 220
Smoked Bone Marrow Butter 53
Smoked Butter 53
Smoked Cod's Roe 40
Smoked Cod's Roe Emulsion 67
Smoked Mackerel 41
Smoked Pollock, Potato Mousse 171
smoking 32
**sorbet**

crème fraîche 246
  sour apple 267
**sorrel**
  Bellini 78
  cultured cream 242
  emulsion 171
  fermented 23
  salt cod brandade 104
  syrup 73
Sour Onions 30
Sour Tomato Jam 50
Spiced Pollock Gougères 101
Spiced Salt 60
**squash** miso 168
**squid ink** dressing 104
stock 61
storage 21
**strawberries**
  jam 254
  mille-feuille 252
Suckling Pig Belly 213
**sugar** syrup 72
**sunflower seeds**
  and lemon nougat 276
  pesto 128
  praline 155
  purée 246
Sussex Alexander 246
sweetcorn 152
Swiss Chard Ferment 27
syrups 72–3

**T**
**tarts** milk 267
**terrines**
  chicken skin 223
  game 232
**thyme**
  cocktail 80
  syrup 73
timing 21
Toasted White Chocolate Panna
  Cotta, Forced Rhubarb 264
**tomatoes**
  and buckwheat pancakes 89
  heritage, sardines and herbs 132
  sour jam 50
Truffle Baron Bigod 92

**V**
**vanilla** sablé 264
Vegan Kimchi 28
**vegetables**
  asparagus and skate 160
  beans 210

borlotti beans 164
braised chicory 202
broad bean and pea salad 166
carrot and caraway pickle 43
fermentation 20–1
fermented chard 27, 192
kale ferment 25
kimchi 28
pickled radishes 45
salsify ferment 27
squash miso 168
sweetcorn, duck hearts,
  polenta 152
*see also* artichoke; beetroot;
  cabbage; cauliflower; cavolo
  nero; courgettes; fennel;
  leeks; mushrooms; onions;
  peas; potatoes; pumpkin
**venison**
  Chart Farm 235
  sauce 63
**vinegars**
  elderflower 66
  shallot 46
Vodka and Coffee Affogato 81

**W**
**wakame**
  fried 182
  pickled 45
**walnuts** and fig bread 90, 92
Weedon, Peter 176
whey 20
**whiskey**
  butter parfait 272
  cultured butter 53
  fat-washed 74
**white chocolate**
  panna cotta 264
  truffles 250
White Peach, Almond Ice Cream,
  Elderflower Jelly 256
Wild Blackberry and Lemon
  Verbena Jam 50
**wild garlic**
  capers 44
  pickle 44
  and sunflower salami 38
  tagliatelle 127
**wood pigeon** roast 202

**Y**
**yoghurt** 142
  horseradish 116

# ACKNOWLEDGEMENTS

To my wife, Sarah, who always keeps me grounded and loved. She brought me Ziggy and has always been my biggest fan. She makes sure we have time outside of the restaurant, lies to me about how long we are on holidays for, and together we know how to have fun.

To true talent... It wasn't until I opened The Dairy that I realised how important, productive and fun it is to share the creativity of menu-planning. Up until that point I always wrote the menus and dictated how things were done. I would always ask for opinions and welcomed input but the opening of The Dairy was different. On day one I wrote the first menu, then asked Dean, Richie and Ben how they thought we should do it. That was the first of millions of brainstorming sessions that happen constantly and paved the way for how we run the business. For the first couple of years, dishes would always have to get the thumbs up from me before they hit the menu, but as we all grew and developed our style, I went on to open other spots, which took me away from time to time and things have to move on. If I'm away from the kitchen for more than a couple of weeks you can be sure that upon my return there will be a few beauties for me to taste. This is a fine example of what happens when people grow and become the creators. The success of every dish and recipe here is down to the collaborative kitchen teams led by Dean, Richie, Ben and Simon.

Restaurants are like theatres: the band and the dancers. My mum told me that if there was an argument between the musicians and cast, the band would up the tempo to create havoc on stage. That story has always stuck with me. We have open kitchens and this has broken the barriers between us. We are a team and that's it – we are a family working towards a common goal. The front of house teams led by Dan, Lewis, Imants, Meri, Alessandra, Becca, Claire and Wesley are a force to be reckoned with. They run the floor with a smile, keeping everyone happy no matter what's broken or any flooding or electrics failing behind the scenes. They are the hardest working band in town!

There are many people who contribute to the success of a restaurant, and many working quietly behind the scenes with little credit. They may add a small contribution but leave a huge impact, so a big shout out to Sarah, who looks after all our wild flower arrangements every week and has been with us since day one, and to Barbara, a huge-hearted character with a potty mouth who taught us how to work with bees and continues to work with bees in our area. And to my mum and Dean's mum, who applied their skills to hand-make our aprons and bread baskets. It's all in the detail!

To all my chef mentors along my travels; Eoin McDonald, Paul from the Na Mara days, Derek Breen, Steve McAllister, Robert Reid, Alfonso Iaccarino, Agnar Sverrisson, Gary Jones and Raymond Blanc.

To Damiano, who was with us from the start, guiding us through the world of wine, committed to being a driving force behind the less-than-smooth opening of The Dairy. We're lucky to still be working with him today.

To Paul Winch-Furness, who has captured what we do so perfectly and made us look good! The best photographer for the job! A natural who just gets it without the need for any direction at all and a dream to work with.

To the wonderful team at Absolute Press/ Bloomsbury, especially Emily and Marie. Thanks for your creativity, complete understanding and patience along the way.

To our brilliant editor, Norma MacMillan, for always keeping us on track throughout this entire process.

Big shout out to Natalie for her beautiful illustrations. She works in The Dairy and has made many badass posters for us too! Watch this space is all I can say!

To all the amazing people that have passed through our doors, come and gone and come back again. Your stamp on the place is still here and always will be.

To our suppliers, who make our jobs a dream. You are the real heroes!

To Emma McGettrick, without whom this book would never have made it to press. She has painstakingly pulled this book together from scraps, recipes in different languages, illegible handwriting, and grease-stained paper. Hats off.

**Publisher** Jon Croft
**Commissioning Editor** Meg Boas
**Project Editor** Emily North
**Art Director and Designer** Marie O'Mara
**Photographer** Paul Winch-Furness
**Photographer's Assistant** Allan Stone
**Illustrations** Natalie Candlish
**Copyeditor** Norma MacMillan
**Proofreader** Rachel Malig
**Indexer** Zoe Ross

**ABSOLUTE PRESS**
Bloomsbury Publishing Plc
50 Bedford Square, London, WC1B 3DP, UK

BLOOMSBURY, ABSOLUTE PRESS
and the Absolute Press logo
are trademarks of Bloomsbury Publishing Plc

First published in Great Britain 2018

Copyright © Robin Gill, 2018
Photography © Paul Winch-Furness, 2018
Illustrations © Natalie Candlish, 2018

Robin Gill has asserted his right under the Copyright, Designs and Patents
Act, 1988, to be identified as Author of this work.

All rights reserved. No part of this publication may be reproduced or
transmitted in any form or by any means, electronic or mechanical,
including photocopying, recording, or any information storage or retrieval
system, without prior permission in writing from the publishers.

Bloomsbury Publishing Plc does not have any control over, or
responsibility for, any third-party websites referred to or in this book. All
internet addresses given in this book were correct at the time of going
to press. The author and publisher regret any inconvenience caused if
addresses have changed or sites have ceased to exist, but can accept no
responsibility for any such changes.

A catalogue record for this book is available from the British Library.

Library of Congress Cataloguing-in-Publication data has been applied for.

ISBN: HB: 978-1-4729-4854-0;
ePub: 978-1-4729-4855-7
ePDF: 978-1-4729-4853-3

2 4 6 8 10 9 7 5 3 1

Printed in China by C&C Offset Printing Co., Ltd.

Bloomsbury Publishing Plc makes every effort to ensure that the papers
used in the manufacture of our books are natural, recyclable products made
from wood grown in well-managed forests. Our manufacturing processes
conform to the environmental regulations of the country of origin.

To find out more about our authors and books visit
www.bloomsbury.com and sign up for our newsletters.